Battle on the Aisne 1914

Battle on the Aisne 1914

The BEF and the Birth of the Western Front

Jerry Murland

Pen & Sword
MILITARY

First published in Great Britain in 2012 by
Pen & Sword Military
an imprint of
Pen & Sword Books Ltd
47 Church Street
Barnsley
South Yorkshire
S70 2AS

ISBN: 978 1 84884 769 9

Typeset in 11pt Ehrhardt by
Mac Style, Beverley, E. Yorkshire

Printed and bound in the UK by CPI Group (UK) Ltd, Croydon, CRO 4YY

Pen & Sword Books Ltd incorporates the Imprints of Pen & Sword
Aviation, Pen & Sword Family History, Pen & Sword Maritime, Pen &
Sword Military, Pen & Sword Discovery, Wharncliffe Local History,
Wharncliffe True Crime, Wharncliffe Transport, Pen & Sword Select, Pen
& Sword Military Classics, Leo Cooper, The Praetorian Press, Remember
When, Seaforth Publishing and Frontline Publishing.

For a complete list of Pen & Sword titles please contact
PEN & SWORD BOOKS LIMITED
47 Church Street, Barnsley, South Yorkshire, S70 2AS, England
E-mail: enquiries@pen-and-sword.co.uk
Website: www.pen-and-sword.co.uk

Contents

In memory of Captain Robert Frank Hawes of the 1st Battalion Leicestershire Regiment who fought and died on the Aisne in September 1914.

A hundred of Thy sunsets spill
Their fresh and sanguine sacrifice,
Ere the sun swings his noonday sword
Must say goodbye to all of this;
By all delights which I shall miss,
Help me to die, O Lord.

W N Hodgson

Acknowledgements

Once again I owe a heartfelt debt of gratitude to the men who fought on the Aisne in 1914 and recorded their experiences for future generations to read. Without their observations and accounts of the four weeks of the campaign, this book would have been all but impossible to write. In tracking down those accounts I must thank the Institution of the Royal Engineers for permission to quote from the *RE Journal*, the Imperial War Museum, the British Library, The Grenadier Guards archive, the Royal Air Force Museum, 9th /12th Lancers Museum at Derby, the Somerset Light Infantry archive, the Leicestershire Record Office and the National Archives. To Maurice Johnson I must extend my special thanks for allowing me full access to his extensive personal archive of Aisne material and for his advice and opinions on numerous questions which arose during the writing of the book.

No book of this nature could be written without first covering the ground on foot and following in the footsteps of those who fought in the valley nearly 100 years ago and in which respect my thanks must go to Dave Rowland, Paul Webster and Bill Dobbs who spent three days with me in March 2012 walking the battlefield and sampling the local brew, and to my wife Joan who first discovered the steep hillsides and valleys of the Aisne with me in 2008. Thanks must also go to the myriad of Great War Forum members who have answered questions, corrected my errors and sent me material. In particular I must thank Doug Lewis, Keith Iles, Stuart Cole, Adam Llewellyn, Jonathan Saunders and John Etheridge who have gone out of their way to collect or transcribe material for me. Sebastian Laudan in Germany pinpointed exactly which German units were involved in the fighting on the British front. Rebecca Jones of Glory Designs in Coventry has again made sense out of my sketches in producing some excellent maps and The History Press very kindly gave permission to quote from *Tickled to Death to Go*. The photograph of Jock Marden is courtesy of his grandchildren John, Stephen, Tom and Richard Espley through his daughter Hazel. My thanks also go to Jon Cooksey who has once again edited this volume with his usual diligence and enthusiasm. In all instances every effort has been made to trace the copyright holders where any substantial extract is quoted. The author craves the indulgence of literary executors or copyright holders where these efforts have so far failed.

Jerry Murland
Coventry 2012

Introduction

The question has often been posed whether the trench stalemate would have come to pass if France had possessed a Napoleon.

Basil Liddell Hart – *A History of the First World War*

The First Battle of the Aisne officially ended on 15 September 1914. It was an encounter which, to all intents and purposes, began three days earlier when Brigadier General Hunter-Weston's 11 Brigade crossed the river under the cover of darkness at Vénizel and very nearly caught the German defence above Bucy-le-Long off-guard. After 15 September the nature of the fighting changed as the two sides paused for breath and began to consolidate their respective positions. As the spade became the most sought after weapon along the British lines, the notion of trench warfare reared its head for the first time and with it, the war of movement, which had characterized the first weeks of the Great War, slowly ground to a halt. For the British Expeditionary Force (BEF) this 'stalemate' continued for another three weeks until units of the French Army began to relieve them in early October 1914 to facilitate the move to Flanders where the last great battle of 1914 was to be decided.

This book does not aspire to be a definitive account of the First Battle of the Aisne – Edmonds' *Official History* already serves that function well enough. When I began researching the primary source material for this book, however, I determined to take a fresh look at a battle which has, over the years, been almost forgotten; overshadowed as it was then and is now by the Retreat from Mons and the First Battle of Ypres. My primary intention in re-examining the battle is to give voice to those who took part in the fighting, lived through it and chronicled their experiences in diaries and letters at the time. Consequently the text leans heavily on their written accounts. Needless to say, it is through these accounts that the personal stories of battle allow us to temporarily share the hardship and terror of warfare and the brutality of the battlefield. Perhaps more importantly they provide us with a glimpse of the irrepressible humanity of man which was occasionally allowed to surface – no better illustrated than in Captain Guy Ward's journal of 18 September 1914 when he records going out under fire with several men of the South Wales Borderers to help bury thirteen Cameron Highlanders because they couldn't bear to see them lying out in the open so pitifully. Consider too, the action of 23-year-old Lieutenant George Hutton of 3/Signal Company who drowned swimming across a swollen River Aisne attempting to take a telephone cable to the north bank. Hutton refused to allow an enlisted man to do so on the grounds that the man was married and Hutton was not. Greater love hath no man.

In those early weeks of the war the BEF was fighting very closely alongside its French allies but, given the size of the British force, it was a very minor player on the wider strategic canvas then unfurling across France and Belgium. That said, this account of the fighting in the Aisne valley focuses solely on the men of the BEF and the German units they were in contact with and only describes the actions of French army units where it is necessary to provide an appreciation of the wider strategic picture. To place the role of the BEF in perspective, by the time the British arrived on the Aisne in September 1914 the battle line stretched some 150 miles from Noyon in the west to Verdun in the east and it was only along a tiny 15-mile sector in the centre which the British were engaged.

The geography of the valley of the Aisne was very much on the side of the defending German Army and held few, if any, advantages for the British whose efforts were directed at pushing the enemy off the northern rim – the Chemin des Dames ridge – a hog's back feature which acquired its name in the eighteenth century when it was in frequent use by the two daughters of Louis XV when visiting Françoise de Châlus, a former mistress of the king at the Château Boves, near Vauclair. The Chemin des Dames commanded – and in places enfiladed – the whole valley, the river itself was deep and unfordable and for most of September 1914 was swollen to full capacity by almost continuous rain. It flowed through numerous bends along a wide valley which was enclosed by a succession of steep spurs, between which ran deep ravines bordered by woods and dense copses. It was the ideal place for an army to stand firm, an opinion echoed by the Northamptonshire regimental historian, 'The battalion was confronted by hostile forces determined to stand their ground and to maintain their hold upon the strong natural position they had occupied'.

There were three battles on the Aisne during the Great War and the focus on each occasion was the Chemin des Dames ridge. The 1914 Battle of the Aisne came about as a direct result of the German retirement from the Battle of the Marne as the huge conscript armies of France and Germany jostled for position over great swathes of Belgium and France. In 1914 the German Army held onto its positions along the Chemin des Dames and although the French gained ground during the Nivelle offensive of April 1917 and established themselves on the Chemin des Dames, they lost heavily in both casualties and morale. (In the first week's fighting alone the French suffered 96,000 casualties of which over 15,000 were killed). The French gains were short-lived as their efforts were reversed in the German Blücher-Yorck spring offensive of 1918 when many of the British Regiments which struggled on the Chemin des Dames in 1914 were represented again by legions of fresh-faced youngsters in the ranks of IX Corps.

When war was declared on 4 August 1914, overall command of the BEF was placed in the hands of Field Marshal Sir John French; his chief of staff was Lieutenant General Sir Archibald Murray, with Major General Henry Wilson as his deputy. The principle staff officer with responsibility for operations (GSO1) was Brigadier General George Harper, and GSO1 (Intelligence) was Lieutenant Colonel George Macdonogh. This core group of senior staff officers formed the nucleus of the British General Headquarters (GHQ) whose task it was to exercise overall command and control of the BEF. Sir John French was 61-years-old in September 1914 and had made his reputation commanding the British Cavalry Division in the South African War. Nevertheless, this brave and resourceful soldier was not in tune with the management of strategic command. He was one of the few senior officers in the BEF who had not attended the Staff College at Camberley and in the opinion of many – including Sir Douglas Haig – lacked the intellectual focus necessary to exercise effective command and control over a force as large and complex as the BEF.

Exacerbated by fears in England of a German invasion of the home country and the recent trouble in Ireland over Home Rule, the British Government was initially cautious and had committed only four of its six available infantry divisions and one cavalry division. Consequently the fighting strength of the BEF was made up of I Corps (1st and 2nd Divisions) commanded by Lieutenant General Sir Douglas Haig, II Corps (3rd and 5th Divisions) commanded by Lieutenant General Sir James Grierson and the Cavalry Division under the command of Major

General Edmund Allenby. In addition there were five infantry battalions designated for the protection and maintenance of the lines of communication clustered together in 19 Brigade. Sadly Grierson died from a heart attack on the way to Le Cateau on 17 August and was replaced by General Sir Horace Smith-Dorrien two days later. The 4th Division would arrive just in time to take part in the Battle at Le Cateau on 26 August and the 6th Division would make its first appearance on the Aisne in mid- September.

Almost immediately upon the declaration of war nearly 70,000 reservists began to pour into regimental depots across the country as the smooth machinery of mobilization organized Britain's army for its first war on the continental mainland of Europe in almost 100 years. Screened by the ships of the Royal Navy, embarkation began on 11 August and was completed nine days later when the BEF assembled near Maubeuge. By 22 August – the eve of the Battle of Mons – the BEF was in position on the left of the French Fifth Army. Smith-Dorrien's II Corps lined the canal between Mons and Condé facing north while Haig's I Corps was posted along the Beaumont–Mons road facing northeast. To the west Allenby's cavalry and units of 19 Brigade guarded the canal crossings as far as Condé. The battle along the canal at Mons on 23 August was the BEF's first clash with the German First Army commanded by General Alexander von Kluck. The outcome was inevitable, outnumbered and out-manoeuvred and with General Charles Lanrezac's French Fifth Army already retiring on his right flank, Sir John French had little recourse but to retire. It was a retirement which eventually saw the BEF reach a position south of the River Marne and drew attention to Sir John's shortcomings as a commander-in-chief.

In fairness to Sir John and his commanders, they were faced with a huge task in August 1914, a task which placed a massive burden of responsibility on men who had very little experience of manoeuvring such large masses of troops over extended periods of time. Even so, at Le Cateau, Horace Smith-Dorrien defied an order from GHQ to continue the retreat of II Corps and stood his ground with three divisions along the line of the Le Cateau-Cambrai road. History agrees that this decision was not only courageous, but the correct one in the circumstances; nevertheless it did add fuel to the long-held animosity between Sir John and Horace Smith-Dorrien.[1]

The retreat from Mons was an episode from which the BEF emerged by the skin of its teeth. It was not handled well by GHQ which was conspicuous by its absence and achieved notoriety for the ambiguity of its operational orders. To the eternal credit of the British soldier the end of the retreat and the subsequent advance to the Marne was seen as an opportunity to hit back at the enemy, Exhausted and footsore they turned to pursue what they understood to be a thoroughly demoralized German Army. Brigadier General Count Edward Gleichen noticed an enormous difference in the spirits of his men as the BEF moved north, a mood which was unfortunately not replicated at GHQ where senior officers were still hesitant to engage the enemy. Even after it became obvious that the German Army was in full retreat British staff officers handled the logistics of the advance badly due to inexperience. The daily operational orders which issued forth from GHQ gave little direction to the fighting units and even within divisions staff officers failed to deliver effective movement orders or to prevent instances of friendly fire as divisional boundaries became blurred in the move north. The end result was inevitable; the German Army escaped and proceeded to withdraw in an orderly fashion to the Aisne while the BEF struggled to pursue them, leaving an astonished Lieutenant Alexander Johnston to express surprise that they had not 'tried anything in the nature of a night advance or night attack, particularly when the Germans are in retreat'.

The BEF advanced to the southern heights above the Aisne Valley expecting the German Army to be in headlong retreat. The Germans, however, having been reinforced with troops and artillery from the fall of Maubeuge, found themselves in a stronger position than previously thought and were thus determined to hold the line of the Chemin des Dames if at all possible to give them time to reorganize. They were still a formidable fighting force and never far from the thinking of the strategists at German General Headquarters (OHL) was the possibility of outflanking the Allied armies by moving west – a strategy which was mirrored by the French and British – and as the Aisne fighting lurched into stalemate, so the sidestep movements towards the channel coast to the north gathered pace.

Expecting to advance in pursuit of a beaten enemy, GHQ had neglected to order any advanced technical reconnaissance by Royal Engineers officers to make assessments as to the equipment required to effect temporary crossings of the Aisne. The heavy bridging trains were still at least a day's march behind the main body of the BEF and there appeared to be a naivety overshadowing the ability of GHQ to consider that the situation ahead of them was fluid and could change at any moment. Yet there was a least one reconnaissance north of the river conducted before the main body of the BEF arrived. Lieutenant Archibald Harrison and trooper Ben Clouting of 4/Dragoon Guards crossed the river on 11 September and reconnoitred as far as the village of Moulins where they apparently remained until the British arrived in the village a few days later. Rather frustratingly Clouting does not disclose if any useful intelligence was gathered and to whom it was delivered and we can only speculate as to why GHQ failed to appreciate that the situation north of the river on the nights of 11 and 12 September was entirely different to that of 13 September. Had Operational Order No. 22, issued on 11 September, been notice of a co-ordinated plan of attack – instead of one of pursuit – and had Sir John demanded a vigorous assault, there may have been a different outcome to the battle. In fact none of the operational orders issued at this time ever disclosed the intentions of Sir John French.

But although we should be wary of censure, the wording of GHQ orders cannot be ignored. The executive order 'pursuit' had an immediate effect upon the military formation adopted by units; pursuit implied marching in column while 'attack' demanded a different and broader formation. Thus on 13 and 14 September units began the day's pursuit in column of route covered by advance guards, which goes some way to providing an explanation as to why the attack north of the river was conducted in such a piecemeal manner – one example being the advance of 6 Brigade on 14 September up the Braye valley. Here the 1st Battalion Royal Berkshire Regiment (1/Royal Berks) acting as vanguard, marched up the valley with the 1st Battalion King's Royal Rifle Corps (1/KRRC) on each flank. Lieutenant Alan Hanbury-Sparrow's account describes the battalion's reaction to the unexpected response from the enemy as they passed La Metz Farm, which together with that of Lieutenant William Synge, commanding a platoon of the King's Liverpool Regiment, illustrates the confusion which overtook the brigade as it struggled to respond to an entrenched enemy.

As the BEF crossed the Aisne and began its advance it committed all of its divisions to the fight leaving no reserves available except 19 Brigade, which, after 14 September, came under the temporary command of Brigadier General Haldane on the left flank. Thus at the crucial moment on the I Corps front when reserves were required, none were forthcoming. In this respect more use could have been made of the cavalry brigades; they appear not to have been given a definite role in the battle and apart from sporadic interventions such as supporting the left of Haig's 2nd Division on 14 September and coming to the aid of the West Yorkshires on 20 September, they could have been used far more effectively. In this respect Second Lieutenant Jock Marden's diary provides us with a very different picture of the Aisne campaign than Lieutenant Jack Needham's account. Needham was an officer with the Northamptonshire Regiment and fought on the Chemin des Dames with his battalion where he was involved in one of the 'white flag' incidents which so infuriated British troops. Marden, an officer with the 9/Lancers, spent much of his time in reserve and, apart from short periods of action in the front line, was able to find time on 15 September to sleep all day at Soupir Château and bathe in its fountain.

As British units became engaged all along the BEF front on 13 and 14 September, so the casualties mounted. German shell fire proved to be remarkably accurate and powerful and it was some time before the British gunners could begin to mount an effective reply. The Battle of the Aisne marked the beginning of the ascendancy of artillery as the major weapon of warfare but initially on the British side it was simply not up to the job. Handicapped by the geography of the Aisne valley and confined to some extent by an outdated tactical manual, British artillery was unable to provide the infantry with the firepower it required to take the Chemin des Dames or indeed fully support infantry attacks elsewhere along the valley. Major John Mowbray, the brigade major of the 2nd Division Artillery, shares his frustration in the pages of his diary at not being able to support the infantry effectively; a frustration undoubtedly felt by Cecil Brereton, a subaltern with 68/Battery when he and his gunners suffered badly at the hands of their German counterparts above Bucy-le-Long.

But with the advent of aerial observation carried out by Royal Flying Corps (RFC) pilots the balance began to swing in favour of the British. The work of Lieutenants Lewis and James in developing the use of wireless transmissions from the air to artillery batteries on the ground was the start of an 'air to ground' partnership which continued to develop through the war. This growing partnership is evident in the diaries of Lieutenants William Read and Kenlis Atkinson, from whom we get a first-hand account of flying above the valley under fire whilst directing artillery fire onto enemy batteries.

The lack of support from the guns of the artillery had profound effects on the infantry advance, particularly on the units which had been engaged at Mons and Le Cateau. At Vailly the 3rd Division's attack was doomed to failure as the much depleted battalions of Hubert Hamilton's division attempted to storm the heights of the Jouy spur. 8 Brigade, which had fought so doggedly at Mons on 23 August in the Nimy salient, had not a single machine gun between them on 14 September and had to rely solely on rifle fire. On the Chivres spur the 5th Division was still in possession of some of their machine guns but had left a significant proportion of their artillery behind at Le Cateau.

Their attack, which went ahead in a rather piecemeal fashion and without supporting fire from the gunners, had the commanding officer of the East Surreys, Lieutenant Colonel John Longley, tearing his hair out in frustration at being ordered to withdraw.

However, there were some commanders who seized the initiative and took opportunities presented to them to forge ahead once they had crossed the river. Sadly these audacious moves were unsupported and thus made little difference to the outcome of the battle. The crossing of the bridge at Vénizel by 11 Brigade and their march across the water meadows to Bucy-le-Long was a masterful stroke which might have taken the brigade onto the Chemin des Dames early on 13 September. But 11 Brigade was far in advance of the remainder of the BEF and at dawn on the 13th was the only full brigade across the river. Once on the heights they were considerably isolated and in the circumstances one has to accept Brigadier General Hunter-Weston's decision that halting the brigade at this point was the best course of action. Isolation and poor communication was probably at the core of the judgement by Brigadier General Richard Haking to withdraw his units of 5 Brigade after they had reached the Chemin des Dames ridge late in the evening of 14 September without encountering any serious opposition. Haking argued that he was in great danger of being cut off by the enemy – and he may well have been correct – but was it really necessary to retire all the way back to Verneuil and would a more daring commander have taken more of a risk?

There was a further bold action on the right flank taken by the Connaught Rangers. By the early hours of 14 September the battalion, under the command of Major William Sarsfield, was over halfway to the brigade objective, in occupation of La Cour de Soupir Farm and in position on the high point of Croix sans Tete, albeit several hours before the Grenadier Guards arrived; yet this advance was not exploited. Ultimately all of these isolated movements only served to draw attention to the lack of effective command and control which dogged the British on the Aisne in those crucial early hours of the battle.

The unsung heroes of the Aisne Campaign were undoubtedly the men of the Royal Engineers and the Royal Army Medical Corps (RAMC). The crossing of the river was in itself a feat of arms which is rarely afforded due credit. The bridges the sappers constructed – often under infantry rifle fire and shell fire from German batteries – were indeed 'bridges over troubled waters'. The diary entries of Second Lieutenant Kenneth Godsell and Lieutenant Bernard Young give us some idea of the effort required to transport troops across the Aisne on temporary pontoon bridges and improvised rafts. Not only did the engineers repair the two bridges which had been partially destroyed at Vénizel and Vailly, but they enabled I Corps to cross over the hastily repaired aqueduct at Bourg. Had the Bourg aqueduct been destroyed completely it is unlikely I Corps would have been in a position to attack the Chemin des Dames on 14 September. It is a fitting tribute to the bravery and tenacity of the sappers that one of their number was awarded the Victoria Cross for his work on the river.

A Victoria Cross was also awarded to Captain Harry Ranken, the medical officer attached to 1/KRRC who sacrificed his own life while attending to the wounded. On the Aisne, as there had been at Mons and Le Cateau, battalion medical officers in the finest traditions of the profession were conspicuous by their devotion to the wounded and dying and the number of medical officers who were tragically killed attending the wounded is a tribute to their gallantry and sacrifice. Whereas it was the battalion medical officer who provided the wounded with initial treatment in the front line, it was the RAMC staff in the forward dressing stations which dealt with the bulk of the wounded and dying after they had been evacuated. We are fortunate that Lieutenant Henry Robinson, a doctor working with 8/Field Ambulance, kept a detailed account of the time he spent at Vailly. Robinson's diary is harrowing in its detail and description and his rationalization of the moral dilemma confronting the medical staff over hastening the death of a fatally injured soldier is thought provoking to say the least. The Aisne also saw the long overdue introduction of motor ambulances which eased the suffering of the wounded and speeded up the evacuation to field hospitals south of the river, an evacuation which had to be carried out under the cover of darkness and usually under the constant threat of German shell fire which searched the approach roads.

Despite the lack of progress and the hoped for continuation of the advance, the BEF and its Allies did frustrate any intentions the Germans may have had in launching a new offensive from the Aisne in 1914. Despite the German superiority in fire power the men of the BEF were steadfast in defence and an even match for the German infantryman, yet there is no doubt that the Battle of the Aisne in 1914 was an opportunity missed for both the British and the French. As early as dawn on 13 September, General Louis Conneau's French cavalry corps was opposite a 10-mile gap in the German line and after crossing the river they rode some 12 miles north to Sissone. Incredibly the French cavalry were at this point 15 miles north of the German Second Army and some 40 miles behind the line of the German Third

Army! One hesitates to imagine what the outcome of a move to the east across enemy lines of communication may have been. As it was the French were ordered to retire to the river to avoid being cut off!

For the British the prospects of breaking through and taking the Chemin des Dames was never greater than on the morning of 13 September. Thanks to the Royal Engineers and the initiative of some brigade and battalion commanders, the passage of the Aisne had been achieved on both flanks and information supplied to Douglas Haig still indicated that the gap between von Kluck and von Bülow was susceptible. The opportunity was lost owing to the failure of GHQ to fully appreciate the situation ahead of them as far back as 10 September, a situation which by the evening of 13 September had changed completely. German reinforcements were known to have arrived and were entrenching on the Chemin des Dames, yet there was no further directive from GHQ other than to continue the pursuit. As a result divisions blundered into the battle piecemeal and without adequate artillery support and out of their failure to make progress grew the trench lines of what became known as the Western Front.

The fighting on the Aisne was going to be very different from anything experienced by the BEF up to that point. All five of its infantry divisions would be engaged along a wide front against a formidable opponent which held the advantages of position and superior artillery. This was not going to be an encounter such as those which had unfolded at Mons or Le Cateau but a sustained campaign that would see lengthy casualty lists and great swathes slashed through the ranks of some of Britain's finest regiments. Moreover, as a situation of 'stalemate' began to set in, the landscape of the Aisne would witness the digging of trench lines which would all too soon run from the North Sea coast of Belgium all the way to the German/Swiss border. Britain was not prepared for a war in Europe in 1914 and the price for failing to do so became more and more evident on the Aisne battlefields. It is a failure which has been captured poignantly in the diary accounts and letters of the men who fought on the slopes of the Chemin des Dames where the bloody concept of the Western Front was born in the autumn of 1914.

Chapter 1

The Marne

I'm afraid that our nation in its headlong careering towards victory will scarcely be able to bear this misfortune.

Helmuth von Moltke – writing on the
German retirement from the Marne.

For Major Tom Bridges and the officers and men of the 4th Royal Irish Dragoon Guards their first encounter with their German adversaries, in what was to become known as the First Battle of the Marne, came on 6 September at the small hilltop village of Pécy, northwest of Provins. Having been in retreat since 23 August after the BEF's clash with the German First Army at Mons, the regiment was now south of the Marne River and under orders to move north as advance guard for the 2nd Cavalry Brigade. After an opening skirmish with units of Alexander von Linsingen's II Corps, during which 24-year-old Sergeant Evelyn Whiteman and Lance Corporal William Ticehurst, both of B Squadron, were killed by shell fire, Bridges and his men were astonished to see 'the enemy column wheel round in the road and retire to the north.'[2] Bridges admits that their own response to this unexpected enemy retirement took the form of a rather 'impotent sniping', and by nightfall they had lost the opportunity to strike back at an enemy who had been pursuing them for two weeks.[3] As the regiment moved north towards Coulommiers they were completely unaware that Allied forces were now embroiled in the Battle of the Marne and that the wider strategic plan would conclude with the German retreat to the heights of the Chemin des Dames which ran along the northern edge of the Aisne River valley.

The First Battle of the Marne was fought between 5 and 11 September 1914. It was, in the opinion of Holger Herwig, 'the most significant land battle of the twentieth century,' and the most decisive since Waterloo.[4] Why? Because the Marne was the final stroke which brought the German operational strategy – masterminded in 1905 by the Chief of the German General Staff, Count Alfred von Schlieffen – to an end and changed the course of European history. Schlieffen's master plan was for a war on two fronts but not at the same time: a rapid forty day advance through Belgium and Northern France to encircle the French armies concluding in a victorious entry into Paris before unwieldy Russian forces in the east were able to mobilize effectively against them. Although more recently some historians have argued that there was in fact no 'Schlieffen Plan', the balance of evidence does not support this rather blinkered view of German military aspirations in the years preceding 1914. That there was a German war plan for 1914 is not in dispute, the original Schlieffen blueprint for war was inherited by Helmuth von Moltke when he was appointed Chief of the General Staff in 1906 and it was a version of this plan which the German OHL used in its preparations for war in Europe. Unquestionably the Schlieffen Plan had been modified by von Moltke – who admittedly had reservations about some of its aspects – but the fundamental goals were similar: the French armies would be ruthlessly and rapidly crushed in a battle of encirclement or *Kesselschlacht*.

German military planners were confident that the strike against France would be concluded before Russian forces could mobilize effectively against them and with France defeated, German divisions could be transferred quickly to the Eastern Front by rail. The essence of the plan was speed and therein lay its Achilles heel, there was no real alternative plan to fall back upon and success depended almost entirely on maintaining the timetable of advance. The great fear was the prospect of fighting a war on two fronts resulting in the division of resources.

However, despite the initial success in the opening weeks of the war, by the end of August it was becoming increasingly clear that the plan was slipping behind schedule. Contrary to expectations, Belgian forces had vigorously resisted the invasion of their country and the First Army, under the command of General Alexander von Kluck, had unexpectedly encountered the BEF at Mons on 23 August and again three days later at Le Cateau. The German Second Army, under the command of General Klaus von Bülow, had been held up by the French Fifth Army on the Sambre during the Battle of Charleroi, and in the east the Russian Army had mobilized in just ten days which had the immediate effect of drawing off two whole army corps which were

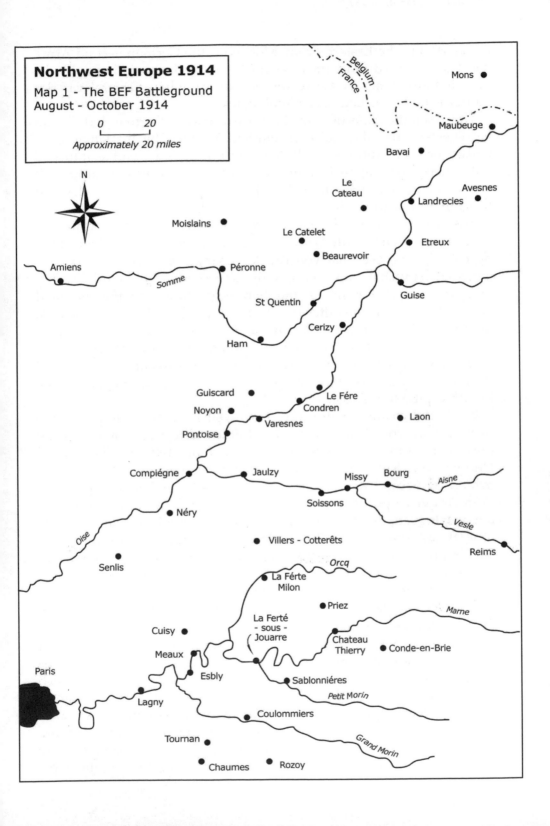

Northwest Europe 1914

Map 1 - The BEF Battleground
August - October 1914

0   20

Approximately 20 miles

N

Belgium
France

Mons

Maubeuge

Bavai

Le
Cateau

Avesnes

Landrecies

Moislains

Le Catelet

Etreux

Beaurevoir

Amiens

Péronne

Somme

Guise

St Quentin

Cerizy

Ham

Guiscard

Le Fére

Noyon

Condren

Laon

Varesnes

Pontoise

Compiégne

Jaulzy

Missy

Bourg

Aisne

Néry

Soissons

Oise

Villers - Cotterêts

Vesle

Reims

Senlis

Orcq

La Férte
Milon

Priez

Marne

La Ferté
- sous -
Jouarre

Cuisy

Chateau
Thierry

Conde-en-Brie

Meaux

Paris

Esbly

Sablonniéres

Lagny

Petit Morin

Coulommiers

Tournan

Grand Morin

Chaumes

Rozoy

transferred to the Eastern Front. Moreover, the German Second Army had been stopped in its tracks again for some thirty-six hours by the French Fifth Army at Guise on 29 August when General Charles Lanrezac had launched his counter attack.

The first indications of a crack in the carapace of German fortune can be detected after the Guise encounter. Alarmed by his situation at Guise, the ever cautious von Bülow sent out urgent – and as it turned out unnecessary – appeals to the First and Third Armies for support. It was von Bülow's appeal for help, which many felt ultimately changed the course of history. The result was a spur-of-the-moment decision by Von Kluck to abandon his sweep west of Paris and change course to confront the French Fifth Army's flank. However, recent evidence cited by Herwig suggests that von Kluck's change of direction had been anticipated by OHL and was not only carried out with the full backing of German high command, but had been built into the modified Schlieffen plan as an alternative strategy.[5] Von Moltke's General Directive of 2 September to the First and Second Armies would appear to support this view – it not only stressed the necessity of driving 'the French away from the capital in a south easterly direction,' but ordered the First Army to follow the Second Army in echelon as it bypassed the French capital to the east.

While the change of direction may well have been built into the overall plan, von Kluck's reply to Moltke's directive was not. In no uncertain terms von Kluck and his chief of staff, the 58-year-old Herman von Kuhl, made it clear that they were unable to follow behind the Second Army if they were to attack the flank of Lanrezac's Fifth Army. To put it simply, von Kluck did not do 'in echelon' with anyone. Indeed, by the morning of 30 August von Kluck and his chief of staff had already come to the decision that the march round Paris was impractical and given the severe wear and tear on his resources and with the French Fifth Army looking vulnerable after its retreat from Guise, he saw the opportunity to strike Charles Lanrezac's army in its exposed flank. Thus, without consultation or approval from OHL, he turned towards the River Oise, a course of action – according to Herwig – which was finally communicated to Moltke on 4 September.[6] Rather than von Bülow's appeal for assistance, it was perhaps von Kluck's refusal to comply with OHL directives which precipitated the Battle of the Marne and changed the course of history.

Of the seven German armies in the field it was von Kluck's First Army which had the task of maintaining the risky right flanking sweep to the west of Paris before turning east to complete the encirclement of the French Army. At 68-years-old he was the same age as von Bülow but there the similarity ended. The First Army commander was essentially more combative in style and, as we have seen, maverick in temperament. At the beginning of the campaign the First Army fielded over 200,000 men and some 750 guns. By the end of August this had been reduced by 20,000 as the toll of those killed or missing in action, together with nearly 10,000 who had simply fallen out with exhaustion, heat stroke and hunger, had reduced many units to below half strength. They had marched over 300 miles in the heat of August, had two serious encounters with the BEF, been in constant contact with British and French rearguard forces and faced the prospect of more of the same. Von Kluck's decision to ignore the OHL directive of 2 September was almost certainly motivated by his personal desire to maintain his role as the right hook which delivered the final blow to the French as they were driven south. This inflexible view – shared it must be said by von Kuhl – was partly responsible for his failure to fully realize the threat of French General Michel-Joseph Maunoury's Sixth Army on his right. But von Kluck was no fool; he had taken measures to protect his right flank by detaching the fifteen battalions and supporting artillery of Hans von Gronau's IV Reserve Corps. The notion that his right flank was wide open is incorrect.

The discovery of a map that had been retrieved from a dead German Guard Cavalry officer on 1 September providentially supplied corroboration of French air reconnaissance reports that German forces were moving east and attempting to outflank the Fifth Army. The captured map showed clearly the German First Army order of battle and the lines of advance. It was all the evidence which was needed to confirm von Kluck's change of direction. Up until this point the idea of the Battle of the Marne had not been conceptualized on the map table of the French commander-in-chief but now General Joseph Joffre realized that if the two armies which formed the German right flank could be enticed into the 'net' which now hung between the 'horns' of Paris and Verdun he could give battle and perhaps achieve the breakthrough all of France had been waiting for. If the Ninth and Fourth French Armies could hold the centre of this 200 mile wide net, the armies on each flank could catch the Germans in a pincer movement. Furthermore, if the French could disrupt the German lines of communication they stood a chance of destroying the invader once and for all.

It was the first time a plan looked coherent enough to suggest success but in order for all the pieces of the allied jigsaw to fit, Joffre required the cooperation of the BEF whose commander-in-chief, Sir

John French was not at his best in these opening weeks of the Great War. He and his staff had been badly shaken by the retreat of the BEF from Mons and it was Sir John's considered opinion that the small British force of five divisions required urgent re-fitting and recuperation before it could re-engage the enemy. Not only did this expose Sir John's overall misunderstanding of the magnitude of the events he and the BEF were now caught up in but underlined his somewhat entrenched distrust of all things French.

By 3 September Joffre's plans for a counter attack were falling into place. Commanded by Maurice Sarrail, the French Third Army faced the German Fifth Army opposite Verdun, the Fourth and Ninth Armies under Fernand de Langle de Cary and Ferdinand Foch held the centre opposite von Hausen's Third Army. Between the Fifth Army – now under the command of the more dynamic General Franchet d'Espèrey – and Maunoury's Sixth Army, a gap existed which Joffre anticipated would be filled by the BEF.

The optimism expressed to his chief by Louis Franchet d'Espèrey went some way to assuring Joffre that the British would take their place on the right of the French Sixth Army and fill the gap between d'Espèrey's left and Maunoury's right. But Joffre still harboured doubts about the commitment of the British Commander-in-Chief. The cooperation of the BEF on the right flank of the Sixth Army was vital and with this in mind General Maunoury was despatched to the British GHQ at Melun on 4 September where, in Sir John's absence, the chief of staff, Sir Archibald Murray, agreed to British involvement – subject of course to Sir John's approval. But even at this juncture there was apparently some confusion as to when exactly Joffre intended to begin his attack. Under the false impression that it was 7 September and that the BEF was required to retire further south to make way for the French Sixth Army to move into position on its left, Murray issued Operational Order No. 16 which instructed the BEF to continue its retirement the following morning.

Later on 4 September Joffre ordered the offensive to begin a day earlier – on 6 September – a decision which did not reach GHQ until nearly 4.00am on the 5th by which time it was too late to prevent some of the British units from continuing their retirement. There was still ample time, however, to halt the movement of the BEF before it concluded its day's march. Despite his apparent enthusiasm it appears very much as though Sir John French was not entirely convinced of the effectiveness of Joffre's plan and was intending to create a buffer zone which would provide the BEF with room to continue the retreat should that be necessary.

However, seizing the opportunity before him, Joffre planned to launch his counter-offensive on the morning of 6 September 1914. The French Sixth Army – which was all that stood between the German First Army and Paris – was poised to strike at the right flank of von Kluck's First Army but still needed time to fall into position. Early on 5 September Maunoury marched his ten infantry divisions to a line northwest of Meaux from where he anticipated engaging the German First Army along the Marne the next day. Maunoury's cavalry screen let him down badly, although they found no German forces along the line of march, they completely overlooked the presence of von Gronau's IV Reserve Corps and the first shots of the Battle of the Marne were fired from the high ground around Monthyon – a day earlier than Joffre had intended. Severely under strength and outnumbered by the units of the French Sixth Army, the German IV Reserve Corps held on for the remainder of the day finally withdrawing that evening northeast towards Puisieux.

Nevertheless, the damage had been done. Not only had Maunoury been prevented from crossing the River Ourcq but the element of surprise had evaporated. Von Kluck now knew his right flank was in serious trouble and typically turned to meet the new threat by attacking across the Ourcq. Orders were dispatched to Sixt von Arnim's IV Corps and von Linsingen's II Corps, now south of the Marne and approaching Pécy, to about turn and march post-haste to add weight to von Gronau's positions which he had now taken up north of the River Thérouanne. It was the execution of these orders which Major Tom Bridges and 4/Royal Irish Dragoons witnessed with incredulity on the morning of 6 September 1914. The British cavalrymen were positioned at the high water mark of von Kluck's advance and, had they but known it, were witnesses to events which began the process of opening a substantial gap between von Kluck's left wing and the right wing of von Bülow's Second Army.

* * *

The so-called gap occurred as von Kluck swung his forces through ninety degrees to face Maunoury and was increased by Bülow whom – without first informing the First Army – pulled back his right flank beyond the Petit Morin River on 7 September, claiming his troops were too tired to take on another frontal assault by the French Fifth Army. It was an altogether surprising move by the Second Army commander; while von Kluck was preparing to attack Maunoury to the west, Bülow was in fact pulling his right flank back northeast. He must have realised he was widening the existing gap and gambled on his First Army counterpart falling into line as instructed by Moltke. In his defence von Bülow cited the OHL directive of 2 September and maintained that the First Army's role was to protect his flank, he was adamant that von Kluck should pull back from his counter offensive against Maunoury and fall into line with the Second Army.

Von Kluck was equally obstinate in his view that the only possible course of action was to destroy Maunoury's Sixth Army before the BEF appeared on the left of Franchet d' Espèrey's Fifth Army and pushed through the gap. It was a concern which was confirmed later on 7 September when German cavalry observed the British vanguard advancing over the Grand Morin River at La Ferté-Gaucher, a movement which served only to galvanize von Kluck in his offensive against the Sixth Army. The morning of 8 September would thus see two battles: von Kluck and Maunoury on the line of the Ourcq and von Bülow and Franchet d' Espèrey on the Grand and Petit Morin.

Reinforcements for Maunoury's Sixth Army in the form of the French 7th Infantry Division began arriving from Paris by rail on the night of 7 September, but mindful of a possible breakdown in the railway network, Joseph Gallieni famously decided to send the 103rd and 104th Infantry Regiments by road using a fleet of several hundred Paris taxi cabs. But it is here that the story which has become a part of almost every account of the Battle of the Marne falters. The true picture of this dash to save the Sixth Army is one of traffic chaos, mechanical breakdown and missed destinations which did little more than create pandemonium on the 30 mile stretch of road between Gagny and Nanteuil-les-Meaux. While it may have been a successful publicity scoop for Gallieni, 'militarily' wrote Herwig, 'it was insignificant'.

Yet despite this the French plan for victory was in trouble. In several places they had been pushed back with heavy losses and Von Kluck's encounter with Maunoury was very much in the balance. Maunoury had already prepared Joffre for a retreat with his declaration that if von Kluck attacked him again he would retire to the west, secretly – as the French *Official History* confirms – he had already issued orders to that effect. But it was now that the fog of war – created by an almost complete lack of lucid communication between OHL and the German First and Second Armies – descended in the form of Colonel Richard Hentsch, chief of the OHL's Intelligence Section.

Doubt and uncertainty was undermining the decision making process at German General Headquarters. Von Moltke was losing his nerve and since 5 September he and the staff at OHL had had no clear idea as to what exactly was taking place on the Marne. Reports from the front were often contradictory and suggested that the First and Second Armies were in danger of being outflanked by the French Fifth Army and the BEF by exploiting the gap between the two. In the mind of von Moltke the worst-case scenario would see von Kluck forced further to the west, surrounded and destroyed, resulting in defeat and a long drawn out retreat. If the line of the Marne was impossible to hold then the First and Second Armies must retire north to close the gap. In a move which was to prove the most contentious of the entire campaign, von Moltke sent Richard Hentsch to the front to establish exactly what was happening.

* * *

Although nothing was ever put in writing, it is almost certain that Hentsch was given full powers by Moltke to initiate a retirement of the German right wing if the First Army's situation demanded it. Hentsch left OHL in Luxembourg to complete a full assessment of the strategic situation, arriving at German Fifth Army headquarters at Varennes-en-Argonne on 8 September. Later that day he motored to Courtisols to confer with the Fourth Army and then to Châlons-sur-Marne where he met Ernst von Hoeppner, the chief of staff for the Third Army. It was only after his arrival in the late afternoon at Montmort-Lucy to hear von Bülow's appraisal of the Second Army's situation, that the cautious optimism generated by his earlier discussions would be dashed.

Von Bülow was unwavering in his criticism of von Kluck's failure to remain in echelon with his Second Army and of the apparently separate battle he was now fighting on the Ourcq with Maunoury's Sixth Army. According to its commander, the Second Army was in no condition to continue its offensive and, he explained to Hentsch, matters were being made worse, by the ever widening gap between the two armies, a gap which was in great danger of being exploited. The Second Army, reiterated Bülow, could only maintain its present line of battle if the First Army withdrew to the east, away from the Ourcq, to link up with Second Army along the northern side of the Marne and thereby close the gap. By the end of the meeting there was no doubt in Hentsch's mind where von Bülow felt the blame for the current crisis should rest: solely and completely with the First Army.

The German Second Army was, in truth, in a potentially difficult position. Franchet d'Espèrey's Fifth Army was hotly engaged with von Bülow's right wing and the BEF had finally put in an appearance between the two armies. Although more of a potential menace than an actual threat, it added to the weight of pessimism which was gripping

German Second Army headquarters. If von Bülow remained in position there was no guarantee that either von Hausen on his left or von Kluck on his right would be victorious. It was this precarious situation which dominated Hentsch's thoughts as he drove over to First Army headquarters early on the morning of 9 September. Yet almost as soon as Hentsch had left Montmort that morning, von Bülow – alarmed by intelligence of allied forces crossing the Marne between La Ferté-sous-Jouarre and Château Thierry – ordered the Second Army to retreat north of the Marne, informing OHL and von Kluck that he was moving north to avoid being outflanked.

At Mareuil-sur-Ourcq, Hentsch met von Kuhl, the First Army's chief of staff, who reportedly greeted him with the words: 'Well if the Second Army's going back, we can't stay here either.'[7] Despite the sour tone of the greeting, von Kuhl brought his OHL colleague quickly up to speed. The French Sixth Army had attacked in force that morning along the Ourcq and aerial reconnaissance had confirmed the BEF's advance into the gap north of the Petit Morin River. Von Gronau's IV Reserve Corps had been reduced significantly by the fighting but, added Kuhl, the situation was now under control with the arrival of the German IV and IX Corps. Incredibly neither officer conferred with von Kluck who was literally within hailing distance at his command post. Kuhl's confidence in the First Army being able to envelop Maunoury's left flank, and the total dismissal of any ability the BEF may have had of endangering the First Army's position, astounded Hentsch. There were too many imponderables at stake and it was clear to him that retreat was a necessity rather than an option. History has subsequently blamed Richard Hentsch for the German failure on the Marne but in reality he didn't initiate the retreat as it had already been set in motion by von Bülow earlier that morning. Reaching for the map which was spread out before them, Hentsch drew on it the lines of retreat which would begin the First Army's withdrawal to the Aisne valley.

Thus the Battle of the Marne was not decided by outstanding generalship or even by von Kluck's change of direction to the east of Paris, it was, as Correlli Barnett points out, a victory handed 'to the French and British by an unjustifiable failure of nerve and resolution on the part of the German command'.[8]

Was the Battle of the Marne over or was the cessation of the fighting phase merely a pause for breath while German forces retired to regroup behind the Aisne River? Herwig suggests that the Marne was the culmination of a series of battles which had begun with the French reversals in the earlier Battle of the Frontiers fought in eastern France and Belgium. There are grounds for extending this argument further and it is not entirely out of the question to suggest that the battles which opened with the German invasion of France and Belgium in early August 1914 were not concluded on the Marne but finally culminated on the high ground north of the River Aisne where the concept and the tangible manifestation of the Western Front was born.

Chapter 2

A Slow and Cautious Advance

*Our pursuit could not be called vigorous,
but then we were still a somewhat jaded army.*

Major Tom Bridges – *Alarms and Excursions*

Although Operational Order No. 16 signalled the final day of the BEF's retreat from Mons it still subjected the British Army to another full day's retirement in the wrong direction. For the officers and men of the 2nd Battalion Oxford and Buckinghamshire Light Infantry (2/Ox & Bucks) the reality of this was a further march of 10 miles which began from the field at Le Fay where they had spent the night of 4 September. That evening as Lieutenant Colonel Henry Davies – now in receipt of orders from 5 Infantry Brigade to advance the next day – surveyed his tired and footsore battalion bivouacked in yet another field northeast of Pézarches, he reflected on the thirteen days he and his men had been in retreat since the encounter at Mons on 23 August.

'Between 24th August and 5th September we did 178 miles in 12 marches and 1 halt day ... Never in my life have I felt anything like the degree of tiredness which I felt on this retreat. Everyone felt like this. I remember that we wondered if we should ever feel rested again and whether it would leave some permanent effect on us. The worst thing was the want of sleep. The next worst thing the heat of the sun and the thirst ... More than half the men were reservists who in spite of the route marches had not got into proper condition for the marching and consequently there were a good many sore feet ... We usually had no ambulances with us so that even the men who fell down unconscious with sun-stroke had to be got along on transport of some kind or on artillery limbers.'

Despite the physical hardships of the retreat, the experience of Davies and his men, who were part of General Douglas Haig's I Corps, had been relatively straightforward. Unlike several other brigades of I Corps they escaped the weight of the pursuing German forces and over the course of the retreat lost only one man.

Saturday 5 September began, for the majority of Lieutenant General Smith-Dorrien's II Corps units as it had for the previous thirteen days, with another long march. The II Corps experience since arriving in France had been very different to that of I Corps; not only had Smith-Dorrien's command fought a defensive battle at Mons but it had also stood again a few days later at Le Cateau on 26 August. To the men of the 1st Battalion Northumberland Fusiliers (1/NF) the news that they were to advance the next day was greeted with both relief and anticipation. At last they were going to get to grips with the enemy again. The Fusiliers had embarked for Le Havre with the 3rd Division on 13 August with 28 officers and 988 NCOs and men on the SS *Norman*. At Mons two companies of Fusiliers had defended a stretch of the Mons-Condé Canal by the lifting bridge at Mariette and afterwards fought a desperate rearguard action through Frameries. A few days later at the battle of Le Cateau they fought at Inchy alongside the three other battalions of 9 Infantry Brigade. Now, having arrived at Châtres after a long night march the battalion adjutant transcribed the names and regimental numbers of every casualty suffered by the battalion from enemy action. It was a long list, the battalion's war diary detailed over ninety men killed and wounded, not to mention those who had fallen by the wayside and were still on record as missing. But this was only the prelude to what was to come.

Casualties on this scale were something the men of the 1st Battalion Hampshire Regiment (1/Hampshire) had only recently been introduced to. Having missed the clash at Mons the battalion had arrived in France with the 4th Division on 22 August in time to join II Corps in its stand at Le Cateau. Deployed to a position southeast of Cattenières the battalion found itself digging in under fire astride the railway line and in the ensuing battle the battalion lost 10 of their officers killed, wounded or missing and nearly 180 other ranks killed and wounded. Although these were regular soldiers it had still been a bloody and shocking introduction to war and one which had had a profound effect upon Private George Pattenden. In his considered opinion, 'we marvellously escaped annihilation, we had to retire and they caught us with shrapnel, it was nearly a wholesale rout and slaughter.' Prone to outbursts of pessimism, Pattenden was a reservist who had served his time with the colours and had been called up in

August 1914. Like so many of the reservists serving with BEF during those fraught days of the retreat he suffered badly, 'my feet are very painful, I can just manage to shuffle along now', he wrote on 1 September, 'it is too terrible, one feels absolutely done up in heart, soul and spirit.' But regardless of his sore feet and the protestations in his diary, he managed four more days of hard marching before 11 Infantry Brigade reached the furthest point of its retreat south of Ozoir la Ferrière. On 31 August the 4th Division became part of the newly formed III Corps under the command of Lieutenant General William Pulteney, which was probably of little interest to George Pattenden and his comrades as they contemplated what the advance might bring.

On the morning of 6 September the three army corps of the BEF turned to take the offensive but because of Sir John French's decision to continue his retirement they found themselves over 10 miles behind the line from which Joffre intended to launch his planned offensive. Brigadier General Colin Ballard, writing with hindsight in 1931, felt that although there had been, 'a real confidence between Joffre and Sir John,' the day spent marching in the wrong direction could easily have been avoided.[9] But even when facing in the right direction the BEF was slow to get going. The *Official History* tells us that the BEF's advance on 6 September was preceded by, 'a wheel to the east pivoting on its right, so that it would come into line roughly parallel to the Grand Morin'. It was a manoeuvre which took up most of the morning and it was not until close to lunch-time that the BEF actually began its advance. Nevertheless the British were now advancing on a wide front with Allenby's Cavalry Division in contact with Conneau's cavalry corps and the Fifth Army on the right. Haig's I Corps was east of Rozay-en-Brie and further west, II Corps and the 3rd and 5th Cavalry Brigades were just south of Coulommiers on the Grand Morin.[10] In touch with Maunoury's Sixth Army on the left was III Corps and like it or not, Sir John French was now committed to playing his part in the Battle of the Marne.

In the strictest sense of the word there was no one deciding battle which could be attributed to victory on the Marne. Indeed there was little actual fighting on the Marne itself, the significant clashes were in the region of the River Ourcq but when the battle was given its name, Joffre chose *Marne* because the rivers of the region amongst which the battle had taken place all flowed into the Marne.[11] For the BEF, the fighting in which it was involved between 5 September up until the point when it reached the Aisne Valley on 13 September, was characterised by a series of seemingly unconnected and often frustrating engagements with German rearguard units as the British advanced towards the gap between the German First and Second Armies. As Captain John Darling of the 20th Hussars (20/Hussars) remarked afterwards, 'it seemed curious to note that we never heard of this battle until it was over.'[12] Yet the fact that the retreat had finally ended and they were now pursuing an enemy which had harassed them since 24 August, provided just the tonic which the weary men of the BEF had been waiting for. 28-year-old Lieutenant Arthur Acland, adjutant of the 1st Battalion Duke of Cornwall's Light Infantry, (1/DCLI) was delighted:

'It was such a joy to know that we were going to push our late pursuers back over their own footsteps. Perhaps what pleased us most was that the Germans were now going to suffer exceedingly for the way they had burnt and pillaged their way south. We had hardly ever held an outpost position or formed a rearguard without having had the hours of darkness lighted by the volume of flames issuing from one of the huge close-stacked hay and straw barns or from some of the perfectly kept farm buildings which those savages had delighted in setting alight ... Perhaps they thought their entry into Paris was a foregone conclusion and that they would never have need of the fodder and food they destroyed.'[13]

The precise *raison d'êtres* behind the much welcomed advance were still unclear in the minds of many in the BEF – the wider strategic movements to the north could only be guessed at – but for Brigadier General Count Edward Gleichen, in command of 15 Infantry Brigade, the turning of the tide brought with it a sea change in the spirits of his men. 'What had happened, or why we were suddenly to turn against the enemy after days of retreat, we could not conceive,' he wrote in his diary but the men 'marched twice as well, whistling and singing, back through Tournans and on to Villeneuve.'[14] It was an observation shared by Brigadier General Aylmer Haldane commanding 10 Infantry Brigade who remarked on, 'the difference in demeanour of the troops now that they had their heads turned towards the enemy.'

As was the case with the British wounded incurred during the retreat from Mons, the German ambulance transport proved to be woefully inadequate for the task now that it was the Germans' turn to retreat. German wounded were experiencing precisely the same trying circumstances which many of the British wounded had had to endure during the forced marching and fighting from Mons to points south of the Marne – that of being abandoned to face the ignominy of captivity.

Yet there was an essential difference; medical staff of the RAMC had generally remained behind to care for the British wounded for whom transport could not be found or who had been too ill to be moved. What was noticeable during the advance towards the Aisne was the almost total absence of German field ambulance staff from the field *lazarettes* attending the wounded. Field ambulance war diaries and personal accounts written by medical officers are punctuated with descriptions of the plight of unattended German wounded. Captain Robert Dolbey, the medical officer with the 2nd Battalion King's Own Scottish Borderers (2/KOSB) noted that, 'all along the roads in ditches, by haystacks, were German dead and wounded; victims, for the most part, of the shrapnel which hurried their flight'.[15] Dolbey also recounts attending to groups of German wounded, 'putting on first field dressings, making them comfortable, giving morphia and leaving instructions to await the field ambulances'.

But regardless of the change in demeanour noted by Haldane, the advance of the BEF was slow and cautious. To be fair it had no easy task to face. What lay ahead were five deeply incised river valleys, all of which, apart from some fordable sections of the Petit Morin, required bridges to be intact or constructed for the passage of troops. If the geography was against it, then the physical condition of the BEF was such that any advance was handicapped by the exhausted state of the men. Many units were very still much depleted by casualties sustained during the engagements of the past two weeks and reinforcements, although dribbling in slowly, were still not enough to replace the 488 officers and 19,532 men who had been lost since Mons.[16] It was not a situation which inspired confidence and was one which Sir John French, for all his lack of effective command and control over the previous weeks, felt keenly. Whilst we may agree that as a commander-in-chief he was almost certainly out of his depth, his apparent reluctance to commit the BEF to further offensive fighting stemmed from an overall – albeit misplaced – concern that his troops were incapable of offensive action.

The BEF's delay in moving northeast did not prevent its units from coming into contact with German forces on 6 September. The 1 Guards Brigade, under the command of Brigadier General Ivor Maxse, came under attack from German artillery and infantry units of Sixt von Arnim's IV Corps and with rumours of additional enemy forces in the area Douglas Haig halted the I Corps advance at Rozay-en-Brie. The sounds of battle were clearly audible to the advance units of the 2nd Division and Lieutenant Charles Paterson, adjutant of the 1st Battalion South Wales Borderers, (1/SWB) was keenly aware that, 'a battle had already begun eastward.' His frustration at being kept out of the fight is clear from his diary account, 'we move a bit nearer to the fight and then halt again.' Arriving at La Chapelle-Iger there was a further wait of several hours which, Paterson reports with undisguised exasperation, gave the German columns ample time to escape. Even with II Corps in support and RFC reconnaissance reports indicating clear roads ahead, by the time Haig resumed his advance at 3.30pm von Arnim had escaped to the Ourcq to reinforce von Kluck. It had been a poor start and one on which General Franchet d'Espèrey had every reason to vent his anger, particularly when it became apparent that, despite II Corps reaching the south bank of the Grand Morin without opposition, the BEF had only advanced 11 miles. 'A most tiring day,' wrote Paterson, 'though we have not done much.'

Monday, 7 September was hardly an improvement on the previous day. GHQ did not issue its orders for the day until 8.00am, prompted, it must be said, by delays in maintaining contact with adjacent French forces, but nevertheless the BEF was not underway until 11.00am that morning. Still concerned at the possibility of outrunning Conneau's cavalry corps on the right flank, GHQ's orders brought the BEF to a standstill by early afternoon with most units only moving forward 8 to 10 miles. II Corps, which had already reached the Grand Morin river hardly moved at all. At 5.00pm Lieutenant Alexander Johnston, the signalling officer with 7 Infantry Brigade, was still kicking his heels at Faremoutiers on the south bank of the Grand Morin wondering why they were not chasing the enemy hard:

> '*Surely our duty is according to Field Service Regulations "not to spare man or horse or gun in pursuing the enemy etc" ... Just heard that we are a long way ahead of the other divisions while we are well in front of our own which accounts for the delay as others have to catch us up. Also hear that, had our I Corps pushed a bit more, we ought to have cornered those Germans last night.'*[17]

Eventually his brigade moved east to Coulommiers where the four battalions of 7 Brigade collected their reinforcements at the railway station. That evening the only British forces across the Grand Morin were the 3rd and 5th Cavalry Brigades.

There was one piece of news on 7 September which was more positive and it came from the cavalrymen of Brigadier General Henry de Lisle's 2 Cavalry Brigade. Since Mons, de Lisle's men had been involved in countless skirmishes with enemy cavalry during the course of the retreat, although not all could be counted as having a satisfactory outcome. At Audregnies on 24 August 4/Dragoon Guards and 9/Lancers had charged the massed infantry and guns of the German

7th Infantry Division during a rearguard action which saw the 1st Battalion Cheshire Regiment (1/Cheshire) reduced to 7 officers and 200 other ranks and the surviving cavalrymen of 2 Cavalry Brigade scattered far and wide. This disastrous cavalry action was in complete contrast to the rearguard action at Cerizy four days later when Brigadier General Phillip Chetwode's 5 Cavalry Brigade put to flight a strong column of von Richthofen's 1st Cavalry Corps with an effective combination of dismounted rifle and machine-gun fire and mounted action.

Yet, to date, there had been no cavalry action between British and German cavalry which had involved lance against lance and as George Paget correctly points out in his *History of the British Cavalry*, the fight at Moncel and Vieux Villers on 7 September was unique in that it was probably the first and certainly the last occasion during the Great War in which British cavalry used their lances against an opponent similarly armed.[18] The action occurred between two troops of Lieutenant Colonel David Campbell's 9/Lancers and a squadron of the 1st Guard Dragoons commanded by *Rittmeister* von Gayling. Campbell's description is typically short and to the point:

> '*I put the two troops behind a haystack ... when I heard some firing from the east of the village and galloped over with my trumpeter to see what it was. At the north end I saw some lancers firing into a wood to the east ... I left my trumpeter and went out towards the wood and when about four hundred yards from it saw 100 to 120 German cavalry begin to mount.*'

Clearly intending to charge, the Guard Dragoons moved towards Campbell who galloped back to his haystack and brought his much smaller force into line and charged the advancing Germans. Campbell's horse being much fresher quickly outpaced the others and the colonel found himself a good 100 yards ahead of his men:

> '*It was, however, too late to wait, so I rode straight on, hoping for the best! As I approached the Germans, they closed in on their troop leader and their long iron lances presented a very disagreeable-looking wall. I directed my horse towards the troop leader, and when I got level with him I shot him as he was in the act of cutting at me with his sword. The next thing I remember was being carried very slowly over the tail of my horse to fall in a field. Both the Germans and our own men passed right over the top of me, but marvellous to relate not a single horse trod on my body.*'[19]

After the charge, during which Campbell and six others were wounded and three others killed, both sides withdrew just as the 18th Hussars arrived at Moncel in time to administer the *coup de grâce* with dismounted rifle and machine-gun fire. It was hardly a major action or one which contributed much to the advance, but at least someone had got to grips with the enemy and had inflicted some damage.

* * *

The orders issued by GHQ for 8 September were lacking in any clear directive other than for all three British corps to continue the advance and attack the enemy wherever they were found. In contrast to previous days, British units were on the road by 6.00am which soon put them in touch with the German rearguards on the Petit Morin. At Sablonnières the 5th Dragoon Guards (Queen's Bays) were caught off guard by the size and strength of the German rearguard. Lieutenant Algernon Lamb was with the troop which successfully took the railway bridge but was prevented from carrying the river bridge by a barricade:

'*A force of Germans were holding the village of Sablonnières. The 1st Cavalry Brigade took up positions on the south side of the valley of the Petit Morin River, opposite Sablonnières. The brigaded machine guns did a lot of firing across the valley which is very wooded, and the slopes held on the far side by the enemy look pretty high and steep. Later, we galloped on down the road under rifle fire from across the river, and came into another position without losing any men, close to Sablonnières station.*'[20]

It was a similar story all along the Petit Morin, German rearguards had effectively brought the cavalry to a standstill and any further progress was on hold until the infantry arrived.

By 9.30am the advance guard of the 1st Division, the 1st Battalion the Black Watch (1/Black Watch), was 2 miles to the east of Sablonnières at Bellot. Here it found French cavalry in possession of the village and, like the British cavalry to the west, unable to make progress. Undeterred, the Black Watch pushed on through the village and into the wooded slopes of the valley on the north side and with the sound of firing quite audible to the west, the battalion turned towards Sablonnières where it came under heavy fire from elements of the *Garde Jäger battalion* and the *Garde Kürassiere Regiment*. This was a strong rearguard and it was not until the arrival of a company of the 1st Battalion Queen's Own Cameron Highlanders (1/Camerons), supported by dismounted troopers of 4 Cavalry Brigade, that the heights were eventually taken at 1.00pm and the rearguard evicted.

Although Sablonnières was a relatively minor skirmish and one of a number of similar episodes along the Petit Morin that morning, the casualties had not been insignificant. Algernon Lamb noted, 'a lot of German wounded and dead lying about' and plenty of prisoners. In addition to their eighteen wounded, the Black Watch lost two of their officers, 31-year-old Captain Charles Dalglish and Lieutenant Ewen Wilson together with eight other ranks, while the Cameron Highlanders lost Privates Ford and Davidson killed and Privates Macdonald, Hay and McShane wounded. Most notable amongst the cavalry casualties was the loss of 38-year-old Captain John Norwood who had won the Victoria Cross whilst serving as a second lieutenant with the Queen's Bays in South Africa fourteen years previously. Nineteen casualties of the action now rest in a quiet corner of the riverside communal cemetery at Sablonnières.

While some had to fight their way over the Petit Morin others had little or no contact with the enemy on 8 September. Brigadier General Edward Gleichen observed that the noise of battle, although 'going on just ahead of us or on both flanks,' never got within striking distance of 15 Infantry Brigade. They crossed the river at St-Cyr-sur-Morin, sweating profusely as they climbed the steep hill out of the valley towards the Montapéine crossroads:

'We were in a curious position, for there was a big fight going on amid some burning villages in the plain far on our left – I don't know what division – probably the 4th – and a smaller fight parallel to us on the right, not two miles off; and we were marching calmly along the road in column.'[21]

Gleichen was correct about the division to his left. Pulteney's III Corps had met little resistance until late morning when it had reached the south banks of the Marne at La Ferté-sous-Jouarre, at which point the advance units discovered the bridges destroyed and a strong German rearguard on the north bank. As 9/Field Company, Royal Engineers, approached the Marne at La Ferté with 10 Infantry Brigade, Lieutenant Bernard Young idly wondered what condition he would find the main road bridge to be in. Less than a week previously, during the retreat south, 26/Field Company had successfully blown one of the stone arches of the bridge, now here they were again attempting to re-cross the Marne and would most probably have to construct a temporary bridge to get III Corps across!

As dusk fell on 8 September the BEF had only averaged around 12 miles and apart from III Corps had not yet reached the Marne. However, the next morning the advance guard of II Corps, which was further east, found the Marne bridges intact and after some initial dithering were on the north bank by 9.00am. I Corps was across by lunchtime but there the advance sputtered to a halt in the face of determined German rearguard actions and from what appeared to be 'a lack of determination' on the part of brigade commanders. At La Ferté-sous-Jouarre, practically the whole of III Corps was stationary. Lieutenant Cecil Brereton, a gunner officer with 68/Battery, arrived at La Ferté to find:

'The infantry were lining a street and the officer commanding told me anyone who showed their nose round the corner was as good as dead. Decided not to do so. All the houses on the north bank were loopholed and the place and hill opposite bristling with machine guns which were skilfully concealed.'[22]

The town was scoured for enough material with which to construct a pontoon bridge and Bernard Young and his sappers got to work:

'We moved down to La Ferté to bridge the river; street fighting and sniping was still going on and we didn't get near the river till noon at the earliest. It was then still impossible to bridge and eventually infantry were ferried over to clear out machine-gun posts which still covered the only possible bridge site near the destroyed road bridge … However we were far from idle and collected barrels, scantling and planking etc for the bridge. Barrels were collected from nearby cellars, their contents being run to waste; we found quite a lot of Bosche in the process, many dead drunk. I am glad to say none of our men succumbed to such temptation; all realized there was too much to be done.'[23]

The actual bridge building began at 5.45pm on 9 September and was completed by 6.30am the following day. In 12 hours the engineers had built a 218 foot long bridge constructed largely from local materials and boats found on the river. As Bernard Young commented in 1933, if III Corps had got its act together and anticipated the crossing by bringing the Bridging Train up quickly, 'the Marne – as far as we were concerned – could have been bridged in a quarter of the time'.

Young's confidence in his bridge was not entirely shared by the men and wagons of 20/Field Ambulance who crossed the pontoon bridge later that day. Lieutenant Travis Hampson felt the bridge appeared to be a little flimsy and was quite relieved when he was safely on the other side:

> 'The pontoon bridge didn't look too strong. It was made with RE bridging pontoons (needless to say the road bridge had been blown up) but there were not enough to span the river, and some oddments of civilian boats had to be used as well. After all that had gone over it already we had another wait while it was strengthened, and even then is sagged a good deal as our heavy GS wagons went over one by one. The ordinary bridges had all been blown up, and there was nowhere else to cross anywhere near. Here we saw the results of the shelling of the town by both sides. Many of the houses were complete ruins, and all showed rifle bullet and shrapnel holes.'[24]

George Pattenden, by now travelling with the battalion transport as his feet had given up on him, crossed over the pontoon bridge at La Ferté-sous-Jouarre at 9.00am: 'Today we are now on the German line of retreat, the state of the place is awful. It is impossible to describe the state of affairs, houses upside down, bottles in thousands'. Pattenden was very much aware of a new tempo being injected into the advance once they were across the Marne, a change of pace induced by GHQ, which, encouraged by the retirement of the German First and Second Armies, now appeared to throw caution to the wind and ordered the BEF to pursue the Germans with all haste. Von Kluck was at this time moving east across the British front and Sir John French, all too late, finally realised there was a real chance of outpacing him.

Although 10 September was perhaps the most successful day of the advance so far with II Corps in contact with the enemy for most of the day, the shortcomings of poor communications were amplified by several 'friendly fire' incidents. Not only did the 1st Divisional artillery open fire on the Royal Sussex and Loyal North Lancashire battalions, but to make matters worse they were joined by the 2nd Division artillery and units of the Royal Horse Artillery. The Royal Sussex war diary rather generously attributes the incident to the fact that it was raining hard and the battalion were wearing their rain capes, the 'artillery thinking apparently we were Germans'. At the time the battalion were engaged with a strongly entrenched enemy at Priez and finding themselves under fire from both sides, Brigadier General Edward Bulfin who was commanding 2 Brigade was forced to order a temporary retirement. It is not clear how many of the seventeen killed and eighty-three wounded were the result of friendly fire. Not to be outdone, the 3rd Divisional artillery shelled the Royal Berkshires and King's Royal Rifle Corps at Hautvesnes later in the morning,

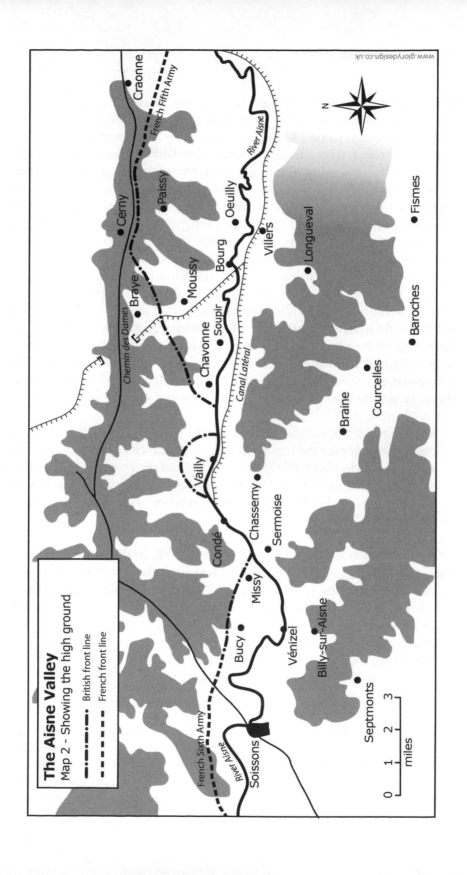

The Aisne Valley

Map 2 - Showing the high ground

—··—··— British front line

— — — French front line

N

French Fifth Army

Craonne

Cerny

Paissy

River Aisne

Oeuilly

Chemin des Dames

Brave

Moussy

Bourg

Villers

Longueval

Fismes

Chavonne

Soupir

Canal Latéral

Courcelles

Baroches

Vailly

Braine

Chassemy

Sermoise

Condé

Missy

Bucy

Vénizel

Billy-sur-Aisne

French Sixth Army

River Aisne

Soissons

Septmonts

0   1   2   3

miles

wounding four men. It was, wrote Sergeant Reeve of 16/Battery RFA, 'an unfortunate occurrence', and one which Douglas Haig took seriously enough to halt I Corps near Neuilly and regroup.

10 September was the last chance the BEF forward units had of catching the retreating Germans and by nightfall it was painfully obvious that this was not going to happen. An RFC reconnaissance report logged by Captains Robert Boger and Robin Grey from 5 Squadron on 9 September, confirmed long columns of von Kluck's 5th Division moving northeast through Ocquerre but fresh orders from Joffre, which turned the direction of advance of the BEF and the French Fifth and Sixth Armies to the northeast, were too slow in materializing.[25] Thus on the morning of Friday, 11 September, British divisions found themselves sharing overburdened roads, not only between themselves but with the French. The new direction had effectively narrowed the BEF frontage and an already overstretched staff now had to face the challenge of squeezing the army into their new positions. Cecil Brereton's battery of six 18-pounder guns was not the only unit to feel the burden of Operational Order No. 21:

> '*Roused at 3.00am but did not move until about 5.30am. How we wished the staff would take the trouble to work out time and space problems. Had a longish halt in the middle of the morning and then continued on our way along evil smelling roads till we were again blocked by the French near Dammard – our division and a French division were apparently allotted the same road.*'[26]

To make matters worse it began to rain heavily in the afternoon and as the long columns of British and French units dragged themselves slowly northeast, the German Army retired practically unhindered to the Aisne. Brereton was not alone in cursing the congestion on the roads, Lieutenant Alexander Johnston and 7 Infantry Brigade soon found themselves sharing the same road as 5 Infantry Brigade and it was not until they passed through Neuilly St Front that they finally got clear. Johnston's diary continued to reflect the frustration he felt at the pace of the advance:

> '*As I have feared, we have let the Germans get clear away with very little loss. Even though we may have got ahead of the other divisions on our right and left, and might have even risked getting an advanced guard knocked about, surely we should have harried the enemy as much as possible. I expect we shall find that the enemy will have been able to retire more or less*

unmolested on to a strong fortified position somewhere further north which will give us a great deal of trouble.'[27]

Little did he realize exactly how far his prophetic diary entry would reflect a future reality.

As the rain continued to pour it exacerbated the already poor state of the roads and the growing congestion which caused delay after frustrating delay and misery for the marching infantry. For Captain James Pennyman, the machine-gun officer with 2/KOSB, Saturday 12 September was,'cold with incessant rain', during which he spent 'a wretched day listening to much gunning southeast of Soissons and wondering what was up.' It was little different for the men of 16 Battery. It was raining when they got up at 3.30am and continued to rain for the remainder of the day. That evening after a difficult day, Reeve and his men managed to find dry billets somewhere near Brenelle:

> *'The village square was in a state of chaos. Cavalry riding through on one side, transport held up on the other, and infantry trying to get along in the centre. Officers shouting orders and the answering back in the pitch darkness added to the confusion and to crown it all it was pouring down a deluge … after struggling through this mass and getting boots full of water we found a billet in a farmyard.'*[28]

Accordingly, on the evening of 12 September the only British units to reach the heights above the south bank of the Aisne were the vanguard of III Corps and a few isolated advanced cavalry patrols. North of the Aisne the German Army – having blown most of the bridges – consolidated its defensive positions on the high ground overlooking the river valley. Their geographical positions may have been formidable, but the gap between the German First and Second Armies which had opened up during the battle of the Marne remained and what's more it was now positioned partly on the British line of advance.

Chapter 3

Parrying the Blow

It is easier to hold ground than to take it.

Carl von Clausewitz

Before we continue with the advance of the BEF over the Aisne we should take a moment to consider the deployment and movement of the German Army after its retreat from the Marne. As far as British and French forces were concerned the German Army was in full retreat and, 'nobody doubted the beginning of the end had come'. The enemy, reckoned Christopher Baker-Carr, 'had shot his bolt and we had him on the run.' Baker-Carr was a former officer of the Rifle Brigade who had retired as a captain in 1906. On the outbreak of war in 1914 he went to France with the BEF as one of the twenty-five civilian volunteer drivers with the Royal Automobile Club Volunteer Force whose task it was to chauffer senior officers of the staff around the front. Baker-Carr's judgement of the state of the enemy retreating in front of him was one also held by Second Lieutenant Jack Hay, an intelligence officer attached to GHQ. Hay was sure that the Germans would, 'have to fall right back, away past St Quentin and Le Cateau … to the line of the Sambre, where they'll want more shifting.' The 'hardest job' he felt was going to be pushing them back past the line of the Rhine.

Whether this view had been influenced by GHQ – which was now convinced the Allies would chase the Germans all the way back to the Rhine – is anyone's guess but it did point to the new wave of optimism abroad at GHQ; an optimism which General Horace Smith-Dorrien tempered with a little more caution. Writing on 10 September, Smith-Dorrien went as far as admitting that, 'today is the first that has made me come to the conclusion that there is real evidence of our enemy being shaken,' but he went on to add:

*'The roads are littered and the [German] retreat is hurried; but I still
realize that the main bodies of the German Corps in front of us may be in
perfect order and that the people we are engaged with are strong
rearguards, who are sacrificing themselves to let their main bodies get far
enough away for fresh operations against us.'[29]*

The roads were indeed littered with all manner of debris, Captain
James Pennyman remembered marching through, 'unsavoury German
remains' and 'debris of all kinds along the roads, consisting of wagons
and things they had got rid of in order to hasten their progress, a dead
horse every 10 yards and a fair number of soldiers'. Many British
accounts of those wet and exhausting days before the line of the Aisne
was reached tell of the large numbers of empty wine and spirit bottles
left by the retreating Germans, citing this as another indication of the
moral collapse of what must be a drunken German Army. But 'Jim'
Pennyman was sure that had the Germans been drunk, as the number
of empty bottles would seem to have suggested, 'we should have
caught them.' The scattered bottles pointed, he thought, to an,
'organized distribution of liquor rather than indiscriminate looting'.

As we now know, there was no moral collapse on the part of the
retreating German Army or indeed a relentless pursuit! The Germans
may have drunk an inordinate amount of alcohol but the BEF only
came into serious contact with the enemy rearguards sporadically as it
moved north – sandwiched as it was between the French Sixth and
Fifth Armies. Correlli Barnett attributes this almost entirely to, 'good
German staff work and limp leadership and sheer exhaustion on the
allied side'.[30] Barnett's belief that good German staff work was evident
during the retreat to the Aisne contrasts greatly with the poor quality
of staff work in the BEF, a running sore which would remain to haunt
the British for some time to come.

The staff corps of an army is akin to the middle management of a
large organization and without an effective staff an army cannot
function. It is the staff officer who is responsible for everything from
troop movements to supply to the distribution of mail from home and
there is no doubt that the skill of its staff working in conjunction with
senior officers gave the German Army a decisive edge on the
battlefield. With sixty years of successful battlefield encounters behind
it, the German Army of 1914 could field over twenty-five regular army
corps and sixteen reserve corps which were serviced and administered
by a core of trained and experienced staff officers. When war was
declared in August 1914 it is estimated that the British Army had only
447 qualified staff officers who had passed the two-year staff course at

Camberley and as a result could put '*psc*' after their name. Moreover, by the end of 1914, when the officer shortage became desperate, many of those qualified staff officers who were not already serving with fighting units returned to their units to fill much-needed vacancies at battalion level.

This deficiency of good staff officers in the BEF had an enormous impact when war came in 1914. There were simply not enough qualified staff officers available to fill the void which existed, and those who were available were largely inexperienced when compared to their German counterparts. Indeed, when it came to the logistics of managing a land force the size of the BEF, not one of the senior core of British commanders had experience of handling more than a single division in the field; and although there were some very capable individuals serving on the staff, the lack of regard held by many regimental officers towards their counterparts on the staff was still in evidence and part of British Army culture.

This contrasted hugely with the prestige which accompanied graduation from the three–year staff course at the German *Kriegsakademie*. By 1871 the contribution of staff officers trained at the *Kriegsakademie* to victories on the battlefield had been linked directly to their extensive training in the art and science of war. German staff education can be traced back to 1765 when Frederick the Great saw the need to educate officers who advised him on military matters. It wasn't until 1801 that any similar education was established in England for the training of staff officers and it was only the *débâcle* of the Crimean War which accelerated the opening of a dedicated Staff College at Camberley in 1858 where students undertook a two-year course. If further evidence of efficient German staff work in 1914 was required one only had to look at the huge turning movement ordered by von Kluck when he swung his forces through ninety degrees to face Maunoury's Sixth Army on the Ourcq during the Battle of the Marne. Such a huge and extremely efficient movement of a vast body of troops should be seen in contrast to the painstaking manoeuvring of the BEF during the advance to the Aisne.

In many ways the British Army of 1914 was still torn by a conflict generated by its relatively new role as part of a European alliance and its continuing colonial responsibilities; a clash which manifested itself, for example, in the tactical doctrine used by the artillery – something which will be examined a little more closely in Chapter 12. Although politically the BEF was committed to a role in Europe and, 'as divisional units they trained for the continent; as part of the old colonial system they trained drafts for the army overseas'.[31] It was this dual role of battalions based in Britain which was principally responsible for the large number of reservists being called in August 1914 up to bring the home battalions up to war strength. To a certain extent the home battalions were always under strength whilst the overseas battalions were usually at full complement. In reality, despite the political will, the British Army of 1914 was not designed for a European war, hence as the junior partner in 1914 the learning curve of the BEF was a steep one, as historian Paddy Griffith pointed out:

> 'Despite its enviable regimental cohesion ... the BEF of August 1914 was scarcely an instrument for total war. It was in no sense designed to act as the dominant partner in the main battle against the main enemy in the main theatre.'[32]

Not only had the retreat from Mons been a close-run affair for the BEF but it had also highlighted the limitations in command and control exercised by Sir John French and GHQ. Now, faced with the German Army entrenching on the higher ground above the north bank of the River Aisne, the line of its learning curve was about to become steeper.

* * *

The Prussian military theorist, Carl von Clausewitz, held a simple view of defence: 'A battle is defensive', he opined, 'if we await the attack – await, that is, the appearance of the enemy in front of our lines and within range'.[33] But while he makes the point that defensive warfare is intrinsically stronger than the offensive, he goes on to say that, 'it would contradict the idea of war to regard defence as its final purpose'. His treatise on defence, which he put together in the early nineteenth century, may almost have been written with the Aisne in mind:

> 'It is self evident that it is the defender who primarily benefits from the terrain. His superior ability to produce surprise by virtue of the strength and direction of his own attack stems from the fact that the attack has to approach on roads and paths on which it can easily be observed; the defender's position, on the other hand, is concealed and virtually invisible to his opponent.'[34]

Of course students of Clausewitz were not confined to the German Army, despite the optimism of British GHQ with regard to the retiring Germans. There were several individuals marching towards the Aisne who had already come to the same conclusions as the German strategists: if the German Army could hold its position along the heights of the Aisne Valley it would be in a very strong position to parry the blow which was approaching and perhaps build on their defensive positions by transforming defence into a new offensive action.

By nightfall on 12 September the pursuit of the German Army had effectively been concluded; its units were across the Aisne and consolidating their positions north of the river. *Hauptmann* Walter Bloem's account confirms that the German 10 Infantry Brigade crossed the Aisne on 12 September near Soissons and marched via Bucy-le-Long up the valley to Chivres, where it was informed of the intention to reform on the northern heights of the Aisne valley.[35] The brigade had marched with von Kluck's First Army since it had left Frankfurt on 7 August 1914. Between 17 August and 12 September it had marched over 400 miles through Belgium and France with very little, if any, respite. Bloem, a reserve officer with the 12th Brandenburg Grenadiers, had already encountered the BEF at Mons on 23 August where his battalion had been severely mauled by 1/Royal West Kents and 2/KOSB at St Gillian. After Mons the battalion had marched continuously, almost to within sight of Paris. 'For three whole weeks', wrote Bloem, 'we had not a single rest day, nor the suggestion of one'. At the conclusion of the battles on the Marne in early September, Bloem's battalion had been reduced to two composite companies, yet regardless of the casualties and the fatigue it was still with a sense of disbelief that they received their orders to retreat:

'At breakfast the next morning came a curious order which further depressed our sorely tried spirits: The regiment will assemble at 7am in the hollow north of Sancy, facing north. North! Backwards in fact! … The men are to be told that the future movements of the corps are in no way to be regarded as a retreat.'[36]

It is unlikely that Bloem and his men had any inkling of the potentially serious nature of the yawning gap which still existed between von Kluck and von Bülow, a gap which on 13 September ran from the eastern village of Berry au Bac to Ostel in the west. Although it was a gap in the defences it was one which was hardly wide open; thrust into the break were three weakened divisions from the 2nd Cavalry Corps under the command of General Georg von der Marwitz.

Although these thinly-spread German units were all that stood between the advancing Allied armies and disaster, they did have the advantage of terrain and a strong defensive position behind them.

However, if the gap could not be held – and the line were to be successfully pierced and exploited by the enemy – then the retreat would in all probability have to continue, the effects of which could easily spell the end of German ambitions in France. In spite of the seriousness of the situation von der Marwitz could spare very few troops to defend this vital piece of ground. The 5th Cavalry Division had already been detached to the Third Army and the 4th Cavalry Division was on the right flank of the First Army northeast of Rethondes at Tracey le Mont. However, by nightfall on 12 September both the 2nd and the 9th Cavalry Divisions were in place north of the Chemin des Dames – the 2nd at Filain and the 9th at Chavignon – while the Jäger battalions of von Richthofen's 1st Cavalry Corps were under the command of III Corps to the north of Condé and at Vailly.

Nonetheless, to fully appreciate the extent of the troop movements required to reinforce the defences on the Aisne we must return briefly to 7 September when von Bülow pulled back his right flank behind the Petit Morin River and in effect increased the gap between himself and von Kluck. The response from OHL was to order the German XV Corps and the 7th Cavalry Division from the German left in Alsace to move post-haste to the extreme right of the German advance to outflank the French Sixth Army which was threatening von Kluck. Ordered to join them, and form the nucleus of a new German Seventh Army was the VII Reserve Corps, consisting of the 13th and 14th Reserve Infantry Divisions, which had been laying siege to Maubeuge.

The retreat of the BEF and the French Fifth Army after the Battle of Mons in August had left the fortress at Maubeuge and its important railway junction isolated. The town sat close to the border between Belgium and France on the River Sambre and was defended by fifteen forts and gun batteries totalling some 435 guns. The permanent garrison of 35,000 troops was initially strengthened by its selection as the advance base of the BEF but with the subsequent retreat of the BEF and the French Fifth Army on 23 August 1914, the town came under siege by the Germans on 25 August. Initially it was thought the garrison might delay the German advance but instead, in keeping with the timetable demands of the Schlieffen Plan, von Bülow detached General Hans von Zwehl and VII Reserve Corps to besiege Maubeuge, leaving the remainder of the army to continue the advance into France. The bombardment of the forts surrounding Maubeuge began a few days later on 29 August and by 5 September the heavy artillery of VII Reserve Corps had reduced four of the key forts to rubble and broken the outer ring of defence. Two days later the garrison surrendered.

The 63-year-old Hans von Zwehl had been recalled from retirement to command the VII Reserve Corps in 1914. During his career, which began in December 1870, he had commanded both 30 Infantry Brigade and the 13th Infantry Division and despite his age was still a formidable commander. Initially von Zwehl had been under orders to move towards Antwerp when three battalions of British marines had been landed at Ostend on 27 and 28 August as part of the ill-fated operation to relieve the beleaguered port. But with the crisis developing on the Marne these orders had been rescinded and, leaving five battalions to garrison Maubeuge, the remainder of VII Corps departed on 10 September to march to La Fère where it was to join the Seventh Army.[37] Events on the Aisne conspired to alter these orders yet again. At 9.40am on 12 September, VII Reserve Corps was redirected to Laon which von Zwehl's Corps reached at 6.00am on the morning of 13 September, rested for three hours – during which time its commander was appraised of the situation on the Aisne – and completed the final 12 miles to the Chemin des Dames. During the course of 13 September von Zwehl's men had marched over 40 miles and lost some twenty-five percent of its strength to fatigue.

Captured documents give us some idea of the relentless nature and urgency of the march south; the war diary of the adjutant of the 3rd Battalion of the German Reserve Infantry Regiment 53 (3/RIR 53) places the 14th Reserve Division 1 kilometre south of Crecy-sur-Serre at midnight on 12 September. Having had very little sleep during the previous twenty-four hours the battalion was once more on the road at 12.50am on the morning of 13 September en route for Laon:

> 'The 3rd Battalion, 53rd Regiment followed by Machine Gun Company advance to within 1 kilometre south of Montigny where it joins up with the 16th Infantry Regiment. Order of dress – sturm anzug (storming order). Iron rations and all cartridges. March via Chery-les-Pouilly-Laon-Festieux. Halt 10.11 at Bievry-Montberault-Chamouille. Division to be placed in a position of readiness on the heights of Chamouille.'[38]

OHL had placed von Bülow in overall command of the First and Second Armies as well as the Seventh; his orders were for the VII Reserve Corps to move with all speed into the gap on the left of the First Army. Leaving Laon, von Zwehl's Corps moved southwest towards Chavonne, the 13th Reserve Division deployed towards Braye-en-Laonnois and the 14th Reserve Division to Cerny. Yet another change of orders issued at 11.00 am on 13 September ordering the VII Reserve Corps to Berry-au-Bac where the right of von Bülow's Second Army was being threatened by

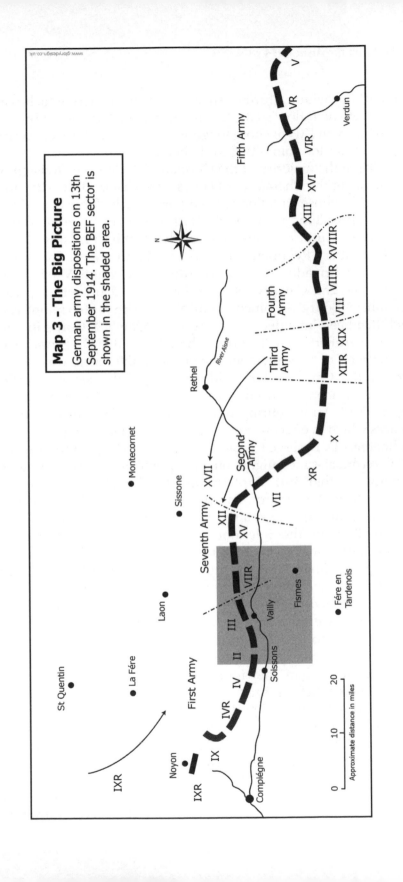

Map 3 – The Big Picture

German army dispositions on 13th September 1914. The BEF sector is shown in the shaded area.

N

First Army

Second Army

Third Army

Fourth Army

Fifth Army

Seventh Army

River Aisne

St Quentin

La Fére

Noyon

Montecornet

Sissone

Laon

Rethel

Compiégne

Soissons

Vailly

Fismes

Fére en Tardenois

Verdun

IXR

IXR

IX

IVR

IV

II

III

VIIR

XV

XII

XVII

VII

XR

X

XIIR

XIX

VIII

VIIIR

XVIIIR

XIII

XVI

VIR

VR

V

Approximate distance in miles

0   10   20

www.glorydesign.co.uk

the French, provides a further snapshot of the anxiety which was still prevalent at von Bülow's HQ. It was – unfortunately for the British – an order which von Zwehl chose to ignore. As far as he was concerned his troops were far too committed to change direction.

By 2.00pm the majority of the German 13th Reserve Division was in position along the Chemin des Dames northeast of Braye, the adjutant of 3/RIR 53, whose battalion formed part of 27 Reserve Brigade, found himself approaching Cerny with, '11th Company as advanced guard and Machine Gun Company, main body of 10th Company, 2 batteries of Field Artillery Regiment, 9th and 12th Companies'. That afternoon 25 *Landwehr* Brigade – which according to General Maximilian von Poseck,[39] the 2nd Cavalry Division had 'picked up retiring from the direction of Bourg' – joined them along with 1,200 reinforcements which had been intended for the Second Army's X Corps in addition to a horse artillery *Abteilung* from the 9th Cavalry Division.[40] Thus by the afternoon of 13 September the crisis on the Aisne was practically over for the German Army. Moreover, on the same day Belgian operations emanating from Antwerp had come to an end with the Belgian Field Army retiring into and taking cover behind the city's defences which in effect released Berthold von Deimling's XV and Max von Boehm's IX Reserve Corps for immediate duty on the Aisne.

RFC reconnaissance flights on 13 September were again hampered by poor weather but Captain Shephard and Lieutenant Kenlis Atkinson from 4 Squadron based at Saponay, northwest of Fère-en-Tardenois, managed to get airborne despite the, 'tremendous gale and low cloud', with the intention of observing the fighting east of Soissons, but it was to be a short flight as the wind proved to be to strong for the flimsy BE2, forcing them down near Orme. There was more success later when Atkinson was again observing with George Raleigh and this time they were airborne for 'a little over an hour and saw the whole German position, no emplacements yet dug, so they are just getting into it'. Unfortunately whilst over Cerny, Raleigh accidentally switched the engine off, forcing them to glide down and land at Revillon where they found a brigade of French infantry which, much to their relief, 'did not fire ... but were very nice to us'. What Raleigh and Atkinson had probably seen was the vanguard units of the German VII Reserve Corps arriving and preparing positions on the Chemin des Dames; not only had the gap been closed but it had also been strengthened by relatively fresh troops which had not taken part in the retreat from the Marne.

The question inevitably arises; how close did the British and French come to exploiting the gap and establishing themselves firmly on the

Chemin des Dames? The *Official History* tells us that there was a difference of some two hours between the first units of VII Reserve Corps arriving and the initial contact with British cavalry patrols. This may very well be the case but as I Corps was in no position to advance at the time it is of little consequence. Despite the reconnaissance report from 4 Squadron, which presumably reached GHQ at Fère-en-Tardenois sometime on 13 September, it was obviously still not clear to Sir John French that German troop movements from the north had in fact reinforced von der Marwitz. A further indication of substantial German troop movements had been observed on 12 September by two pilots from 2 Squadron who were forced to land behind enemy lines in a small field near Anizy-le-Château after their machine developed a fault. Incredibly Lieutenants Leonard Dawes and Wilfred Freeman landed their damaged aircraft between two large German columns which were on the roads either side of them and hid until nightfall in a nearby wood. Evading capture they navigated across country and swam the river eventually returning to their unit on 14 September, by which time the intelligence they had to report was of little use. If – as was probable – they had observed fresh units moving towards the Aisne and successfully reported their information it may well have encouraged I Corps to press forward with more haste on 13 September.

However, British intelligence on 13 September, devoid of the 2 Squadron report, suggested that the gap had not been substantially reinforced and there was little in front of I Corps but a strong force of cavalry and five batteries entrenched on the Chemin des Dames. Up until lunchtime this estimate was essentially correct, which together with the news that the French 35th Division had crossed the Aisne at Pontavert and that Conneau's cavalry were already pressing the enemy at the eastern end of the Chemin des Dames, made the possibility of a break-through a realistic prospect to Douglas Haig at I Corps HQ.

It was not to be. By 1.00pm on 13 September the advance guard of Haig's I Corps – 2 Infantry Brigade – had reached the top of the spur north of Bourg enabling patrols from C Squadron, 15/Hussars, to press on beyond Moulins and Vendresse and to reconnoitre towards the Chemin des Dames. Major Frederick Pilkington soon reported contact with the enemy in the form of, 'large numbers north of Vendresse with artillery in position'. Later that afternoon another RFC reconnaissance flight sighted German columns moving towards Bourg from the direction of Chivy and, potentially more worrying for GHQ, the concentration of yet more enemy forces north of Courtecon. This time there could be no doubt that a fresh army corps was moving towards the Aisne and that substantial troop movements were taking place along the Chemin des Dames. Major Archibald 'Sally' Home was at Troyon on 13 September with 2 Cavalry Brigade and recalled seeing 'masses of German cavalry moving all along the skyline on the main Rheims-Soissons road, we watched them for about two or three hours and estimated them to be a strong division'. He does not put a time on these observations but they may very well have been units of the 2nd and 9th German Cavalry Divisions.

The war diary of I Corps on 14 September indicates that the I Corps divisional commanders were aware that RIR 56 and RIR 53 were in position in the 'Cerny-Troyon neighbourhood' together with two *Landwehr* regiments, but it would not be for some days before the complete picture of German forces opposing them on the Chemin des Dames became apparent.[41] What was not clear to the British at the time was the extent to which German units were being trawled from elsewhere and diverted towards the Aisne in order to bolster the forces already engaged along the Chemin des Dames. Consequently it was the arrival of fresh German units such as the mixed detachment from von Kirchbach's XII Saxon Reserve Corps, 50 Brigade from the Fourth Army's XVIII Corps and the five battalions from von Deimling's XV Corps which would finally put an end to any hopes of a breakthrough.

The strength of German forces facing Smith-Dorrien's II Corps was never in doubt. Von Lochow's III Corps consisting of the 5th and 6th Infantry Divisions and 34 Brigade from IX Corps with two field artillery brigades were firmly in position by last light on 13 September; whilst in front of the British 4th Division the 3rd and 4th Infantry Divisions of von Linsingen's II Corps, supported by 3 and 4 Artillery Brigades, were digging in above Bucy-le-Long. Overall this was still a formidable fighting force and despite the attrition of the previous weeks there were at least 100 – albeit under strength – German infantry battalions opposing the seventy-two tired and weakened infantry battalions of the BEF, a figure which would only be increased to eighty-four with the arrival of the 6th Division on 19 September.

Von Bülow was now nominally back in charge on the German side and this time he was clearly on the offensive. His orders for 14 September were for a general attack to consolidate the line of his three armies with the end result of pushing the Allied armies back over the Aisne. Even so, there was still doubt at OHL as to the successful outcome of the decision to stand and fight on the Aisne heights. Von Bülow entered the fray on 14 September with the OHL directive still on his desk: 'If the First Army cannot hold the Aisne valley, it should retire in good time in the general direction of La Fère, behind the river valley'.

Chapter 4

Bridges over Troubled Waters

The temporary pontoon bridge the Engineers had put up, further down the river, had just been blown up by a shell, and the only way for me was the canvas raft which, by chance, might still be intact.

Captain Robert Dolbey – describing his passage across the Aisne.

A t 4.30am on 11 September, after completing their mammoth task of bridging the Marne at La Ferté-sous-Jouarre, the officers and men of 9/Field Company together with their weary contemporaries in 7/Field Company were told to lift their bridging equipment and move to the head of the 4th Division column in order to be available to bridge the Aisne should it be necessary. It was another case of divisional staff officers writing out orders and expecting them to take effect immediately. The sappers were quite used to this by now, during the retreat orders and counter-orders had, on more than one occasion, placed them in some considerable danger. More to the point perhaps, was that often many of these orders were very confusing and despite the high level of complaints from senior RE officers, the staff at divisional level still failed to align the vital work of bridging with the movement of troops.

As Lieutenant Bernard Young and his colleagues well knew, marching with all their equipment to catch up with and then attempt to pass the divisional column was 'no light undertaking'. Not only did they have to share the road with numerous motorised supply columns, which inevitably overtook them and then met them again on their return journey, but also there were also ambulance convoys to pass before they came into contact with the main body of marching troops which made up the 4th Division. A division on the march in 1914 occupied some 15 miles of road and included over 5,000 horses and seventy or more artillery pieces – and that was without including the slow-moving divisional ammunition column which took up another one and a half miles of road. Add to this sundry other forms of transport which seemed to attach itself to divisional columns and which contributed to, 'making life extremely difficult for everyone' and some perception of the task facing the engineers begins to emerge. Is it any wonder that Young later suggested – rather politely in the circumstances – that the bright spark who had opined that, 'bridging equipment should be kept well to the rear and rushed up in lorries when wanted,' should have tried the exercise for himself, particularly as lorries never seemed to be available!

Young's exasperation at finding himself at the rear of the column was not an experience generally shared by the cavalry. During the advance to the Aisne the cavalry corps was usually at the forefront of any action and in the bad weather preceding the crossing of the Aisne itself – with the RFC effectively grounded at Saponay– the cavalry was the only means GHQ had of knowing exactly where the enemy were. William Read recorded his frustration at being grounded by poor weather, 'low heavy clouds all day, heavy rain from 1pm onwards'. Twenty four hours later he described the damage caused to the squadron's aircraft after a particularly violent storm on the night of the 12 September. 'A sudden squall got up and turned over five BE's and two Henri's. They were all badly smashed up. Sheckleton's [Second Lieutenant Alexander Sheckleton] machine was making love to Fuller's – one was found leaning against the other'. Four aircraft of 5 Squadron were completely destroyed and over half the machines belonging to 3 Squadron 'turned turtle' and were badly damaged. One Henri Farman was blown 30 feet into the air and deposited on top of another and Lieutenant Louis Strange only saved his Henri Farman by pushing it up against a haystack, laying a ladder over the front skids, and piling large stones on the ladder. When daylight eventually dawned there were probably not more than ten machines serviceable.

Bad weather or not, as the BEF pressed ever closer towards the Aisne valley it was essential to have good intelligence on the state of the numerous known crossing points over the river ahead. Along the front facing the BEF – from Bourg to Vénizel – there were seven road bridges, an aqueduct and a railway bridge. Unbelievably none of the divisional staffs, apart from that of the 1st Division, appear to have ordered a technical reconnaissance to be carried out by RE officers ahead of the main body of troops. RE officers did carry out a token reconnaissance of the Bourg bridges on 13 September on orders from 1st Division HQ, not that that made a shred of difference to the overall bridging strategy which subsequently evolved. It is true there was a field squadron with the cavalry division – and this could have been used more effectively – but this hardly exonerates the lack of foresight. Had there been more forethought and consultation with senior RE officers, the heavy bridging equipment could have been directed to the crossing points where they were most needed. As it was it was a further twenty-four hours after the first troops arrived on the Aisne before the first bridging train arrived – more of which later.

Pressed into a 15 mile front, the Cavalry Division and Douglas Haig's I Corps were allocated the crossings at Bourg, Pont Arcy and Chavonne, General Gough's Cavalry Brigade and II Corps at Vailly, Condé and Missy and III Corps at Vénizel and Soissons. Apart from the realization that most, if not all, of these bridging points would inevitably be targeted by German demolition teams, the British sappers would have immediately recognized the difficulties posed by the Canal Latéral which ran parallel to a good deal of the river's course on its southern bank. To cross the river east of Condé, the crossings over the canal had first to be secured – providing of course they had not been demolished. The passage of the Aisne was not going to be easy.

Although some of the units of the BEF now heading towards the Aisne valley would have already had a fleeting introduction to its geography during the retreat, it would have been the steep march in the August heat which took them out of the valley towards the Marne that most of the men would have remembered. Now, with the boot on the other foot, there was a fresh opportunity to assess the task which confronted them. Major John Mowbray, the brigade major of the 2nd Divisional Artillery had no illusions about the difficulties which the BEF faced:

'The country on both sides of the river between Soissons and Craonne consists of high ground some 250 – 300 feet above the valley bottom. The direction of the Aisne is east to west – the main valley being about 1 mile in width. The valley bottoms are partly wooded and the slopes are almost entirely wooded with dense copses in which progress is difficult. One notable feature is a layer of limestone running at a height of about 200 feet above the valley which had been drawn upon for building stone resulting in numerous quarries and natural caves. The Aisne is about the size of the Thames at Oxford and unfordable. A feature is the canal running along the valley with a branch to the Oise at Bourg, passing the ridge north of the Aisne through a tunnel. The canal is also an unfordable obstacle. The watershed between the valley and the country further north is a continuous ridge of about 300 feet above the valley stretching from Soissons to*

*Craonne along which runs the Chemin de Dames. From this ridge the
plateau extends down in fingers.'*[42]

The fingers were in fact a series of spurs projecting south towards the
river from the Chemin des Dames ridge. Running left to right from
Crouy to Bourg – a linear distance of approximately 15 miles – some
nine spurs of varying size projected down towards the river. It was
these spurs which were the key to gaining the Chemin des Dames
ridge as Mowbray's professional eye was quick to establish. His diary
betrays his concerns as to the difficulties this valley would pose should
the Germans decide to make a stand on the northern heights along the
Chemin des Dames. In estimating the distance between the two ridges
on either side of the valley as about 6 miles, he recognized that, 'any
point in the valley can be observed from the Chemin de Dames ridge,
as can most of the spurs and valleys and be very exposed to artillery
fire. The whole position on the river lends itself to artillery fire from the
northern side.' In addition he quickly and correctly weighed up the
difficulties infantry and artillery would have in advancing up the
numerous spurs and side valleys, 'all of these positions', he felt, 'were
exposed to cross fire' and were, 'tenable only with great difficulty.'

It would very soon become clear that the width of the valley and the
wooded nature of the slopes severely handicapped artillery batteries in
finding suitable positions from which to mount any form of counter-
battery fire or indeed support the advancing infantry. The standard 18-
pounder gun used by the Royal Field Artillery found the German guns
beyond range and the thickly-wooded slopes prevented artillery
observers from spotting German batteries with any degree of accuracy,
or, in some cases, the British infantry formations they were attempting
to support. Initially it was only the heavy 60-pounder guns which
could make an impression until the field artillery batteries were able to
cross the river behind the infantry. Even then the difficulty in locating
suitable firing positions proved a continual headache for battery
commanders.

In the absence of the RFC, intelligence on the river crossings was left
largely to cavalry reconnaissance, one such patrol of the 4th Queen's
Own Hussars (4/Hussars) which was dispatched on 12 September to
gather information on the Vailly and Condé river bridges, found
themselves up against a German rearguard still on the south bank of
the river. The Hussars were now under the leadership of Major Phillip
Howell who had assumed command after Lieutenant Colonel Ian
Hogg had been fatally wounded during the rearguard action in the
forest north of Villers-Cotterêts eleven days previously.[43] Hard pressed

by the pursuing Germans, the regiment was forced to leave its mortally wounded commanding officer behind in the care of the regimental medical officer near the hamlet of Haramont.

Here, as had happened at Villers-Cotterêts, the Hussars found themselves up against a larger force, but this time they were in no mood to retire. Galloping under shell fire along the narrow approach road to the bridge at Vailly they came under fire on their right flank from German cavalry ensconced in the nearby Château de Bois Morin. With the question as to whether the bridge and its immediate area was occupied now answered, and never one to avoid a fight, Captain John Gatacre led C Squadron in a spirited attack down the length of the winding road to the chateau effectively driving off the Germans who vanished in the direction of the bridge. Howell was later able to report to brigade HQ that:

> 'Gatacre's squadron ('C') comfortably established north end of wood near bridge with two maxims. Bridge appears to be intact and is only about 500 yards from Gatacre. Uhlan patrols attempting to cross have been driven back and except a few men cut off and still wandering about woods, I doubt if any Germans are south of the river in this quarter.'[44]

The bridge observed by Gatacre's men was most likely the canal bridge, as the road bridge spanning the river was certainly not intact by that time as 56/Field Company was soon to discover. However Gatacre's assessment of the Condé Bridge – a mile and a half downstream of Vailly – was correct. The bridge was found to be intact and very strongly held at the northern end, to which any approach was greeted with a hail of well directed machine-gun fire. As darkness fell that night Gatacre and his men were bivouacked on the banks of the river but it would be another day before the marching columns of I and II Corps heading north in the pouring rain would arrive.

Nevertheless, on the left flank of the BEF, the advance guard of the 4th Division had already arrived. At 1.00pm on 12 September Brigadier General Aylmer Haldane and 10 Infantry Brigade were directed to take the high ground above Septmonts and reconnoitre the bridge at Vénizel. According to Haldane's diary the bridge was approached by a patrol of 16/Lancers who reported it had been damaged by the enemy – exactly how and to what extent was unclear. This was reported to Brigadier General Wilson, the acting divisional commander, who, at the time, was standing with Haldane on the heights above Septmonts watching, 'a considerable body of German troops and transport moving northeast along the Laon road'.

That evening the daylight faded quickly as a canopy of rain cloaked the river valley, masking the arrival of the forward units of the 4th Division into Billy-sur-Aisne. Working on his own initiative, Major Charles Wilding, commanding 2/Royal Inniskilling Fusiliers, sent two of his rifle companies down to the bridge at Vénizel, their appearance prompting the German engineers to blow the charges they had prepared on the bridge. The Inniskilling war diary does not note the exact time of this incident but it was after dark and there is a note that the detonation was only partially successful and that a second attempt to blow the remaining charges by the German unit on the bridge was prevented. After this encounter the battalion moved back north of Billy.

There is understandably some confusion as to when the various movements on and around the bridge took place. The three brigades of Wilson's 4th Division were being funnelled into the Aisne crossing at Vénizel in the pouring rain, each brigade ostensibly undertaking its own reconnaissance of the bridge and divisional staff clearly not getting to grips with the logistics of movement.[45] Haldane's record of the 16/Lancers reporting the bridge damaged during the late afternoon on 12 September does conflict somewhat with the Inniskilling war diary account but fortunately the Royal Engineers' historian is a little more precise and places Captain Francis Westland of 9/Field Company on the bridge sometime after 8.00pm on 12 September.

Westland found that only two of the demolition charges had gone off and, in his opinion, the bridge would take the weight of an infantry brigade providing they crossed in single file, thus suggesting the encounter on the bridge by Wilding's men occurred a little earlier. The *Official History* also tells us that 'after dark' Captain Roe of the Inniskillings removed the remaining fuses by torchlight and that German units were entrenched on the opposite bank. Whether this was actually undertaken by Roe or by Westland is not known but what is not in doubt is that by dawn on 13 September Hunter-Weston's 11 Infantry Brigade had received its orders, crossed the Aisne using the Vénizel bridge and was in position above Bucy-le-Long.

* * *

The main body of 9/Field Company arrived at Septmonts at 9.00am on 13 September, 'We had considerable trouble getting the pontoons up to Septmonts', recalled Bernard Young, 'the mud had begun to give us a foretaste of what the winter of 14/15 was to be, and our horses were pretty much done up'. His new commanding officer, Major Desmond Hoysted, having joined the unit on the road near Montigny, was now faced with the task of building a pontoon bridge over the now swollen Aisne. Hoysted was replacing Major John Barstow who had been killed during the retreat whilst attempting to blow the bridge at Bailly on 30 August. Killed during an ambush by a cavalry patrol from the German Guard Cavalry Division, Barstow's body had been left behind as the sappers had beat a hasty retreat. Hoysted was an experienced engineer and no stranger to active service – he had commanded 26/Field Company in South Africa during the Second Boer War – and realizing the urgency of establishing a safe crossing over the river – he and his sappers set about constructing a pontoon bridge alongside the damaged one. Bernard Young recalled that the bridge was:

'Started at noon and finished at 5.00pm; 190 feet in all, three trestles, four pontoons and the remainder made with barrel piers from a convenient oil depot nearby and a superstructure from the village ... As far as we could tell we were in sight of the enemy; in any case, the bridge proper, 50 yards upstream, was on the map; nevertheless these bridges were never hit by the enemy, though he was sufficiently persistent in all his attempts to hit them.'[46]

The road bridge was made safe and repaired in time for 12 Infantry Brigade to cross on the morning of 13 September by Lieutenant Giffard Le Quesey Martel and a troop of sappers using, 'a few Heath Robinson iron flats and bolts and a handy steel-work telegraph pole'.

Three miles upstream at Missy-sur-Aisne, Major George Walker and the sappers of 59/Field Company were faced with a far more difficult task. The company arrived at Serches early on 13 September and after successfully descending the long hill down to Ciry without attracting fire from the opposite bank, Walker despatched Lieutenant James Pennycuick ahead to reconnoitre the road bridge. Walker then continued on to the railway station with the remainder of the company to forage for material which might be of use in rebuilding the bridge at Missy should it be required. At 3.00pm Walker was contacted by Lieutenant Colonel Arundel Martyn commanding the 1st Battalion Queen's Own Royal West Kents (1/RWK), who had arrived with the battalion the previous evening. Martyn explained that his battalion had been ordered to attack and cross the bridge at all costs which was believed to be intact. This information had apparently been provided by a party of 4th Divisional Cyclists which it seemed, had seized the bridge at 1.00am but had been driven off by superior numbers soon afterwards. The cyclists were plainly working in isolation from the patrol of West Kents, led by Lieutenant Moulton-Barrett, which had succeeded in getting to within 150 yards of the bridge sometime during the early hours of 13 September and despite losing a senior NCO had at least ascertained that both banks were being held by a German rearguard but could shed no further light on the material state of the bridge.

Needless to say, it wasn't long before Lieutenant Pennycuick's reconnaissance of the bridge – which had been carried out using field glasses in daylight – served to confirm Walker's initial fears. Two of the three spans of the bridge had been demolished and the river was too deep to ford. It was, commented Walker drily, 'a nice job for a field company with nothing but what they carried in tool carts'. Conveying this information to Colonel Martyn, the West Kent's had little alternative but to push on to the river as ordered and see for themselves. In what was described as, 'a bad day for us' by Lieutenant William Palmer, the OC of C Company, Colonel Martyn deployed B and C Companies in the woods on either side of the road leading to the bridge in support of D Company which had the task of taking the bridge if it was indeed intact. William Palmer watched with some apprehension from the cover of the wooded bank as D Company advanced over the flat, featureless ground which led to the bridge. With no indication of the strength of the enemy rearguard, Captain Frank Fisher and Lance Corporal William Atkins went on ahead but were met with a fusillade of rifle and machine-gun fire, Fisher was cut down immediately and Atkins only narrowly escaped a similar fate.

Despite the loss of their company commander, the advance continued in the face of heavy fire from the far bank – but not without casualties. No. 6 Platoon not only lost their officer, Lieutenant Horatio Vicat, but also their platoon NCO, Sergeant William Burr. Frank Fisher had only been promoted to captain a few weeks earlier on 5 August and had survived Mons, Le Cateau and the retreat, whereas 29-year-old Horatio Vicat, who had only joined the battalion at Tournan on 4 September, served just nine days before losing his life.[47] Their loss was a grievous blow to the battalion and merely added to the lengthening casualty list of twelve officers already killed or wounded in the four weeks since the battalion had embarked for France. That evening saw the battalion in control of the southern bank which enabled Major Matthew Buckle of the West Kents and Major Walker to examine the bridge in more detail. As Walker wrote after the war, with one complete span of the bridge destroyed, 'nothing could be done to make it fit to cross in under two or three days'.

With the bridging train still a day's march away, and faced with the urgency of getting troops across the river, there was little alternative but to try and get the infantry across the river using makeshift rafts. By 5.00pm the German rearguard had been driven off the damaged bridge by the West Kents and 59/Field Company began ferrying the men of 13 Brigade across the river, an operation which took most of the night to accomplish. It was at this hotly contested crossing that Captain William Johnston and Lieutenant Robert Flint spent much of the next day under fire ferrying ammunition across one way and wounded the other. Major Walker later commented:

'When I got near him [Johnston] *he signalled me not to approach. He and Flint were working the raft to and fro … I sat down under cover with Pennycuick and a few men ready to assist and so we spent the day …Johnston and Flint continued this work until 7pm when they were relieved, quite worn out. Johnston received a VC for this and Flint a DSO. I was able to recommend them personally as I saw it all.'*[48]

At 11.00am on 13 September the sappers of 17/Field Company arrived further downstream at Moulin des Roches and began ferrying 14 Brigade across the river. Second Lieutenant Kenneth Godsell described the night's activity:

'On reaching the river we discovered a boat on the far side and a Sapper of my section stripped, swam across, and fetched it back. It was discovered later that there was nobody in front of us and the Germans were holding an entrenched position on the hills just the other side of Missy. By 12 o'clock No. 2 Section had made a pontoon raft and had started ferrying the infantry across. We got 53 men on to the pontoon raft and nine in the boat. Each trip took 8 minutes if the party to board were ready on the bank. Later we constructed a landing bay each side by using the Weldon Trestles which accelerated boarding and reduced the time per trip to 6 minutes. The actual place of crossing was most convenient as it was where a track, which crossed the railway by a level crossing, ran into the tow path along the river bank. The point was sheltered from observation by a belt of trees and a small copse.'[49]

Godsell estimated that, 'the river at this point was some 70 yards wide and flowed at a good rate', but any hopes of a rest were soon dispelled when the advance guard of 15 Brigade arrived at 11.30pm. 'We found ourselves on the bank', wrote Edward Gleichen, 'with a darker shadow splashing backwards and forwards over the river in our front, and some RE officers talking in whispers'. Godsell's diary records an exhausting night with the last man of 15 Brigade crossing just before 6.30am the next morning. 'It was', he felt, 'a very wet night but we were too busy to notice it'.

At Vailly, Second Lieutenant Cyril Martin from 56/Field Company and Major Henderson the officer commanding the 57th, soon discovered that the bridge over the Canal Latéral was undamaged but in contrast the river bridge boasted but a single plank spanning a rather precarious looking gap. Despite making a wide detour to avoid being spotted by German infantry from IR13 on the far bank, Henderson was hit in the elbow by enemy fire. Martin sent Henderson back 'with the man we had with us and then made a rough sketch of the bridge' and headed back to lodge his report. On returning to the bridge to see if the gap was safe enough to traverse by infantry, Martin managed to jump across and secure the plank. 'It was a pretty warm time as the Germans were firing from quite close'. Martin's apparent lack of concern for his own safety had already been demonstrated at Le Cateau, where he won a DSO. He would be noticed again in April 1915 when his stubborn refusal to give up a captured trench resulted in the award of the Victoria Cross. The bridge, Martin felt, was probably not going to take the weight of an infantry brigade, but after a personal inspection by Hubert Hamilton, commanding the 3rd Division, 8 Brigade was ordered to cross the river using the bridge.[50]

What followed was a repeat of the Vénizel experience, a single plank spanned the breach in the road bridge and the Royal Irish and Royal Scots began crossing at 3.00pm on 13 September. Being daylight they were under continual shell fire from German batteries, both battalions taking casualties, however, by 6.00pm they had established themselves around Vailly: the Royal Irish east of St-Pierre and the Scots at Vauxcelles Château, a mile or so northwest of Vailly. That night 9 Brigade followed on using the same precarious plank whilst 56 and 57/Field Companies began the task of erecting a pontoon bridge across the river, completing their task by 3.00am on 14 September.

Further east, the approach to Bourg lay across two canal bridges and a road bridge which crossed the river itself. An initial cavalry reconnaissance reported the village clear of enemy troops but when Lieutenant Robert Featherstonehaugh and a troop of B Squadron, 4/Dragoon Guards arrived, they were met with a hail of gunfire from well entrenched German infantry along the canal bank. Similarly, when A Squadron approached the bridges at Villiers – which had both been destroyed – the canal bank was found to be occupied by an enemy rearguard. Fortunately the two canal bridges at Bourg were intact and taken by the dragoons under heavy fire. Given the task confronting them, casualties were extraordinarily light: only one officer and three men killed. When 28-year-old Captain Gerald 'Pat' Fitzgerald, the machine - gun officer, went down with a bullet between the eyes, Arthur Osburn, the regimental medical officer was only yards away: 'Fitzgerald was unconscious when I got to him, his wound no bigger than a blue pencil mark in the centre of his forehead. Then in a moment he was gone'.[51] Once across the canals it became apparent that although the road bridge had been destroyed, the aqueduct carrying the canal over the river was intact. Apart from an 'uncomfortable quarter of an hour', when the cavalrymen were caught in crossfire, Osburn recorded his relief in watching the defending German rearguard being the subject of some accurate shell fire and eventually retreating towards the wooded slopes of the high ground to the north.

Just upstream of the Bourg bridges 2 Cavalry Brigade crossed the river using the hand-drawn ferry where, despite the obvious dangers from gunfire, the ferry boy was still at work, a deed which impressed Second Lieutenant Jock Marden, an officer with A Squadron, 9/Lancers:

> '6.25, orders to move at once – off in a confusion at 6.35 then we attack Bourg and the crossings of the Aisne and parallel canal – the furthest bridge of the two having been blown up. We go to the right and cross by 6s in a ferry under an irritating sniper's fire from a church tower. Gave the ferry boy a franc for courage.'[52]

With the cavalry across the river, the waiting infantry and artillery units which were gathering south of the Canal Latéral began moving to join them. Lieutenant Evelyn Needham had been on the road since 4.00am with his company of 1st Battalion Northamptonshire Regiment and arrived south of Bourg to find, 'the cavalry and artillery hotly engaged with the enemy on the far side of the river'.[53] Glad of the rest they were held up for three or four hours before the order to advance saw the battalion crossing the aqueduct. 'Oddly enough', wrote Needham, 'I have no recollection of this crossing beyond the fact that we doubled across as fast as we could, so as to get under cover on the far side'. Second Lieutenant James Hyndson who crossed with B Company, 1st Battalion Loyal North Lancashire Regiment (1/Loyals), noticed, 'strong barricades and disguised trenches abandoned by the enemy which, if held, would certainly have cost us casualties'. Corporal J N Perks, a motorcycle rider with the 1st Signal Company, remembered his crossing over the aqueduct vividly:

'The Germans had obviously though we might try and cross this way and had tried to blow up the viaduct but had only succeeded in blowing a small hole in the towpath which engineers soon repaired with wooden faggots ... the reason for the German failure was obvious, as lying by the side of the towpath were 3 dead Germans who had obviously been killed before they could finish the job.'[54]

Perks' assessment of the German failure was almost certainly incorrect; there is no record of a German demolition party being killed and the dead Germans he saw were probably casualties of the earlier fighting. The aqueduct was a massive steel structure carrying the canal and would have required a considerable amount of explosive to destroy it, a task clearly beyond the resources of the German rearguard. After crossing the river on his Triumph Roadster, Perks was nearly pushed into the canal by an artillery brigade who took up most of the available road, 'I only had a few feet to ride between the guns and the edge of the canal, and the towpath was awfully greasy'. To make matters worse just as he reached the junction with the main road – the modern day D88 – German gunners were beginning to get the range of the advancing troops: 'Just in front of me a shell landed in front of a team of horses drawing a gun, killing the leaders but luckily not touching the drivers'.

Frederick Coleman, another of the RAC volunteer drivers, managed to get his vehicle over the aqueduct but almost came to grief in the rain on the muddy towpath attempting to drive up a steep slope. 'No choice remained but to charge it at such speed as one could muster. Near the top the whirring wheels refused to bite and back the car slid towards the river'. Surrounded as he was by units of the 1st Division he eventually 'crawled upwards' and over the crest of the bank to join the advance north towards Vendresse. Also at Bourg, Corporal Cuthbert Avis of the 1/Queen's Royal West Surreys remembered scrambling, 'along girders of a destroyed bridge' and advancing with his battalion in heavy rain up the slopes of the river bank. 'It was an unlucky day', he recorded, 'when the battalion forced the passage of the river with a loss of nearly 100 killed and wounded'.

Meanwhile at Pont-Arcy, 11/Field Company began work on the road bridge which had only been partly destroyed, while a mile and a half upstream the sappers of 5/Field Company started construction of a pontoon bridge which was in use by 5.00pm that afternoon. One of the first battalions to cross the river at Pont-Arcy was 2/Connaught Rangers which, under fire, used the single girder that remained – albeit partly submerged – and took up positions on the north bank where they covered the crossing by the remainder of 5 Brigade over the pontoon bridge. The Connaughts had lost their commanding officer, Lieutenant Colonel Alexander Abercrombie, at Le Grand Fayt on 26 August.[55] Forced into fighting a rearguard action after the battalion's strength was divided, Abercrombie and some 100 officers and men were ambushed as they entered the village, resulting in the eventual capture of the colonel and the majority of the party. The battalion, now under the command of Major William Sarsfield, was ordered into Soupir to take up positions on the northern and western outskirts of the village. At 1.00am Major Sarsfield – on his own initiative – moved the battalion up to La Cour de Soupir Farm which lay at the head of the valley through which the next day's advance would take place. The Connaughts arrived at 5.30am on 14 September and found no sign of the enemy. They were less than 2 miles from the Chemin des Dames ridge.

Further downstream opposite Chavonne, 4 (Guards) Brigade, under the temporary command of Lieutenant Colonel Fielding, was assembled to begin crossing the canal at Cys-la-Commune. They had arrived late and it was not until noon that they were ready to cross. Notwithstanding the information that Chavonne was apparently only lightly held, the approaches to the village were distinctly hazardous for the infantryman. The 800 yard wide stretch of ground between the canal bridge at Cys and the river crossing at Chavonne was devoid of all cover and offered no protection to assaulting infantry. On the northern bank the partially wooded ground rose steeply from the river providing cover for a concealed enemy who had the benefit of excellent fields of fire over the whole area. If the village and the commanding heights above it were held in force and the rearguard determined to resist, a successful crossing would be very much in the balance.

With the three remaining battalions of the brigade in support, it fell to the 2nd Battalion Coldstream Guards (2/Coldstream) to test the strength and resolve of the German rearguard. Captain Gilbert Follett and Number 2 Company soon came under heavy rifle and machine gun fire as he approached the canal bridge, prompting Lieutenant Colonel Pereira to send up two further companies to return fire from the canal bank. Watching the afternoon's events from the high ground south of Cys was Major Lord Bernard Gordon Lennox and the men of 2/Grenadier Guards. He notes in his diary that, 'after a couple of hours they [the Coldstream] ejected the Dutchmen [sic] who were seen scuttling up the hill and over the skyline'.[56]

The 'scuttling' retreat of the German rearguard had been encouraged by the combined firepower of shell fire from the guns of 71/Battery which scoured the ridge above Chavonne and the machine-gun section from 2/Grenadier Guards commanded by Lieutenant Hon. William Cecil which came into action by the canal bridge. By 4.00pm the Coldstream were on the river bank where a leaking boat found by Lance Corporal Albert Milward provided the transport for Number 3 Company to begin establishing themselves on the northern bank. The Coldstream war diary records the, 'considerable opposition from hostile infantry and machine guns and at least a squadron of German cavalry', which was met by the Coldstream's Number 3 Company as it fought its way up onto the heights of Les Crinons above the village. Meanwhile the Grenadiers had begun crossing the river a mile or so east of Chavonne using what the regimental historian describes as, 'three or four boats of doubtful buoyancy'. No doubt it was the onset of darkness and heavy rain which decided Colonel Fielding to withdraw the brigade – except the Coldstream Company established on Les Crinons – to the safety of St Mard and Cys for the nigh; a welcome alternative to a riverside bivouac. Bernard Gordon Lennox and his company officers were fortunate in that they:

> *'Found an obliging farmer, whose daughter had come home from Paris for a fortnight's holiday ... she proved to be an awfully good cook and made us an excellent bouillon of vegetable followed by an equally excellent omelette ...a pouring wet night and were glad to have a roof over our heads.'*[57]

However, the logic as to why Fielding was ordered to withdraw his forces on the north bank remains a mystery, but the orders came directly from I Corps Headquarters. Had Fielding pushed his men over the river and continued the advance that night – as 2/Connaughts did – the stalemate which became synonymous with Cour de Soupir Farm may have had a more favourable outcome.

So by dawn on 14 September the Cavalry Division and the 1st Division were across the river and established between Paissy and Verneuil. Only 5 Infantry Brigade – plus one company of Coldstream at Chavonne – from the 2nd Division had crossed and were occupying a line running roughly from Verneuil to Soupir. Then there was a gap of some 5 miles where 8 and 9 Infantry Brigades were established at Vauxelles, before a further gap of 3 miles occurred – formed by the Condé salient. At Missy two battalions of 13 Brigade, the 1/Royal West Kents and 2/King's Own Scottish Borderers were dug in together with 14 and 15 Brigades. Close by were the three brigades of the 4th

Division occupying positions from St Marguerite to Crouy. South of the Aisne, and not yet across the river, were 4 and 6 Infantry Brigades at Veil Arcy, Cys and St Mard, 3 and 5 Cavalry Brigades and 7 Infantry Brigade at Braine, and the two missing battalions of 13 Brigade somewhere south of Missy. 19 Brigade were at Billy-sur-Aisne.

Both flanks of the BEF were in touch with their French counterparts. On the right General Conneau's Cavalry Corps had fallen back on Jouvincourt in the face of strong enemy resistance, however, on Conneau's right the French XVII Corps appeared to be having more success in their advance towards Corbeny and Craonne. On the left of the BEF, the French Sixth Army advance was held up at Soissons by the demolished bridges and heavy shell fire from the heights between Crouy and Vaurezis. The 55th Division had failed to advance beyond Cuffies and the 56th Division's attempts to cross the Aisne at Pommiers had also resulted in failure. However, the 14th Division had crossed the river at Vic-sur-Aisne and part of the French IV Corps had completed a similar exercise at Berneuil. This piecemeal success was the first sign of the looming strategic nightmare which would halt the northward advance of the BEF and see the name Chemin des Dames pass forever into French consciousness and become part of Gallic military legend.

Chapter 5

The Left Flank – 4th Division

Everything went more or less calmly till 9.30am when our own guns spotted us in our waterproof sheets, as it was still raining, from the opposite side of the river, and thinking we were Germans, started shelling us with lyddite.

Lieutenant Lionel Tennyson – diary entry 13 September, 1914.

11 Infantry Brigade's march to the Aisne on 12 September began later than anyone had expected. Breakfast had been eaten at 2.15am and although the initial orders had been for a 3.30am start, the four infantry battalions did not begin their march for another four hours. Movement along the congested roads was not made any easier by the advance units of two Royal Engineers field companies bustling past them with their bridging equipment and by the time the 1st Battalion Somerset Light Infantry (1/SLI) halted at Montreboeuf Farm at mid-day most of the battalion felt they had already put in a good day's march.

The Somersets had begun their day with the loss of their battalion commander, Lieutenant Colonel Edward Swayne. Gazetted second lieutenant in 1885, Swayne had commanded the battalion from 1913. Disembarking at Le Havre on 22 August he and his battalion had joined the BEF in time to take part in General Smith-Dorrien's stand behind the N43 Le Cateau – Cambrai road. The rigours of the subsequent retreat had clearly taken their toll on the 50-year-old Swayne and his departure on sick leave left Major Charles Prowse in command. The 45-year-old Prowse was an ideal replacement, but unlike his former Commanding Officer, he would not survive the war.

Commanding 11 Infantry Brigade was Brigadier General Aylmer Hunter-Weston. An interesting and somewhat unpredictable individual, he had been commissioned into the Royal Engineers in 1884, and had served in South Africa on the staff and later in command of a unit of mounted engineers. Described as having 'reckless courage combined with technical skill and great coolness in emergency', the 11 Brigade commander – universally known as 'Hunter-Bunter' by the men – was more usually seen on the back of a motorcycle which appeared to be his preferred seat of command.[58]

Whether George Pattenden ever saw his brigade commander on his motorcycle is not disclosed in his diary but he had good cause to remember 12 September, noting rather despondently that they 'marched all day passing through several villages', to arrive at Septmonts at about 5.00pm where he hoped the battalion might have a rest and find something to eat. A rest they were able to take but the expectation of obtaining food was short-lived and before long the exhausted battalions were again on the move, this time heading for Vénizel with the additional weight of another 100 rounds of .303 ammunition per man. Pattenden may well have still been 'in the dark' as to their destination but Lieutenant Gerald Whittuck of the Somersets had a much clearer picture as he approached the Aisne valley. 'Germans were evidently close in front of us as the inhabitants informed us that they had only passed through in the morning'. For Whittuck it was looking more and more likely that they would attempt the crossing of the river that night – an exercise he viewed with some apprehension. The young lieutenant was in temporary command of B Company, his diary recording that they had 'three quarters of an hour's halt in the middle of the day, but otherwise were marching all day'. Concerned that, 'many of the men were suffering with diarrhoea', he was relieved to reach Vénizel about 8.00pm that evening, rather proudly recording, 'they stuck to the march wonderfully'.

Lieutenant the Honourable Lionel Tennyson, the Hampshire and England cricketer and grandson of the poet Alfred Lord Tennyson, was on the 11 Brigade staff. He too had memories of the march to Vénizel: 'after an awful march of 27 miles still in torrents of rain to the village of Roziérés, we were ordered to advance once more just as we got ready to billet for the night, and arrived after yet another drenching at Vénizel'. Any thoughts Tennyson may have had of crossing the Aisne the next morning were dashed by orders for the whole brigade to cross the damaged bridge immediately and move onto the high ground above Bucy-le Long:

> *'The whole of 11th Brigade crossed the river. This was the manner of their crossing, which at the time seemed to us the riskiest and most slap-dash proceeding ever ... In the midst of the inky darkness, and although the men were so tired with their march in the rain that they went to sleep as they*

stood or marched, they crossed the girder one by one. It was sixty feet above the river and quivered and shook all the time.'[59]

As advance guard, 1/Hampshire was the first battalion to cross the Vénizel Bridge, unfortunately without Private George Pattenden whose feet had once again refused to support him. The Hampshires were closely followed by the 1st Battalion Rifle Brigade (1/Rifle Brigade) and the stretcher bearers from 10/Field Ambulance who reached the bridge at 11.00pm and completed their crossing in thirty minutes. Following the Rifle Brigade were the 1st Battalion East Lancashire Regiment (1/East Lancs) and Gerald Whittuck and the Somersets who, 'crossed the Aisne just before light … It was nervous work and took a long time as we could only go in single file'. The men, according to the 1/SLI war diary, were tired and grumpy, but no mention was made of any opposition, presumably the German rearguard had long since retired beyond Bucy-le-Long.

Hunter-Weston's own account of the night's operations describes the small-arms ammunition carts being unloaded and their contents being passed over the girder by hand. Written sometime after the event, and in a rather self-congratulatory tone, his four-page report to the 4th Division does highlight what can be achieved in the face of adversity.

At Vénizel the river forms a wide loop which passes under the steep southern edge of the valley allowing flat, open water meadows to stretch for over a mile to the foot of the high ground. Across this open ground a single road – the present day N95 – ran from the bridge to Bucy-le-Long, a road which was very much exposed to enemy observation and one which in the coming days would become almost impossible to negotiate safely in daylight. Above Bucy-le-Long the high ground took the form of three spurs where it was expected the enemy rearguard would be positioned.

Hunter-Weston's judgement of the potentially dangerous and exposed nature of the Bucy-le-Long road was apparent in his report:

'In order to hold the crossing of the river at Vénizel effectively it was in the opinion of the brigadier necessary to hold the heights above Bucy-le-Long which dominated the bridge and the flat ground between those heights and the river. He therefore ordered the brigade to advance to the attack of those heights and to seize them at the point of the bayonet. The leading battalion, the 1st Hants, were ordered to take the central spur on which is La Montagne Farm. The Somersets were ordered to the left spur, NW of Bucy

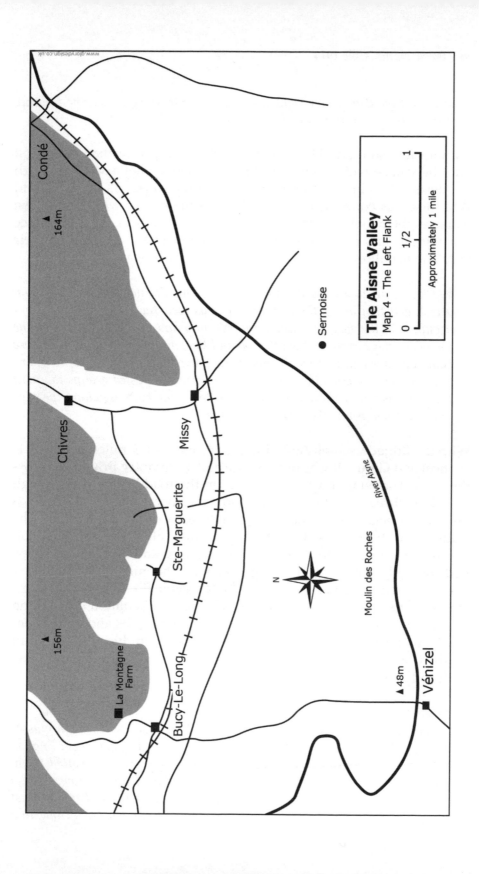

The Aisne Valley
Map 4 - The Left Flank

0   1/2   1

Approximately 1 mile

Condé

164m

156m

La Montagne
Farm

Chivres

Bucy-Le-Long

Ste-Marguerite

Missy

Sermoise

Moulin des Roches

River Aisne

48m

Vénizel

N

and the Rifle Brigade the right spur north of Ste Marguerite. The E Lancs being kept in reserve south of the centre of Bucy-le-Long.'[60]

Captain Johnston and D Company of the Hampshires had been first into the village which they found unoccupied as they passed through the deserted main street on their way up the slope. As far as Gerald Whittuck was concerned the march from the bridge was, 'one of the worst night marches I remember'. After a march of 30 miles since starting off early on 12 September, the men were almost dead on their feet. The battalion reached Bucy-le-Long just as it was getting light:

'We were sent to occupy the high ground. This did not look much like an attack at dawn and I think it was just as well the ridge tops were not occupied, as the men were dead tired. We only saw a party of Uhlans on the top of the ridge as we reached the top and they disappeared at once. Prowse came up later and told me the points he particularly wanted me to guard and gave me direction in case of further advance. I posted groups to guard these points and withdrew my company to a bank running along the edge of a wood just below the crest of the ridge.'[61]

With 11 Brigade established along a frontage of 3 miles between le Moncel and Crouy, it was now the turn of 12 Infantry Brigade to cross the river. The temporary repair work on the road bridge was enough to allow three battalions of Brigadier General Frederick Anley's brigade to begin using the bridge at 6.00am on 13 September. The bridge had been passed fit for light duty after the sappers had manhandled one of the 68/Battery guns across and by 11.00am Anley had the bulk of his brigade – together with the guns of 68/Battery – over the river and moving under heavy shell fire across the water meadows towards Bucy-le-Long, leaving the 2nd Battalion Inniskilling Fusiliers (2/Inniskillings) to bring the remaining guns and equipment of XIV and XXXVII Brigades over the bridge. From his vantage point on the Chivres spur *Hauptmann* Walter Bloem had a grandstand view of the advance of the British 12 Brigade:

'Stretched across the broad expanse of meadows between us and the meadows was a long line of dots wide apart, and looking through glasses one saw that these dots were infantry advancing, widely extended: English infantry too, unmistakable. A field battery on our left had spotted them, and we watched their shrapnel bursting over the advancing line. Soon a second line of dots emerged from the willows along the river bank, at least ten paces apart, and began to advance. More of our batteries came into

action; but it was noticed that a shell, however well aimed, seldom killed more than one man, the lines being so well and widely extended … our guns now fired like mad, but it did not stop the movement: a fifth and a sixth line came on, all with the same wide interval between men and the same distance apart. It was magnificently done.'[62]

Incredibly, in spite of the heavy shell fire from the German gunners casualties were relatively light. Major Christopher Griffin commanding the 2nd Battalion Lancashire Fusiliers put much of this down to good discipline and resolve:

'The battalion advanced across the shell-swept plain to Bucy-le-Long in lines of half companies. This manoeuvre was admirably carried out, largely due to the excellent leading, and disregard of danger, of company officers; the lines moved forward as steadily as if on parade. The casualties, which were few, would have been increased four-fold it there had been any hanging back or hesitation in the advance.'[63]

Meanwhile on the right of Gerald Whittuck and the Somersets, the Hampshires had taken up positions around La Montagne Farm to find the enemy strongly entrenched some 1,500 yards in front of them, while to their right the Rifle Brigade were in place north of le Moncel. The arrival of 12 Infantry Brigade extended the British line on the right whereas further back, a little to the north of Vénizel, were elements of the XIV Brigade guns which, although exposed to the German gunners on the Chivres spur, had little choice but to stand their ground. Up at La Montagne Farm the 31/ and 55/Howitzer batteries were in place providing support to the French advance north of Soissons, whilst at Le Moncel Lieutenant Cecil Brereton and 68/Battery were in support of the Rifle Brigade:

'We were then ordered up to support the infantry at the top of the hill. Found the Rifle Brigade there. We brought a section into action and immediately got shelled like fury from two places. Went back and got another section on the right. Noise appalling and could not make my orders understood. First rounds from the right section hit the crest and by the time we had run these up it was getting dark. The shelling was by now quite furious and we were only 800 yards from the German infantry who turned machine guns onto us as well.'[64]

The advance of the Lancashire Fusiliers was halted briefly at Bucy-le-Long before they moved to Ste Marguerite from where they were ordered to attack the western edge of the Chivres spur. The hoped for assistance from 14 Infantry Brigade which was in position half a mile west of Missy unfortunately did not materialize in time to take part in the attack. Accordingly a rather piecemeal and under-strength attack on the Chivres spur advanced either side of the minor road leading from Ste Marguerite to Chivres with 2/Essex on the left and the Lancashire Fusiliers on the right. The Essex war diarist recording that the 'Lancashire Fusiliers were ordered to attack Chivres covered by fire from the battalion. The attack failed'. Major Griffin's account again:

> 'None of us realized we were about to bump into the enemy, well entrenched and in carefully selected positions ... the task assigned to us was to advance with the Ste Marguerite-Chivres road on our left, and attack the position east of Chivres. The battalion moved through the back gardens of Ste Marguerite almost to Missy, and entered the wood east of Ste Marguerite ... the Germans became aware of our presence, after we had advanced about three quarters of a mile, and opened a brisk fire on us. About this time it was decided to deploy in the open, as it was getting late in the afternoon, and the wood had become practically impenetrable. Woodman's and Fulton's companies deployed on the left, while Blencowe's and Evatt's held the right edge of the wood facing the German trenches, which were only a couple of hundred yards away.'[65]

All four of the Lancashire companies then came under heavy fire from enemy trenches south of the village and from the Chivres spur but continued to press on regardless until it became impossible to make any effective headway. At what point Major Griffin was wounded is not clear but the battalion as a whole suffered sixteen killed including 25-year-old Second Lieutenant John Paulson and another three officers and forty-four other ranks wounded.[66] The battalion was quite clearly distressed by the high number of men who were classed as missing; of these eighty-three missing other ranks the war diary had this to say:

> 'Many under the heading of missing got to within 100 yards of the enemy, and whether killed or wounded, with the exception of 5 or 6 of the latter, who were brought in after dark, could not be recovered, and it can only be hoped that we shall meet the majority restored to health on our arrival at Berlin.'[67]

Apart from the optimistic reference to Berlin, the battalion had just been initiated into the art of the frontal assault against an entrenched enemy and as it withdrew to consolidate the line and await the arrival of the relieving battalion the men had little idea that the line of hurriedly- scraped rifle pits they now occupied would soon stretch from the Belgian North Sea coast to the Swiss border. After dark the relief arrived in the form of 2/Manchesters from Brigadier General Stuart Rolt's 14 Brigade.

The 12 Brigade attack, undertaken without any significant support from British guns and against a position of which they knew very little, made no progress in the face of enemy infantry and artillery fire. As 11 Brigade had already discovered, the British guns established on the heights south of the river were unable to locate and neutralize the German batteries on the high ground to the north of the river and in particular on the Chivres spur. Indeed Hunter-Weston had come to the conclusion, on 13 September, that further progress was unlikely without considerable artillery support. Moreover, the lack of any centralized control of divisional artillery units did not give rise to a culture of close co-operation between the infantry and artillery. This decentralization contributed to several incidents where the 5th Division artillery fired upon the infantry of the 4th Division on the spurs above Bucy-le-Long, adding to the misery of the troops holding the forward positions.[68]

The war diaries of the other battalions which were in the line above Bucy-le-Long on 13 September recount a similar story of stalemate. The Rifle Brigade diary recorded the arrival of Cecil Brereton's 68/Battery guns and immediately sent one platoon from B Company to support the gunners, noting that once the battery opened fire, the enemy counter-battery fire was instantaneous forcing Brereton and his men to retire with six men wounded and fifteen horses killed. Ordered to attack late in the afternoon, the Rifle Brigade advanced with two companies to the crest of the spur where they were met with a withering fire from artillery and German infantry. Tennyson's diary:

'About 30 of our fellows were killed and another 70 or 80 wounded, as well as Captains Nugent, Harrison and Riley, the last named very slightly. Sergeant Dorey,[69] my old platoon sergeant of No. 7 Platoon, when I was in B Company, was killed, and Rfmn Spindler and many others I knew killed. Sergeant Walker, who had done so well at Ligny and had been recommended for the DCM and Médaille Militaire, had his leg almost blown off in this advance, but hanging by a bit of bone. It is hardly credible but he took his pocket knife out and on the field where he lay cut his leg off, and bound his leg up and when it grew dark he was still conscious when he was brought in on a stretcher.'[70]

The Rifle Brigade casualties were – according to the war diary – fourteen killed and three officers and thirty-three other ranks wounded, Tennyson's estimate of the number killed and wounded being a little overstated. The 68/Battery guns were withdrawn under the cover of darkness:

> 'We went down the hill to Ste Marguerite and were told to entrench ourselves back by the Aisne. Major Short suggested we should take up a good position south of the Aisne, but for reasons of 'morale' this was not allowed ... looked at our position and then said to Loch,[71] 'what a terrible place to put up, we will catch it alright tomorrow.'[72]

The Somersets were shelled heavily during the afternoon, losing three men killed and a number wounded, prompting Gerald Whittuck to begin digging the company in with their entrenching tools. 'We were holding a wide extent of front and it did not seem probable to me that we could remain in such a position. We were all expecting a further advance'. Like Whittuck, Brigadier Haldane was also expecting to advance, although by the time he and his brigade were over the river, an element of doubt was apparent in his diary, 'it was uncertain at this time if the enemy intended to stand or continue his retreat'.

Haldane's advance over the river suffered a minor setback when the pontoon bridge put across the river by 9/Field Company was damaged on the night of 13 September. A complete 18-pounder field gun and limber drove over the side into the river causing 'considerable damage to the bridge and it took two hours to get it repaired'. While Lieutenant Young lamented the loss of three horses, he rather gleefully remarked that the 'gun remained on the bottom of the river for three or four days before we could get it out'. The gun and its limber belonged to 122/Battery and was the last remaining gun of Second Lieutenant Clarrie Hodgson's section, the remainder having been destroyed at Le Cateau:

> 'They said we would be able to cross it any minute now, so I had a talk to the fellow doing it and he said, "yes, very well, if you'd like to risk it without side rails." So off we started trying to get across this river along the pontoon bridge. Well, just as the horses and gun got halfway across a German shell pitched into the river. It frightened the horses so much that they slewed off the bridge dragging the gun with them.'[73]

This unfortunate mishap diverted Aylmer Haldane's 10 Infantry Brigade to the damaged road bridge where it too had to cross in single file. 'We did not begin to cross till nearly midnight', commented Haldane, 'and reached Bucy about 1am on the 14th'. Haldane's arrival, almost twenty-four hours after 11 Brigade first entered Bucy-le-Long, at least plugged the gaps in the 11 Brigade frontage which was worrying Gerald Whittuck but it was far too late to make a difference against a strongly-entrenched enemy.

Undeterred by the inconsistent artillery support, the 4th Division was ordered to push on north over the plateau between Vregny and Crouy with the intention of supporting the advance of the 5th Division from their bridgehead at Missy and dislodging the German guns at Clamecy which were effectively holding up Maunoury's advance on the left. But Wilson hesitated. There would need to be a significant increase in the level of artillery support for such an attack to succeed and in Wilson's view, unless the French Sixth Army on the left and the 5th Division on his right could make a decisive move forward, the plan was doomed to failure. And doomed it was, little if any progress was made by the French and the 5th Division made no headway. Haldane's brigade – which was not involved in the attack – suffered badly from shell fire, losing over 100 officers and men as they struggled to find shelter.

On 15 September Haldane was given operational command of the 4th Division units north of the river and those of 19 Brigade yet to cross. Haldane's chief concern was the maintenance of the line on the high ground above Bucy-le-Long but at the back of his mind was always the logistics of a retreat to the river. His diary again betraying his concern:

> 'At first the suggestion that additional bridges should be provided ... was not favourably received in higher quarters ... A retreat, even if carried out at night, would have been a hazardous operation, rendered still more so by the possibility of finding the pontoon bridge at Vénizel destroyed by hostile shells. But before we left the Aisne ... several alternative means of crossing had been made.'[74]

Additional crossing points were also very much on the mind of 10/Field Ambulance which had established a forward dressing station in the school house at Bucy-le-Long. Shortly after crossing with 11 Brigade, the Field Ambulance was joined by Sergeant David Lloyd-Burch, 'we went across the river on a pontoon bridge, the Germans had a commanding view of the river and the flat country from the hills in the distance. Two ambulance wagons were hit getting into Bucy'. Lloyd-Burch had highlighted what was to become a recurring problem for the ambulance units over the next three weeks: the constant shelling from German artillery batteries made the evacuation of the wounded an almost impossible task during the hours of daylight. All that could be done for the plight of the wounded was to make life as comfortable as possible until darkness and the arrival of the ambulance convoys. Evacuation was made even more demanding by the condition of the bridges in the early stages of the campaign which were not really capable of supporting wheeled traffic and the unavoidable congestion on the winding road which ran west-east between Bucy-le-Long and Ste Marguerite. Once the road bridge at Vénizel had been repaired, however, a footbridge was added just downstream whilst on 20 September two more pontoon bridges were built at Moulin des Roches and Missy.

With 10/Field Ambulance firmly installed at Bucy-le-Long, the school house became the main receiving centre for casualties on the 4th Division front, whilst the little church at Ste Marguerite, which stood on the north side of the main street, now acted as the main dressing station for all three infantry brigades. Additional medical staff from 11/Field Ambulance eased the situation a little but the nature of the injuries – mainly from shell fire – was often extensive and put both staff and medical supplies under pressure. It was found, for instance, that the size of the 1914 issue field dressing was woefully inadequate when it came to dressing the wounds inflicted by the razor sharp splinters from high-explosive shell fire. Not only that but also the work of locating, dressing and evacuating the wounded from open ground was severely hampered by continuous shell fire and sniping by the enemy. For the RAMC it was just a taste of what was to become the norm for the next three years.

It was from Bucy that the precarious nightly evacuation of the wounded took place in the horse-drawn ambulance wagons based at La Carrière l'Evecque Farm, just north of Septmonts. A mile further back, at the extensive Château Ecuiry near Rozières, the staff of Number 6 Clearing Hospital opened what was to become the centre for the evacuation of wounded from the left flank of the BEF, mirroring the role Braine was to perform on the right flank. Yet the journey from Vénizel to Rozières by horse-drawn ambulance was slow and tedious and for the badly wounded a painful and uncomfortable experience. Steep roads liberally covered with mud demanded a doubling of the number of horses required to pull each ambulance and the long suffering horses found this more arduous than during the retreat. It was only the arrival of three motor ambulances on 17 September which eased the problem and reduced the journey time significantly.

Nevertheless, enemy shell fire continued to inflict casualties in the British positions. Cecil Brereton was badly wounded on 14 September when German counter battery fire found his gun position:

'We had just got the order to advance again to support the infantry attack, and had sent for our wagons, when the first shell came along. In about 8 minutes the Hun had completely got the range and we were fairly for it. A direct hit on one of Loch's guns finished most of the detachment and a direct hit on one of my guns then finished me and most of my detachment and also poor Wallinger who was observing for his Howitzer battery from behind my limber.'[75]

Earlier in the day the Seaforth Highlanders lost their commanding officer, 45-year-old Lieutenant Colonel Sir Evelyn Bradford. Bradford, a celebrated Hampshire county cricketer, was commissioned in 1888 from Sandhurst and killed by a single shell as he inspected the ground in front of the battalion over which it was expected the advance would continue. It has to be said that German shelling was highly accurate and very destructive. Lieutenant Geoffrey Prideaux, an officer with the 1/SLI, was in Bucy-le-Long on the morning of 15 September:

'The Germans hit a house opposite the church with a high explosive shell of large calibre, completely demolishing the house. It also set on fire the East Lancs' machine-gun limber, which happened to be standing under cover of the house, and killed one horse and wounded another very badly ... the road up to the trenches was blocked with debris in many places, and the church was hit. A wall had been blown down across the road in one place, and a big tree in another place. On my way up I saw a howitzer battery which had taken up its position on the hillside in a field due west of La Montagne Farm, completely put out of action by German 8.4" howitzers. The shells fell amongst the guns with surprising accuracy, in one case lifting an ammunition wagon up in the air and dropping it upside down.'[76]

What Prideaux had witnessed was some very effective counter-battery fire directed overhead from a Rumpler Taube of the Imperial German Army Air Service. The howitzer battery in question was from XXXVII Brigade whose guns had crossed the river before dawn on 13 September and engaged enemy batteries to the north. By noon both the 31/ and 55/Battery positions had been spotted by a Taube and although they too came under heavy shell fire and lost seventeen men killed, it appears none of the guns were damaged. At around 2.00pm on the 15th the German spotter aircraft was back, the brigade war diary recorded the ensuing bombardment:

> *'Shortly after this the batteries were subjected to a heavy fire from heavy guns ... 40 to 50 shells falling amongst the batteries in five to ten minutes. During the firing 31 Battery lost 16 killed, 12 wounded and 33 horses, one shell falling amongst the men, who had been moved under cover of a sunken road, killed 12 and wounded 9.'*[77]

Both batteries were forced to retire to the wooded area northeast of Vénizel Bridge. 31/Battery alone had lost over 30 per cent of its manpower.

Whilst artillery support was welcomed, batteries which were sited too close to the infantry trenches inevitably drew fire and caused further casualties. Gerald Whittuck watched a battery of French 75s come into action in front of his trenches and despite, 'some wonderful shooting, drew fire onto us. We were unluckily just outside our dugouts when they opened fire first'. The first salvo killed Lieutenant Arthur Read[78] and the second severely wounded 21-year-old Lieutenant Arthur Newton. 'Four men were killed and eight wounded', wrote Whittuck, 'but I managed to get stretchers up when the shells were not quite so thick. We buried Read and four others the same night, a parson reading the service'.

Thus as night fell on 15 September the 4th Division held the edge of the high ground from a point south of Chivres running north of Ste Marguerite to La Montagne Farm from where the line moved westwards to Point 151 east of Crouy. South of the river was 19 Infantry Brigade less the Argyll and Sutherland Highlanders whom General Haldane had brought up to Bucy-le-Long as a reserve. The XXIX Brigade guns were all south of the Aisne and firing at extreme range against German batteries which were cleverly concealed and difficult to locate. 125/ and 127/Batteries were in action near Sermoise but after 126/Battery crossed the river and attracted a hail of shell fire, it too was withdrawn across to the south bank. The XXXVII Brigade guns which were subjected to the severe mauling witnessed by Geoffrey Prideaux were now under the cover of the wooded area north of Vénizel, whilst the XIV Brigade guns were about Bucy-le-Long.

The Chivres spur which dominated Condé and its bridge continued to be a thorn in the side of the British attack. The eighteen heavy guns which the Germans had positioned on the spur provided their gunners with an almost uninterrupted view on either side and allowed them to fire on the British positions accordingly. It was the opinion of many that it was the failure to storm this promontory that not only decided the battle on the left flank but made a significant contribution to the ultimate failure to break the deadlock.

Chapter 6

The Centre Left – 5th Division

*When we arrived in the village we were told the most harrowing
tales of how it was shelled every day and sniped into continuously.*

Lieutenant Cyril Helm – describing his first impressions of Missy

R eaders will recall that Sir Charles Fergusson's 5th Division
began crossing the Aisne on the night of 13 September at Missy
and Major General Hubert Hamilton's 3rd Division at Vailly.
The crossing at both points was greeted by German artillery fire from
batteries situated on the Chivres spur, in particular one battery near
the Fort de Condé and two further north at Les Carrières and although
the British artillery was quick to respond, their guns were soon under
heavy counter-battery fire themselves. On the high ground above Ciry,
Major Cecil de Sausmarez, commanding 108/Heavy Battery, was
responding to the enemy fire:

'*Saw Germans on opposite bank of Aisne apparently very busy. Got onto a
target and switched to a place north of wood surrounding Condé Fort from
where hostile battery appeared to be firing … Shells soon began to fall to
with 100 to 200 yards of us. I went to a field on the right where Major
Livingstone-Learmonth*[79] *(65th Howitzer Battery) had his observing post
to confer with him. On my way back I saw shells bursting close to my
observing party … The shells which were from large howitzers began to
burst all round.*'[80]

In the face of this bombardment from German 8-inch howitzers,
Sausmarez pulled the battery back 600 yards leaving nine horses
killed. He was fortunate that not a single man was touched.
Nevertheless the German heavy howitzers appeared to have had the
upper hand and from their positions north of the river clearly

outranged all the British artillery with the exception of the heavy batteries.

The 5th Division artillery had lost heavily at Le Cateau on 26 August. Holding the right flank of II Corps on and around the Montay spur southwest of Le Cateau, they lost a total of twenty-seven guns to enemy action. By far the hardest hit in terms of losses was XXIII Brigade which left sixteen of its guns behind and XV Brigade which was reduced to just eight guns. But it was not only guns which were lost. At least 22 officers and 180 NCOs and men were killed or captured in addition to 257 horses that became casualties. 108/Battery was more fortunate, positioned close to the Bois Marronnier near Reumont it was to the south of the main action and only lost one of its heavy 60 pounders – not to enemy action but to a French drainage ditch which overturned the gun and its limber! At nearly 5 tons in weight and with the German Army expected any moment, there was no time for any attempt at recovery.

Back on the river at Missy, 13 Brigade was slowly establishing itself on the north bank. By dawn on 14 September both the Royal West Kents and 2/KOSB were across the Aisne and entrenched on the northern bank, taking up a position between the damaged bridge and the village of Missy. Jim Pennyman, the KOSB machine-gun officer, recalled the crossing vividly and the scene which greeted him on the other side:

> *'The engineers* [59/Field Company] *had made a raft which had a nasty trick of sinking, and when we got there we found three drowned men being brought round by Sergeant Major Fuller. For some reason, the Germans weren't opposing the crossing so the boat went back and forwards unmolested. I got leave to take my party across at once, as it would soon be light, and I thought we might be wanted. As soon as I landed I did a scout round on my own and found as follows: On our left the broken bridge, and a road to the village of Missy. The village was half a mile off and, I think, in the hands of the Germans. Immediately to the right of the bridge was an old farm house with a depression behind it which afforded a certain amount of cover. All along the river bank was a thinnish wood thirty yards wide, sloping down to the river … to our front we could see about half a mile of open park like country and then wooded hills, which we knew to be full of Germans.'*[81]

Lieutenant Palmer of the West Kents was soon soaked through by the rain as his battalion crossed over amid the ricochets from enemy rifle fire which he recorded were, 'unpleasantly thick'. The crossing was not without incident. Second Lieutenant Kenneth Godsell, working with 17/Field Company at the Moulin des Roches crossing point, had problems with Brigadier Gleichen's horse, 'Silver', which, 'jumped out of the raft and swam up and down the middle of the river for over ten minutes whilst the batman threw fits on the bank'. It was perhaps a much needed moment of amusement in a situation which was somewhat uncertain for all concerned.

At Missy, Captain Robert Dolbey, the KOSB medical officer, felt their position, 'was a perilous one from a military sense'. The two 13 Brigade battalions were only in occupation of the Missy road and the wooded area on the north bank. 'Both our flanks were in the air', wrote Dolbey, 'we had no line of retreat save the damaged bridge, why we were not rushed we could never understand'. Pennyman agreed and felt that the ,'position was an extremely unpleasant one' and if it came to retirement they would have to swim for it.

According to Godsell's diary, at 8.45pm on 14 September a section of the 2nd Bridging Train (2/Bridging Train) finally appeared at Moulin des Roches to construct a pontoon bridge capable of taking heavy traffic which, to Godsell's delight, was in place by midnight. The two bridging trains had been sent up to the front by train from Le Mans on 9 September and after detraining at Chaumes two days later, began the march towards the Aisne. Each of the two bridging trains carried forty-two pontoons on specially adapted wagons and on the march was pulled by some 350 horses. Cumbersome and requiring a great deal of road space, the two bridging units had, like their steam-driven namesakes, spent an inordinate amount of time and effort being 'shunted' around northern France since their arrival in late August.

2/Bridging Train had disembarked at Le Havre on 20 August, one day later than the 1st Bridging Train which had already landed at Boulogne. Having loaded their equipment onto several trains, both bridging units were transported by rail to Cambrai where orders were received on 23 August to unload and proceed by road to Amiens. Events at Mons and the subsequent retreat had now caught up with them and instead of advancing they then had to retire with the rest of the BEF in the face of von Kluck's First Army. One of the complaints the Royal Engineers voiced in the early months of the war centred on the apparent inability of the staff to grasp the effort and time required to carry out certain orders. There was an expectation that once an order had been committed to paper by a staff officer, the effect would be almost immediate. The war diary of 2/Bridging Train gives an indication of the time and physical effort it took to unload the pontoons and equipment:

'Detraining began immediately but was slow owing to the difficulty of off loading the pontoon wagons sideways. Each wagon had to be lifted by hand before it could be sufficiently turned to run off the trucks ... the first vehicle came off at 10pm and the last at 3am. The whole train was in bivouac at the station by 4am.'[82]

Both units reached Amiens by noon on 26 August – the same day that II Corps was fighting its rearguard action at Le Cateau 75 miles to the northeast. At Amiens fresh orders directed them to Rouen where the war diary wearily records them arriving on 30 September and being ordered on to Evreux where they were to entrain for Le Mans. Questionable staff work was most likely behind the reason they were not deployed to bridge the Marne at La Ferté-sous-Jouarre on 8 September; an oversight which meant that that particular burden fell on the shoulders of 7/ and 9/Field Companies.

In the space of twenty-five days the two bridging units had travelled over 700 miles by train and road and yet had still arrived two days after the first Royal Engineer field companies reached the Aisne. The arrangement at the time appears to have been to hold back the bridging trains until the first reconnaissance had been completed and then order them up as required. Thus poor staff work, together with a failure to fully appreciate the bridging logistics required to move five infantry divisions across a major river inevitably contributed to the stalemate on the Aisne. There is a strong argument to support the view that the vital heavy bridging units should have been allocated to the leading divisions and made available to bridge the river much earlier, thus enabling the infantry to cross in greater strength and creating the conditions necessary for more co-ordinated attacks. Certainly this may have given British units the opportunity to gain a secure foothold on the Chivres spur and may have altered the course of the battle.[83]

* * *

Although the advance of the 5th Division ran parallel with that of the 4th Division on its left, the two British units were separated by the Chivres spur on which the German 5th Infantry Division was very securely entrenched. This promontory, referred to by Edward Gleichen as, 'that horrible Chivres spur', not only separated the two British divisions physically but appeared to check any attempt at co-ordinating their offensive planning. From very early on in the battle it became apparent that the key to any advance on the left of the British front lay in gaining possession of the spur. The high ground of the spur, with the old Fort de Condé on its summit, dominated the valleys on either side and whilst it remained in German hands, any significant advance was unlikely. Accordingly a two-pronged attack was planned for 14 September: 14 Brigade would attack from the direction of Ste Marguerite and, when Missy was cleared of the enemy, 15 Brigade was to advance and attack the spur from the southeast. Artillery support was provided in the form of XV Brigade and the heavy howitzers of 37/ and 61/Batteries, all of which had been brought up to Bucy-le-Long.

The mist and rain which greeted the troops at dawn on 14 September did not prevent the German gunners on the spur from shelling the valleys on either side as soon as it was light and against this backdrop the 1/Duke of Cornwall's Light Infantry (1/DCLI) and the 1st Battalion East Surrey Regiment (1/East Surreys) advanced towards the wooded western slopes of the spur. The line of advance, described by the East Surreys war diarist, was, 'open and rather across the enemy's front and casualties commenced very soon', but by noon both battalions were in possession of the northern edge of Missy. It was a different story on the left of the DCLI where 2/Manchesters, came under heavy fire from the direction of Chivres, the village was held by the German 52nd Infantry Regiment, (IR52) and against their resolute defence could make no further progress. The Manchesters had crossed the river the day before and been in action above Ste Marguerite in support of the 4th Division, relieving the Lancashire Fusiliers at dusk that evening. It was from their positions west of Chivres that they attempted to advance on 14 September, the war diary rather brusquely recording that the Manchesters 'took up a position of defence on the west of Chivres wood and remained there a week'.

Meanwhile 15 Infantry Brigade which had crossed the river just before dawn on 14 September, courtesy of the Royal Engineers of 17/Field Company and their leaking rafts, made their way via Bucy-le-Long to Ste Marguerite, now held by 12 Brigade. With the 1st Battalion Dorsetshire Regiment (1/Dorsets) left in reserve in the shelter of the sunken road north of the village, the three remaining battalions of Gleichen's brigade moved on towards Missy with orders to clear the Chivres spur from the southeast and push on to Condé. It was, felt Edward Gleichen, 'rather a large order'. Even the process of actually getting to Missy along the winding road which skirted the high ground to the north was no easy matter:

'The road thither was spattered with bullets, and shells were bursting all along it. However, by dint of careful work we moved out bit by bit, cutting

through gardens and avoiding the road, and taking advantage of a slight slope in the ground by which we could sneak to the far side of the little railway embankment which led to Missy station.'[84]

Gleichen met Stuart Rolt on the way and agreed with 14 Brigade's commander to join forces and attack the Chivres spur with a combined force. One company of the Bedfords together with another of the East Surreys had already advanced some way up the wooded spur beyond the village where they consolidated their position and awaited the arrival of the main force. Gleichen's diary summarised the situation they were in:

'The difficulty was that it was already getting late – 4.30pm – and that there was insufficient time for a thorough reconnaissance, though we did what we could in that direction. However my orders from the divisional commander had been to take the ridge, and I tried to do it. I had got together three companies of the Norfolks, three of the Bedfords, two Cheshires (in reserve), two East Surreys (14 Brigade) and two Cornwalls (12 Brigade who had arrived via the broken bridge at Missy) – twelve companies altogether.'[85]

Although reconnaissance had established the presence of wire netting and wire entanglements in the woods, a number of battalion commanders were more concerned at the level of support available to the attacking infantry. Lieutenant Colonel John Longley, the 47-year-old commanding officer of the East Surreys, was not entirely comfortable with the plan of attack. The battalion war diary recorded his concerns and the subsequent advance:

'It was not apparent to the commanding officer where the necessary support was to come from in his attack on the spur, and in his report on the situation he pointed this out … The battalion crossed the entanglements unopposed, with the Norfolks on its right and the Bedfords on its left. After passing the wire it had a short steep climb before emerging on to a wide grass track leading up through the wood. The battalion was crossing this track with some of the Norfolks when a very heavy fire was opened on us from our right front, where on some rising ground was a German trench not 70 yards away. It was almost dark now which increased our difficulties, but the line of the track however was made good.'[86]

After conferring with the Norfolks and the leading company of the Bedfords, Longley was about to instigate a flanking attack when orders arrived from Edward Gleichen to retire. The Norfolks did so immediately leaving one company of Bedfords in support of the East Surreys. From Gleichen's diary it appears that a number of men were under the impression that they were being shelled by British artillery and had taken it upon themselves to retire, he also makes reference to groups of British infantry firing at their own men in the confusion of the wood. 'This may have been true', wrote Gleichen, 'for some shells were bursting over the wood; but whether they were English or German I do not know to this day'. There was undoubtedly some confusion of direction amongst some units in the gathering dusk which finally gave way to an equally confused retirement. The Cheshire's regimental historian described the action:

> 'Battalions on the left swung unconsciously to the right, and right in front of the Germans there was the most glorious jumble imaginable. Everyone blames everyone else and the Germans took full advantage of it all, as can be imagined. Men fell in every direction whilst officers and NCOs strove, by word and whistle, to reduce this chaos to some sort of order.'[87]

As to the incident of friendly fire noted by Gleichen, Major Cranley Onslow of the Bedfords described the proliferation of shell fire in the wood which could easily have led to the impression that British batteries were firing upon their own troops:

> 'Then the enemy shelled our end (south) of the wood and our guns shelled the north end – so we went back to the village where there was evidently a German telephone as it immediately began to rain shells in the village and most of the houses were brought down, so we took up a position south of the village as it was now getting dusk.'[88]

While Missy was subjected to a furious bombardment the stream of men retiring from the spur increased, leaving three companies of East Surreys and one of the Bedfords on the spur. Onslow's reference to a German telephone reflects the widely held belief at the time that the British lines were riddled with spies who were directing German artillery fire. Spies there certainly were and a number of German soldiers were discovered *in situ* behind British lines doing exactly that, but on the night of 14 September the artillery barrage which fell on Missy was directed by the enormous advantage of direct observation the German gunners enjoyed from the high ground.

Back on the spur Colonel John Longley redistributed his men and pushed forward Lieutenant 'Monty' Montanaro with B Company only to have him withdraw to the track again after he found that the German line had been reinforced. Interestingly, there is an undercurrent of implied disapproval running through the East Surreys account of the action in their war diary. Longley would have been quite justified in believing his position – albeit insecure and just 50 yards from the German trenches – was still manageable and with support could be held overnight. The orders from 14 Brigade to retire to Ste Marguerite must have bewildered him a little, particularly – as he correctly predicted – the attack would be continued the next day. Even more galling was the idea that the hard won ground upon which he was now standing should be given up to an enemy who would spend the hours of darkness strengthening their positions. Reluctantly, Longley withdrew his men to Ste Marguerite as ordered.

Before we continue with the attacks of 15 September, we should return to the plight of the battalions at the Missy bridge. The original plan of attack for 14 September included the KOSB and the West Kents from 13 Brigade who were north of the Missy Bridge. But any thoughts of advancing further towards the Chivres spur were prevented by the volume of fire which effectively kept them pinned down on the north bank. Jim Pennyman's diary account describes the fight which was taking place along the wooded fringe to the east of the bridge:

> *'An increasing rifle fire was directed on to our wood, but no shell fire. The task allotted to the Borderers was to line out in the wood in order to prevent the Germans from sneaking down to the river bank, rushing the wood and taking in the rear the troops on our left front. Our front line had its right on the river and its left about the middle of the little salient wood.'* [89]

Aware that the enemy were indeed intending to attack their right flank, Pennyman, who was commanding D Company in the wood, deployed Second Lieutenant Gilbert Amos with his platoon to prevent any enemy intentions in that direction.

> *'The bullets kept plumping in here in the most alarming manner, but we daren't leave it unoccupied. After about a quarter-of-an-hour the message came down from Amos to say he had already had five casualties. So we withdrew his platoon into the middle of the salient and bent our own left flank to join up with them. This seemed to be successful.'* [90]

With casualties mounting in the wood Captain Robert Dolbey decided his presence was required on the firing line. Accordingly he took whatever medical supplies he had to hand and crossed the river to establish his dressing station. It was a journey fraught with danger which began in a leaking raft:

> *'A climb up the bank; a rush across the road; a swift tumble down the other side, and we were in the wood; a wood which seemed alive with death. How thankful I was that we had come in time; for there were wounded men everywhere and one didn't know where to begin. Then a corporal spoke to me and I turned aside to a little hollow; and there lay young Amos.'*[91]

Gilbert Amos died almost immediately after he was hit. The 18-year-old former Wellington College schoolboy had only just joined the regiment from Sandhurst and was the youngest subaltern in the battalion. He had fought at Mons, Le Cateau and during the advance from the Marne. Mourning his death, Robert Dolbey was under no illusion that, 'life was very short for all the officers in this battalion; and if death had not come now, it would have surely have overtaken him in the next three months'.

German snipers up in the trees on the high ground to the right of the KOSB were exacting a heavy toll on the men. Pennyman himself had a close shave shortly after Amos had been hit when a sniper's bullet 'went into the ground very close' to where he was firing a machine gun. But it was the second bullet that got him:

> *'I thought it might be a sniper who had seen us, so we moved three of four yards to our right. The next thing I remember was a sensation like a blow with a cricket ball in the chest. It knocked me clean down, and I remember shouting as I fell bleeding profusely at the mouth. I felt quite certain I was a gonner, but managed to get up again and give some directions to the gunner, then I flopped down again.'*[92]

Fortunately Robert Dolbey was on hand and his prompt action undoubtedly saved the young officer's life. 'Pennyman was brought in all limp and grey and cold; there was blood on his shirt in front and my orderly seeing the position of the wound, said too loudly that he was gone ... but the age of miracles was not past'.

* * *

After the retirement from the Chivres spur the previous day Edward Gleichen was summoned to a riverside meeting with Sir Charles Fergusson at the Missy Bridge. 'We got there eventually and crossed the river, sliding down steep slippery banks into a punt, ferried across, and up the other side'. Fergusson ordered a fresh assault on the spur led by the 1st Battalion Norfolk Regiment (1/Norfolks) with the Bedfords in support. On this occasion the attack was preceded by a thirty minute artillery barrage which did little to suppress the enemy sniper fire that greeted the arrival of first light. Major Cranley Onslow had good reason to remember that morning very well:

> *'Stand to Arms at 3.30am and await orders which arrived about 5.00am. Snipers in the village and orchards began plugging – I was going along to see everybody had got their rations when I got what was called a German ticket to England in the shape of a bullet from a sniper in my left loin about 6.00am. I got this dressed by a couple of men and lay where I was behind the parapet and eventually got to the dressing station by the haystack where I spent last night.'*[93]

The Norfolks pushed on up the spur but were soon brought to a standstill in the wood where the German positions had been strengthened overnight.

Ordered to advance up the valley to the east of the Missy-Vregny road, 1/DCLI soon came under fire from the spur. Lieutenant Arthur Acland described the valley as, 'a death trap, cross-fire from machine guns, infantry and artillery, no troops could have got further than ours, unsupported as we were from our artillery'. Such was the confusion brought about by the strength of the enemy defence that the rear battalions of 15 Brigade and the DCLI crowded into Missy where the congestion was spotted from above by a German Taube with the inevitable result. At around 10.00am German artillery drenched the village with shells forcing a temporary evacuation. The attack had been a total failure and it wasn't long before Colonel John Longley was ordered to move to Missy from his battalion's dugouts at Ste Marguerite to relieve 15 Brigade which had retired to the northern edge of the village. The Surreys' war diary takes up the story, noting rather dryly that the 15 Brigade attack had 'apparently' not progressed very far:

> *'The commanding officer called at Brigade Headquarters en route in order to arrange for some support from the two battalions of 13 Brigade who were still in position as yesterday S E of Missy, as it seemed to him one battalion only might be insufficient to hold the line previously held by a brigade ... The night was pitch dark with incessant rain so it was not to be wondered at that a searchlight from the German lines was much in evidence or that the posts of the 15 Brigade were in a hurry to be relieved. Hurry, however, on such a night was impossible.'*[94]

It was well past midnight before the last of 15 Brigade left Missy to cross the river via the new pontoon bridge erected by 2/Bridging Train at Vénizel. Gleichen recalls leaving the village during a heavy German artillery bombardment accompanied by, 'German flare lights and searchlights', whilst John Longley observed rather sardonically that it had been, 'a very trying night'. That evening command of all 5th Division troops north of the river was placed in the hands of Brigadier General Rolt.

Longley's request for support arrived on the evening of 16 September in the form of the 2nd Battalion Duke of Wellington's Regiment (2/Duke of Wellington's) which had originally been intended to be part of the attack on the Chivres spur but had not been able to get into position owing to the weight of fire from the direction of Condé. The delay occurred on the river at the pontoon bridge built by 9/Field Company. Having repaired the bridge on 13 September it was badly damaged again next day by a French ammunition limber. 'It was a very extraordinary feeling', wrote Lieutenant Bernard Young, 'as the bridge gradually sank, the decking opened out and through and down we went'. Consequently the two waiting battalions of 13 Brigade were forced to take to the water in rafts. In the event it was only the Duke of Wellington's which crossed the river that night, the 2nd Battalion King's Own Yorkshire Light Infantry (2/KOYLI) were caught by the breaking dawn in full view of the enemy gunners. Lieutenant Cyril Helm, the battalion medical officer, described the consequences of being caught in the open by German artillery in his diary:

'We started off about 3.00am and marched down to the river through the village of Sermoise to within a few hundred yards of the river. Here we halted whilst the Adjutant went on to reconnoitre. Half an hour went by and we could not work out what was the matter as the first signs of dawn were appearing in the sky. We all knew that if we were still there when day broke, we were in full view of the Germans, without any cover, and only a few hundred yards from them. Well! Day broke and we were still there ...The men were spread out along a single line of trees and told to lie down. We knew that we had been seen by the German observers and almost immediately four high explosive 5.9 shells burst together, exactly over our heads. They were beautifully timed and only a few yards above us. The scene after that was appalling ... the groans of the wounded was too nerve racking for words. Men started to get up and run to a flank but this was no good as there was no cover.'[95]

Helm describes how his own terror manifested itself with a strong desire to run away but realizing it was up to him and the other officers to set an example to the men he contained his panic and encouraged those around him to remain where they were:

'My thoughts were indescribable as I realized that lying on my belly, the next shell might blow me to smithereens. A minute afterwards, another salvo came and my orderly corporal, who was with me, only a few feet away, was frightfully shattered; one of his legs being completely blown away ... that morning twenty were killed and about fifty wounded.'[96]

The battalion eventually crossed the river on 24 September and relieved 2/Duke of Wellington's at Missy.

The arrangements for the evacuation of the wounded from Missy relied upon the bridges at the village and the winding road which led steeply up to the dressing station at Sermoise. Casualties for the 5th Division alone on the 13 September were 16 officers and 728 other ranks killed and wounded and of these, 11 officers and 560 other ranks were wounded. As the majority of these men were in action on the north bank of the river, and the available bridges were in constant use by troops, it is not surprising that very few casualties reached Sermoise that evening. The next day enemy shell fire prevented any movement by the field ambulances during daylight to a great extent and it was only under the cover of darkness that 15/Field Ambulance was able to begin bringing out wounded men from Missy. Even above the river, the road between Ciry and Serches was heavily shelled, disrupting movement between the dressing station and the divisional collecting station at Mont de Soissons Farm. 5th Division horse drawn ambulance trains suffered the same difficulties as their counterparts in the 4th Division, the steepness of the roads leading out of the river valley severely taxed the flagging strength of the horses and it wasn't until 20 September that motor ambulances put in an appearance to lighten the load.

Mont de Soissons Farm was described by Major Frederick Brereton as, 'a commodious place', with beds for between 300 and 400 casualties:

'A barn here, floored with straw, an outhouse over the way with palliasses [straw-filled mattresses] ranged along beside the walls, stretchers in the wash house, more palliasses upstairs, and, thanks to the willing assistance of the farmer and his spouse, actual beds in one part of the dwelling – real, comfortable beds for the very severe cases, for those who had needed operations, perhaps for the dying.'[97]

It was here that Cranley Onslow was brought after being wounded at Missy, although his journey from the front line was not in one of the new motor ambulances:

> 'Three miles being jolted in a Maltese Cart then four miles in a horsed ambulance wagon to a clearing hospital at Mont Des Soissons Farm where my wound was dressed again and I had some soup and milk and slept in a bed until daybreak.'[98]

Onslow remembered 'a journey in a motor lorry of about fifteen miles' before he was put onto an ambulance train at Ouchly-le-Château , arriving at St Nazaire on 19 September. Onslow was in all probability at the farm on the day Jim Pennyman arrived in a 13/Field Ambulance wagon:

> 'We crossed the Aisne somewhere by a pontoon bridge and fetched up at a large farm called Pont-de-Soissons (sic) in the early morning. I recognized it as a place we had been to on the previous Saturday (12th). I lay there all the morning and was given a glass of egg and milk to comfort me. Our heavies were shooting from a place close to the farm – very inconsiderate of them, as shells aimed back might easily have hit us.'[99]

Pennyman was also taken by what he described as a 'springless motor lorry' to the railhead at Oulchy and arrived at Number 8 Clearing hospital at Rouen late on 19 September.

As far as the Chivres spur was concerned it had become very apparent that its capture was beyond the current strength of the BEF. To the left and right of the British front the French were also in the same position and as the 5th Division commenced its consolidation of the line it clung to from Missy to Ste Marguerite, the battle entered a new phase.

Chapter 7

The Centre Right – 3rd Division

I slowly raised my head to see that the shell had exploded precisely over the hollow and killed every one of the wounded.

Corporal John Lucy – *There's a Devil in the Drum*

Between Missy and the 3rd Division bridgehead at Vailly the Condé salient drove a dangerous wedge through the British front. Originally allocated to the 5th Division as one of two crossing points over the river, the reader will recall that the bridge at Condé was discovered to be intact on 12 September by a patrol of 4/Hussars led by Captain John Gatacre. A hail of fire from the northern end of the bridge greeted his patrol as they had crossed over the River Vesle and headed towards the road bridge over the Aisne. At the time the approaches to the Condé bridge were said to be too exposed and the bridge too heavily defended to allow a direct infantry assault. From all accounts it would seem that this was never actually put to the test and the bridge remained in German hands for the whole of the British campaign, something which Douglas Haig – on hearing the bridge had not been taken – felt required an explanation. The terse note in his diary regarding 'the action of the 2nd Corps and particularly the 3rd Division (H Hamilton) on 13th September, will want a lot of explaining', was probably aimed at Simth–Dorrien's failure to secure the Condé Bridge. Bearing in mind the location of the bridge in relation to the Condé spur he did have a point!

At Vailly, Second Lieutenant Cyril Martin's reconnaissance had established that the bridge spanning the Canal Latéral was intact but the river bridge was badly damaged and the light railway bridge a mile upstream destroyed. Nevertheless the 3rd Division began to negotiate the river crossing on 13 September using a single plank to span the gap which the Germans – according to the *Official History* – had apparently left behind. The high ground north of Vailly is divided by the Jouy Valley up which the D14 now runs to join the N2. On the left of the D14 is the Jouy spur and on the right, the larger Ostel spur with the St Précord spur running south from La Rouge Maison Farm. Hamilton's plan of attack for the 3rd Division was to keep McCracken's 7 Infantry Brigade in reserve and deploy Doran's 8 Brigade to advance up the Jouy spur and Shaw's 9 Brigade to the Ostel spur, where it was hoped to join up with the left of the 2nd Division advancing north from La Cour Soupir Farm.

Yet even before 8 Infantry Brigade had reached the river they came under fire from German batteries. Arriving at Chassemy, which overlooked the river below, German gunners were quick to greet them with a heavy barrage. Despite the grey and wet start to the day, the single road – the D14 – which led down to the bridge at Vailly was clearly visible to the Germans on the Chivres spur and as the 2nd Battalion Royal Irish Regiment (2/Royal Irish) left the security of the wooded slopes they came under shell fire sometime after 8.15am. 26-year-old Lieutenant Frederick Rushton immediately ordered his men to take cover on either side of the road, noting that, 'a battery of our guns took up a position in [the] wood in rear of open space. Enemy shelling the edge of wood steadily. Range absolutely correct. Each shell overhead, bursting in rear'. The British battery seen by Rushton and his men was 49/Battery from XL Brigade which had unlimbered, not in the wood, but in the open and commenced firing across the valley. All too soon it was silenced by the greater fire power of the German howitzer batteries, putting two guns out of action and forcing the gunners to abandon the guns, or as Frederick Rushton rather benevolently put it, 'our gunners have moved back, leaving [the] guns ready to fire when required'.[100]

At 10.00am, under the cover of the guns of 48/Heavy Battery which had come into action north of Brenelle, the 2nd Battalion Royal Scots (2/Royal Scots) began working its way downhill through the woods to the right of the road to reach the canal a little to the east of the bridge. It was followed by the Royal Irish and the 4th Battalion Middlesex Regiment (4/Middlesex), all of which were successfully over the river and established on the other side by 4.00pm on 13 September. It is worth noting here that 8 Brigade was without the 1st Battalion Gordon Highlanders, which had suffered badly at Le Cateau on 26 August, losing over 700 officers and men killed or taken prisoner and in the process practically ceasing to exist as a battalion. It was only at the end of September that the battalion attained its full strength again and rejoined the brigade.[101]

After dark, Shaw's 9 Infantry Brigade crossed the river. The 1st Battalion Lincolnshire Regiment (1/Lincolns) historian described the passage which took place in the pouring rain:

> *'It was near midnight before the Lincolnshire began their hazardous crossing. The advance was by sections, each section first crossing the bridge over the canal and then over the single plank spanning the gap in the broken bridge over the river in single file. A false step left or right would have meant certain death from drowning. Every now and then a bursting shell would throw the weird scene into prominence but not a single man was hit, neither did anyone fall into the river. Progress was very slow, but once across the men had to double several hundred yards to where the battalion was forming. When the last man had joined, the battalion marched off through the town of Vailly at a rapid pace and wheeled right up a narrow lane and then across a large tract of cultivated land on to a high ridge to the southwest of Rouge Maison Farm.'*[102]

The crossing, 'took the best part of two hours and we had a weary wait in the pitch darkness', wrote Captain Gerard Kempthorne, the medical officer attached to the battalion. As the battalion moved up above Vailly onto the southern slopes of the Ostel spur they found themselves in what Kempthorne described as a, 'vast turnip field' where they found the men of the 4th Battalion Royal Fusiliers, (4/Royal Fusiliers) already in place having completed their crossing by 11.30pm. The Lincolns extended the line to the left of La Rouge Maison Farm and the medical officer and his team dug in behind the firing line alongside one of the A Company platoons:

> *'We were in a trench with about 30 men, all cold, hungry, and shivering and caked with mud from head to foot. The ground rose a little, 100 yards in front of us, and all that was to be seen was wet turnips, on either side, and to the rear.'*[103]

At dawn on 14 September two companies of the Royal Scots advanced up the Jouy spur through the mist and rain with the Royal Irish on their left and the Middlesex on the right. Artillery support, such as it was, provided little to assist the advance and as the Royal Scots historian remarked, 'the German fire by this time was positively murderous'.[104] The German trenches were on the reverse slope of the crest and as soon as the British troops came into range they were effectively stopped in their tracks by machine-gun and artillery fire. Major Hamilton Finch, advancing with the Middlesex, was alarmed to find they were, 'for a short period under fire from several directions', as German machine-gun teams managed to establish a firing line on the British flanks. 'An effort was made by some to take their machine guns', wrote Finch, 'but it was a hopeless attempt and our men got back with wonderfully few casualties'. B Company of the Royal Irish found themselves involved in heavy fighting in the wooded slopes and shortly after being reinforced by half of A Company, Lieutenant Frederick Rushton was killed at the head of his platoon. Pushed back, the Royal Irish took up a new position on the minor road running east of Vauxelles towards Vailly, with the Royal Scots and the Middlesex on their left.

The lack of fire power offered by the attacking 8 Brigade would certainly have given encouragement to the German counter-attack which was launched just before 9.00am. It was well timed and the British were in no position to respond effectively, although they did manage to hold on for close to an hour; long enough for the enemy attack to peter out. At around 10.00am the brigade began to fall back. Major Finch's account:

> 'Now came the moment for us to retire, and this might have been a very unpleasant experience as the enemy's guns were very busily at work on the bend of the road we had to follow before we could get on the high ground. However, we reached another ridge with, I believe, no casualties, by doubling round the bend at about 20 paces interval. The order then came that we were to hold on there (on the north side of the river) at all costs; this was about 4.00pm.'[105]

In many ways the attack had had little chance of success from the outset. On 14 September 8 Brigade had to rely very much on the fire power from its rifle companies as the three battalions had not a single machine gun available between them.[106] Moreover, the combined manpower of the three battalions only numbered some 1,500 officers and men, a state of affairs which can be traced directly to the brigade's action in the Nimy salient at Mons on 23 August and the subsequent encounters at Le Cateau and on the Marne. At Nimy the Middlesex and the Royal Irish had fought a desperate rearguard action as they had retired towards Cuesmes – which incidentally was held by 1/Lincolns – both regiments losing heavily in the process. Le Cateau further depleted the ranks with the loss of the Gordon Highlanders, as did the rigours of the retreat. It was only after the arrival of the 1st Battalion of the Devonshire Regiment (1/Devons) on 15 September that the brigade could put two machine guns in the firing line! Little wonder then that the attack on the Jouy spur failed.

* * *

On the Ostel spur at La Rouge Maison Farm the morning mist had concealed the presence of the German positions which were only 600 yards away just below the crest of the ridge. It was from these trenches that the German attack was launched at 7.30am. Somewhat taken aback by the ferocity of the supporting shell and machine-gun fire, the appearance of waves of enemy infantry initially put the British on the back foot, prompting Brigadier General Shaw to reinforce the line with the Northumberland Fusiliers and the three battalions – although ordered to counter attack – were eventually pushed back almost to the edge of the spur. Throughout the morning the Germans continued the attack; wave after wave advancing against the British line. According to the Royal Fusiliers' war diary, they managed to hold their sector of the line for 'some time' until the regiment on the right gave way, forcing them to retire to a sunken road about 200 yards south of La Rouge Maison Farm. The regiment in question was 1/Lincolns which had come under attack from German machine gunners who had managed to get into La Rouge Maison Farm and were pouring heavy fire into A and C Companies. At the same time German infantry were attacking their right flank from the woods near Folemprise Farm. It was an unenviable position.

Calling for support, four companies of Royal Scots Fusiliers – two companies to the right flank and two to the left – were ordered up to the firing line. Advancing through turnip fields on the right of the besieged Lincolns, the Scots came under heavy machine-gun fire from the woods on their right flank, which, in the absence of supporting fire from the British artillery, eventually forced Captain George Briggs to order a gradual withdrawal. Tragically Briggs was killed during the retirement along with seven other ranks, the battalion recording sixty-seven wounded and ninety missing. It had been a costly morning for the Scotsmen.[107]

Exactly when the Lincolns retired is unclear, the battalion war diary covers the whole action in eight lines but notes that 7 officers and 184 other ranks were reported as killed, wounded or missing. Kempthorne's diary sheds some light on the story at the point the Lincolns began to pull back:

'After a time it became obvious our flank was threatened as the bullets began to hit the traverses instead of the parapet and we had to pull our

*wounded under their protection. Then I saw a section of our men retiring
... but we hung on, and continued our work, till to my disgust I sighted
the whole German line advancing over the skyline 200 yards away. It was
obviously hopeless to make a bolt in the open over slippery turnips and still
clay so we carried on. When they were about 50 yards off I climbed out of
the trench brandishing a very dirty handkerchief and they made no attempt
to fire on me. By this time the brigade must have made good their retreat
down the line to the river for all was quiet.'*[108]

Simpson, in his history of the Lincolnshire Regiment, confirms that the
battalion not only retired to Vailly but continued over the river
crossing by the light railway bridge! No mention of this retirement is
made in the war diary or in the *Official History* although there is a short
reference to British soldiers from 9 Brigade, 'filing back over the
narrow passage towards the southern bank'.[109]

The situation had now become critical. With the retirement of the
Lincolns, the right flank of 9 Infantry Brigade was wide open,
increasing the gap between them and the left of the 2nd Division on the
spur above Soupir to a distance of one and a half miles. To add to
British woes the Guards Brigade along with the Connaught Rangers at
Cour de Soupir Farm came under a furious attack which began at
10.30am and threatened to push the division back to the river. As far as
the 3rd Division was concerned the mist and fog which clung to the
hillsides had rendered the artillery batteries on the southern heights of
the river practically useless for a large part of the day and at this point
in the battle there was a real possibility of a strong German counter
attack splitting I Corps on the right flank from the remainder of the
BEF. Hamilton was now in need of his reserves but the only troops that
were on the northern side of the river and available to plug the gap
were those of 5 Cavalry Brigade who had crossed early that morning
and were now at Vailly. Infantry reserves in the form of McCracken's
7 Brigade were still in the process of crossing the river.

* * *

On 13 September the 3rd and 5th Cavalry Brigades had been formed
into 2nd Cavalry Division under the command of Major General
Hubert de la Poer Gough.[110] 'Goughie', as he was universally known,
had demonstrated his maverick streak during the retreat from Mons
when he had all but detached himself from Major General Edmund
Allenby's command and acted independently. Many commanders
exhibiting similar behaviour would have been sent home but Gough,
basking under the aegis of Sir Douglas Haig, was rewarded with

promotion and divisional command. That said, as far as 5 Cavalry Brigade was concerned, on the particular misty morning in question, it was still answerable to Brigadier General Chetwode.

When Captain John Darling, the signalling officer with 20/Hussars, crossed over the pontoon bridge with his regiment, the Scots Greys and 12/Lancers had already arrived and had dismounted at Vailly:

> 'The whole valley, including the bridge, was under hostile observation and artillery fire. It was a misty morning, and to this alone could be attributed the fact we had got so far without drawing the enemy's fire. As the regiment reached the bridge the fog lifted, the German gunners spotted us and started firing. Pontoons are not intended to carry cavalry at a trot, at least this one was not, so the Colonel dismounted the regiment and gave the order to lead over in single file. This we did.'[111]

Gunner Myatt from 109/Battery was close enough to observe the cavalry crossing the bridge:

> 'The Scots Greys came along in fours and the Germans' first shell knocked their machine gun, horse and men all in the river, so they had to gallop for it. The 12 Lancers came across in single file and did not lose a single man, and my word did the RHA gallop across like mad and came through safely.'[112]

Myatt may have been mistaken about the RHA galloping across the bridge, the J Battery war diary records the battery being stopped by Brigadier Chetwode about 400 yards short of the bridge, 'as the village of Vailly was full of cavalry who could not get on as the infantry attack was held up'. The battery retired and came into action east of the Chassemy road about a mile from Vailly where it opened fire on a German battery.

The individual responsible for controlling the movement across the bridge on the morning of 14 September was Captain Theodore Wright, the 57/Field Company officer who had been awarded the Victoria Cross for his bravery at the Mariette Bridge during the Battle of Mons on 23 August. Wright and Lance Corporal Alfred Jarvis – also 57/Field Company – had both won the coveted cross for their work in blowing the canal bridges at Mons. Tragically, controlling the movement of the cavalry across the pontoon bridge at Vailly was to be Theodore Wright's last act, he was killed by shell fire whilst assisting wounded troopers to shelter. The three batteries from XL Brigade which had crossed with the cavalry decided on a safer passage over the river and eventually recrossed at Pont Arcy.

Meanwhile, 7 Infantry Brigade was attempting to cross the river. Lieutenant Alexander Johnston's anxiety over the accuracy of the German artillery batteries which, 'seemed to be in some strength', was relieved somewhat by orders to cross further up the river, using the repaired light railway bridge which took him away from the shrapnel torn crossing at Vailly. This delay, however, almost certainly contributed to the difficulties 9 Brigade was experiencing on the spur. Even before McCracken's brigade had crossed over, elements of 9 Brigade were already seen to be withdrawing.

Corporal John Lucy reached the railway bridge at 3.30pm with the rest of C Company of the Royal Irish Rifles, just as the German shell fire increased:

'We were making for the railway bridge east of Vailly, which at that moment was being recrossed by an English regiment retiring out of action from the northern side of the river ... As we approached the bridge we saw that it was completely wrecked; a tangled mass of ironwork, most of which was submerged, with a dead horse held against it by the current, and only a line of single planks, which sagged in the middle, as a means of getting over.'[113]

Lucy felt the whole business of getting over the river was, 'a nasty proposition', remarking angrily that a shrapnel bullet had penetrated his haversack and torn into a folded towel inside. Reforming, his unit followed the 1st Battalion Wiltshire Regiment (1/Wilts) – which had crossed before – up towards the St Précord spur and as the battalion moved steadily uphill and came within range of the enemy the casualties began to accumulate, 'a good many men were knocked out, but we did not miss them in the excitement'. The German riflemen, thought Lucy, were generally rotten shots:

'Their rifles cracked sharply now, and the whistle and whine of bullets passing wide changed to the startling bangs of bullets just missing one. The near rattle of machine guns sent our hearts thumping ... Our own shells were bursting a short distance ahead, just beyond the crest line clearly visible to us. This line marked the near edge of a large plateau, and as we made it in a last rush we found this plateau edge forming a small continuous cliff of chalk giving good protection from bullets and fair cover from shell fire.'[114]

24-year-old Lieutenant Gerald Lowry was a platoon commander in C Company of the Irish Rifles and despite his diary account being inaccurate in places, he recalled:

'We had a splendid fight that day, taking the hill and the wood on its summit before evening. The position was at the Maison Rouge Farm ... our flank here swung round into a wood, and we lined a bank fronting a stubble field which led upward at a gentle slope.'[115]

The Irish Rifles had established themselves on the left of the Wiltshires and as the remainder of 7 Brigade crossed the river, 8 Brigade fell back to the southern edge of the Jouy spur. Fortunately for the BEF the line was now relatively stable, there was no German counter attack and the British guns on the heights at Chassemy finally managed to get into action. 130/Battery fired some 200 rounds at enemy infantry on the Ostel spur and 48/Heavy Battery did have some success in silencing machine gun positions near Folemprise Farm, although it was probably this battery which fired on D Company of the Royal Irish Rifles after their advance in the afternoon. However, other artillery units such as XL Brigade on the Brenelle plateau and XLII Brigade, east of Chassemy, failed to come into action all day.

The 600 or so rifles which 5 Cavalry Brigade could have mustered were never called into action. The two pages of the 12/Lancers regimental history devoted to the fighting on the Aisne merely mentions that after being, 'pushed across at Vailly', they were, 'unable to debouch and had a most unpleasant return passage across the two canal bridges'. Quite why they were not deployed to shore up the line is anyone's guess – the *Official History* rather lamely explains they were not required as the situation had improved, but at least they were kept in reserve with the Greys until the situation above Vailly had been stabilized. The 20/Hussars on the other hand did an immediate turn-about on reaching the village after being told they were not needed. John Darling again:

'Once more we had to face the ordeal of leading over [the bridge] *in single file under heavy shell fire. By now the Boche had got the range pretty well, and it became an unpleasant manoeuvre, especially for the last squadron, B. The marvel is that we did not lose more men. The total casualties in the regiment were only ten.'*[116]

One suspects that the infantry battalions of the 3rd Division which had been engaged that day above Vailly would have been only too glad to report ten casualties.

The fighting on the 14th was concluded with an unsuccessful night attack on the British line at 10.00pm, an attack which Alexander Johnston was made aware of by the rifle and machine-gun fire which resounded, 'all along the line for some time'. Although Johnston, who had been commissioned into the Worcestershire Regiment in 1903, was on the staff of 7 Brigade, many of the comments he makes in his diary reflect his infantry pedigree and background and one suspects he would preferred to have been on the firing line rather than within the relative safety of brigade headquarters. He was clearly concerned about the outcome of this attack, writing, 'it was a nasty situation as one cannot tell in the dark what strength we are up against'.

Overall it had been a frustratingly difficult day, a day which had begun in anticipation of a general advance and for the 3rd Division one which almost ended in disaster. As the rattling of rifle fire died away in the darkness the line held by the division traced a rough semi-circle around Vailly. The position was hardly secure; the gap between the 3rd and 2nd Divisions was only covered by outposts and there was still uncertainty as to the intentions of the German Army. Johnstone's diary entry for 14 September merely stated what most of his contemporaries were thinking, 'this is no rearguard action we are fighting now but I should say is part of a big attempt by the Germans to hold the line of the Aisne'.

* * *

Dawn on 15 September was again wet and cold and for the Royal Irish Rifles – established a little to the south of La Rouge Maison Farm – the morning began with a scouting patrol of D Company under the command of Lieutenant Charles Dawes. Lieutenant Colonel Wilkinson Bird was anxious to discover the exact whereabouts of the enemy and it wasn't long before Dawes' patrol found them just below the crest. A sharp fire fight ensued during which one man was killed and Dawes and another wounded before they retired under fire. Not content with the outcome, and still unsure as to whether the enemy had retired or not, Bird ordered A and C Companies to advance. Gerald Lowry was with them:

'There was practically no cover, and the ground was hard and bare, so we proceeded by short rushes. The Germans were, however, waiting for us, and when we got to within a few hundred yards of their line they opened a perfect hail of machine-gun and rifle fire and shrapnel – a veritable tornado of flying, shrieking metal, well directed. Part of the company on our left got into the first line of German trenches, but was ultimately compelled to retire, as it was obvious that not only were the Germans dug in, but were in full force. Captain Bowen-Colhurst, who commanded this reconnaissance,

was badly wounded in the assault, whilst two officers[117] were killed and half the men killed or wounded; the machine-gun and shrapnel played havoc amongst us as we were getting back across the open valley.'[118]

The Lincolns, we are told, returned to Vailly and after spending the night of 14 September in the village square, 'marched to the top of the hill again and were kept in support the whole of the day, and at dusk lay alongside the road'. This was presumably the minor road which still runs northeast from Vailly towards La Rouge Maison Farm.

It was now clear that the Germans were no longer retiring and any notion that they were purely on the defensive was dispelled by another attack on the British line at 5.00pm, an attack the Irish Rifles' war diary tells us, 'ceased about 9.15pm'.[119] The battalion war diary does not record the casualties sustained between 14 and 15 September but during the eight days following their arrival on the spur the battalion lost 3 officers and 44 other ranks killed and 12 officers wounded along with 226 other ranks. It was a similar story with the other battalions, over the two days they had been in action the Royal Fusiliers lost 5 officers and nearly 200 other ranks killed, wounded or missing and the Northumberland Fusiliers had 3 officers killed and 9 wounded together with 5 other ranks killed and over 85 wounded. The Royal Scots Fusiliers, who had been brought up to support 9 Brigade, lost 8 killed, 67 wounded and recorded 90 of their men as missing.

Casualties from the fighting on the spurs above Vailly were brought down to the advanced dressing station established by 8/Field Ambulance in the twelfth century church which bordered the village square. Lieutenant Henry Robinson's diary provides a detailed and rather distressing account of his stay in the village:

'We went northward through the main street of Vailly, in which many of the houses were burning, and up to the Brigadier's office (sic) at the north end of the town. Here we found an empty house which we broke into, and after establishing the men in the shelter of a very high bank, we went to sleep in the house. This would have been about 2 or 3 am on September 15th. Soon after dawn we were roused by firing, and found bullets were coming through the walls of the house we were in, so we beat a hasty retreat, and took over a dressing station in the church and in some neighbouring buildings.'[120]

The village had suffered a good deal from German shelling but fortunately it was only the lower end of the town near the river which bore the brunt of this so far, the northern end, which included the church, was still under the lee of the steep, high ground of the Ostel spur behind. It wasn't until after 15 September that the church and the square were shelled. Robinson was the medical officer with responsibility for the casualties brought to the church:

> *'I, more or less, took charge of the church, though others used to come and assist whenever they had a spare moment … The scene in that church was one which defies all description. It was a large church for the size of the town, and the whole of the floor space was covered with mattresses; we even had to place them on the altar steps. Wounded men, covered in mud and blood were everywhere, and space was so precious that we could not even keep gangways through the rows of mattresses. To get to our patients we had to step over others. Many of the wounds were very serious, and my bottle of morphia was in constant request, in fact it was soon empty and I got a fresh stock from a chemist in the town … During the three nights I spent in Vailly I slept altogether about five hours. Fresh batches of wounded were coming in all hours of the day and night, and the work was absolutely incessant.'*[121]

As with the casualties at Bucy-le-Long, it was not until nightfall each evening that the wounded could be moved across the pontoon bridge and onto the ambulance trains waiting to transport them to Braine. Parties of stretcher bearers from 7/and 8/Field Ambulance were sent across the river each evening and all those wounded who were able to be moved were carried or assisted to walk down through the town and over the river. The Germans of course were well aware of this nocturnal evacuation and shelled the bridge on average every twenty minutes; this led to a deadly game of chance as the bearers waited for the interval between each shell to traverse the bridge. 'But if one happened to be going down with wounded to the bridge and no shell had come for a good many minutes', wrote Robinson, 'there was always a chance of catching one just as the bearers got to the bridge'.

Many of the casualties were the result of German shell fire which subjected the troops to some quite horrific injuries, some of which Henry Robinson and his doctor colleagues knew instinctively to be fatal. In the early months of the war the absence of the clear-cut triage process which was adopted later by casualty clearing stations, often placed medical officers working in forward dressing stations such as Vailly with difficult professional dilemmas:

> *'A soldier was taken into Dr Lancry's house suffering from a horrible wound of the abdomen. A piece of his abdominal wall about as big as a*

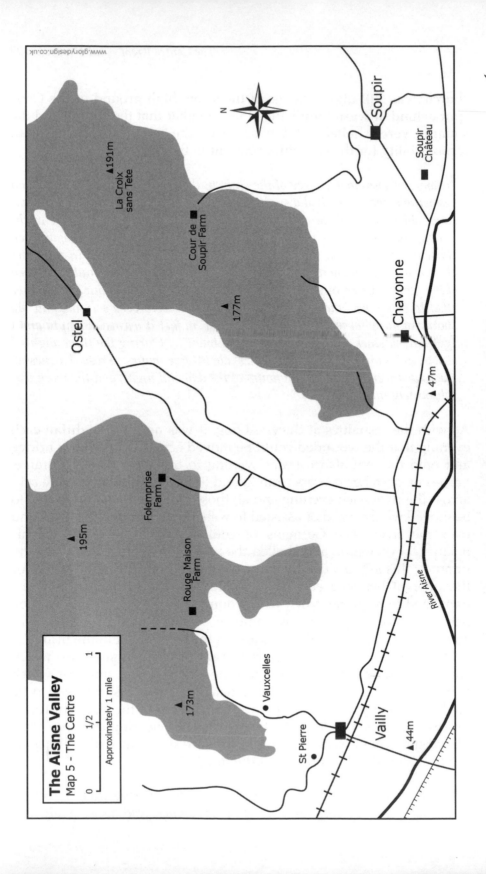

The Aisne Valley
Map 5 - The Centre

0   1/2   1
Approximately 1 mile

N

195m ▲

173m ▲

Folemprise Farm ■

Rouge Maison Farm ■

La Croix sans Tete ▲191m

Ostel ■

Cour de Soupir Farm ■

177m ▲

Soupir ■

Soupir Château ■

Chavonne ■

47m ▲

• Vauxcelles

St Pierre •

Vailly ■

44m ▲

River Aisne

pudding plate had been shot clean away, and one could see two or three broken ribs, a large piece of his liver, large intestine, small intestine, and omentum[122] *in the cavity. Although men have recovered many times in this war from wounds which apparently must have been fatal, in this case it was indisputable that recovery was totally out of the question. I advised that the man should be given a poisonous dose of morphia at once; I was overruled, and the man lingered on for two or three days occupying a bed which had better have been given to somebody less seriously wounded.'*[123]

Whereas Robinson makes the point that no doctor is justified in deliberately killing a patient, he felt in those circumstances that the man, who was unconscious the entire time, could have been treated in what he terms as a more humane and defensible manner.

On 17 September, two of the hard-worked trio of medical officers were relieved and Robinson and his colleague Lieutenant Greenfield were sent back to Braine, to be followed shortly afterwards by Major Raymond Foster. Over the course of the brief period that Robinson had been at Vailly, nearly 500 wounded officers and men had been successfully evacuated: 11 officers and 238 other ranks on the night of 15 September and another 6 officers and 241 other ranks the following night. Under the circumstances the medics had every right to feel proud of their efforts.

Chapter 8

The Right Flank – 2nd Division

His death salute was the artillery thunder,
Praise be to God for such an Englishman.

Edward Tennant – written in memory of Percy Wyndham.

We left the bulk of Fielding's 4 (Guards) Brigade south of the river on the night of 13 September leaving 5 Infantry Brigade, including 2/Connaught Rangers, in position on the north bank. The Connaughts subsequently moved up to La Cour de Soupir Farm arriving at 5.50am on 14 September, more of which later. GHQ operational orders for 14 September – issued at 6.00pm the previous evening – anticipated a general advance on the right flank over the Chemin des Dames with the advanced units of the BEF occupying a line from Laon in the east to Suzy, some 6 miles to the west. 2nd Division orders for the morning of the 14th were for 6 Infantry Brigade and the guns of XXXIV Brigade to form the advance guard under the command of Brigadier General Richard Davies and cross the Aisne at Pont-Arcy at 5.00am to press forward through the 5 Brigade outpost line which had been established north of Moussy. The Guards Brigade was to cross by the same pontoon bridge at 7.00am together with the XXXVI Brigade batteries and advance through Soupir village and up the Soupir spur, followed by the remainder of the division. Like so many plans it looked good on paper and at one point in the day it appeared as though it might just succeed.

Despite being at the bridge on time, the four battalions of 6 Brigade did not complete their crossing until 8.00am, the narrow pontoon bridge put across by 5/Field Company only just able to cope with the large number of troops and artillery batteries. Commanding a section of the 71/Battery guns was Lieutenant Arthur Griffith, who was relieved to find there was no shelling during the crossing, 'owing, no doubt, to the thick mist', he thought. The last men of 1/Royal Berks were clear of the bridge by 5.00 am and advancing up the valley towards Braye-en-Laonnois with two companies of 1/KRRC on each flank. No doubt Lieutenant Colonel Edward Northey, commanding the KRRC, felt a little uneasy about splitting his battalion but complying with orders, detailed B and C Companies under Captain Frank Willan to the right with instructions to maintain contact with 5 Brigade and A and D Companies under Major Edward Armitage to the left of La Bovette Wood to get in touch with the Guards. The Braye valley also hosts the l'Oise à l'Aisne Canal, this waterway – running north-south through the centre of the 6 Brigade advance – cuts into the main ridge of the Chemin des Dames just south of Braye and effectively bisects the valley. Lieutenant Alan Hanbury-Sparrow had a clear picture of the ground as he advanced with the Berkshires towards La Metz Farm:

> *'Immediately on our west hand lies the Oise-Aisne Canal crossed by a small bridge at the large Ferme de Metz, and this is to be our right boundary. Beyond it is the country road running north and south, along which a few refugees are hastening. After a cannonade of some duration we move down towards this bridge, and see for the first time shells exploding in enormous clouds of black smoke – eleven inch, as we afterwards learn. As we approach, a young woman dragging a child by each hand rushes out of the farm and with terrified countenance scurries down the road.'*[124]

At around 9.00am the forward company of the Berkshires had reached a line running eastwest of Le Moulin Brulé – about halfway between Moussy and Braye – when their advance was checked by heavy shell and rifle fire from both the Chemin des Dames ridge and the wooded areas on the sides of the valley.[125] The delay in responding to the enemy fire suggests that the brigade had been, to some extent, taken aback by its intensity and while the 1st Battalion King's Liverpool Regiment (1/King's) was brought forward on the Berkshires' right, the XXXIV Brigade guns were hurriedly brought into action on the southern slopes of the Moussy spur. Thus reinforced, the 6 Brigade attack was launched at 10.30am with 1/King's on the east side of the canal and the Berkshires on the western side, flanked by the KRRC on the edges of the two spurs bordering the valley.

The attack was badly organized and hurriedly launched before the troops on the Moussy spur had time to get into position; the Berkshires advancing up the valley soon outstripped the King's who in turn found themselves ahead of the KRRC flank companies. Hanbury-Sparrow's account is almost breathless with tension as he describes his platoon's forward movement:

'Advance then with a rush! Down! Again! Down! Still no sight of the
enemy, still this fire. You are on the crest of a small billow of ground. Fifty
yards ahead the canal, bordered by leafy trees, turns left handed and crosses
your front. Advance by section rushes to the canal. Get on, Corporal, damn
you! You are on the edge of the canal, concealed by its border of trees. The
Germans are no longer firing at you. In fact their infantry seem to have
ceased fire altogether. For the first time since the advance started you are
able to look around undistracted by acute fear.'[126]

The sector given to the King's was from the canal to the top of the
Moussy spur, Lieutenant William Synge in B Company remembered
the attack was, 'arranged on the map' and the, 'factor of time
prevented a systematic reconnaissance of the position'. Synge and his
company were tasked with taking les Grelines Farm which lay in the
valley below the final slope up to the Chemin des Dames:

'In the foreground was an open field, and on the right-hand side a wood, the
end of the Bois des Grelines, running up the hillside. About 300 yards in
front of me was another small wood, and a gap of about 50 yards between
it and the Bois des Grelines. Through the gap it was possible to see that the
ground sloped down and then up again in an open space about 800 yards
across. In this dip the ground appeared to run up a little into the Moussy
spur ... all the hillside was thickly wooded and beyond these woods, and
about a mile and a half away, the ground sloped up again to the Chemin
des Dames.'[127]

The wooded nature of the ground and the haste in which the attack
was planned was a recipe for confusion, William Synge continues the
story:

'In front of us the wood got even thicker, but there was an overgrown path
leading through it. There was a lot of argument here, as to who was on the
right line and who was not. It seemed to me that D Company ought to have
been higher up, and A [Company] lower down. However, as both
company leaders concerned were senior to me, they followed each other
along the narrow path, whilst I waited for my commander to come up and
give me orders.'

The battalion war diary describes the King's advance taking place on
both sides of the road from Moussy to the canal towards what Captain
Hudson, the battalion adjutant, describes as the Marval Ridge.[128] This
would confirm Synge's recollection that they were on the eastern side

of the canal and approaching the ridge above les Grelines Farm which leads directly onto the Chemin des Dames. In his account Hudson acknowledges that the Berkshires got in front of them and describes how the King's worked along the edge of the Beaulne Spur to the point where they came under fire from behind. After reporting to his CO, Lieutenant Colonel William Bannatyne,[129] who was with D Company, Hudson was sent to find Major Charles Steavenson commanding B Company, who also had part of C Company with him:

'[They] *were being fired into from behind. I went back to try and find out what it was and found our infantry were firing into the Germans who had not been cleared off the ridge above and behind our advance. A Company had pushed on, on the right, in the open; all through the advance the companies had been under very heavy rifle and artillery fire from field guns and big howitzers. C Company had got badly handled on the right and Major S. had managed to pull them back, to B Company.'*[130]

Hudson's assessment of the situation was probably the correct one; the enemy fire from the edges of the Beaulne spur was the result of the King's getting too far ahead of the the KRRC troops who were on the right flank. However, William Synge was unsure as to who was firing at them, 'someone said that it was our own people who were firing down on us from the hill top. Whether this was so I do not know, and probably never will know'. Whoever it was – friend or foe – the King's were now under fire from German infantry to their front and from the rear. Synge tells us his company then withdrew but at some stage during the advance an attempt was made to take the trenches on the ridge ahead of them, this time with the support of a platoon of 2/Worcesters. The attack was unsuccessful:

'It *was impossible to get on until the high ground on our right had been cleared and Major S. then pulled the whole of the companies back. As the fire from behind made it nearly impossible to get forward ... Capt. Tanner and Ferneran were wounded. We took 5 Germans prisoners. Our losses were 2 officers killed and 90* [other ranks] *killed and wounded.'*[131]

Even so, after crossing the canal just south of Braye, the Berkshires got a toehold on the small spur which runs down from the Chemin des Dames east of the village and by noon had two companies engaging a well dug-in German 28 Reserve Regiment established on the steep slopes rising to the Chemin des Dames road. Under heavy fire Alan Hanbury-Sparrow, who confesses freely to his fear of being killed, is driven on by what he terms as a 'duty' prompting him to, 'take the initiative':

> 'You hesitate, hesitate, hesitate – doubtful, doubtful. You don't know what you'll do. Ten black devils chant, "You'll be killed" and ten red devils curl their lips and sneer, "You're afraid of being killed." What will you do? One way or the other you must make the choice, now, at once, instantly.'[132]

At length the order reached him to retire and he noted with some anger that the men of his platoon were quick to obey it. Yet even as the brigade fell back in the face of a well dug-in enemy, Douglas Haig, in consultation with Major General Charles Munro the GOC 2nd Division, was planning a late-in-the-day push up the Beaulne spur in the hope of gaining the ridge before nightfall. It was an advance which was planned in conjunction with the 1st Division – considered in more depth in Chapter 9 – and as far as the infantry battalions of 5 Infantry Brigade and Brigadier General Richard Haking was concerned, it achieved its objective. Haig described the advance in the I Corps War Diary:

> 'The forward movement began about sunset, and the men, of whom many had been fighting hard since before daybreak, answered readily to my demand. They were met everywhere by very heavy rifle and gunfire. The 4th (Guards) Brigade found itself pinned down by a counter attack against the exposed left, and again the danger on this flank checked a great part of the line. The 1st Division on the right gained some ground, but could not maintain itself in the face of the opposition encountered. Only in the centre, the 5th Brigade moving along the eastern slopes of the Beaulne ridges, was able to get forward and continue its advance until it reached the ridge about Tilleul de Courtcon. In the dark General Haking failed to get in touch with the 1st Division, but his patrols found German outposts on both flanks. He consequently drew back his troops under cover of darkness to the neighbourhood of Verneuil.'[133]

Moving ahead with 5 Brigade was Lieutenant Colonel Northey and half the 1/KRRC which reported reaching the Chemin des Dames at Tilleul de Courtcon from where they moved west to Malval farm. On arrival, instead of finding British troops, 'they tumbled into a mass of Germans collecting near a large signal lamp'.[134] The war diary gives no further information except to say they withdrew at midnight to Verneuil. The 2nd Battalion Highland Light Infantry (2/HLI) were also on the Chemin des Dames ridge at midnight but quite where and at what time the Worcesters gained the ridge is clouded by their war diary account which reported their retirement at about 9.00pm after taking a few German prisoners – all pointing to a general confusion taking place in the darkness. It was during the early part of this advance that a Highland Light Infantry reservist, Private George Wilson, single-handedly captured a German machine gun, turning it on the enemy before returning to his company with both the weapon and its ammunition. His award of the Victoria Cross took the total number of VCs won by the infantry on 14 September to three.

Nevertheless, despite the failure of 3 Brigade to establish a presence on the Chemin des Dames, a substantial body of British troops from 5 Brigade did set foot on the ridge that night, a feat which throws up a number of questions, not least of which is why did General Haking order a retirement all the way back to Verneuil and not seek to consolidate the line further forward? In mitigation it has to be said that being on a rain swept Chemin des Dames ridge in the dark would not have been conducive to establishing clear communications between bodies of tired troops. Haking presumably felt isolated – as indeed he was – and without support on his right from 3 Brigade he was in a precarious position, however, he appears not to have encountered any serious opposition apart from the German outposts. So was this an opportunity lost or a necessary tactical withdrawal? One wonders what the officer commanding 11 Brigade – Brigadier General Hunter-Weston – would have done in these circumstances.

* * *

The Guards Brigade was on the move by 4.50am and after a march of 2 miles, 'in the pouring wet', they were over the pontoon bridge by 8.30am. Here a disgruntled Major Bernard Gordon Lennox felt he, 'had to wait a long time before getting across as various artillery and other units had to get across [before us]'. The 2/Grenadiers were the leading battalion and moved off towards Soupir leaving the remainder of the brigade to cross behind them. Major Gordon Lennox:

'In Soupir we turned to our left, and after about a mile or so, turned up the hill. It was not known whether these wooded heights were held or not – it was our job to find out – we soon did. No. 1 and ½ of No. 2 [Company] formed the vanguard, and on barely reaching the top the advance party was fired on: we pushed on and two more platoons of No. 2 were sent forward. Being second-in-command I had to stay behind. Pretty steady firing was now going on, and we – the main body – got heavily shelled as we came up *the road, the Dutchmen apparently having the range to a nicety. At the top of the hill was the farm of La Cour de Soupir – a building we were to become intimately acquainted with during the next few days – held or rather occupied by a regiment, which shall be nameless.'[135]*

The 'nameless' regiment was of course 2/Connaught Rangers which had occupied the farm and pushed out their outposts onto the high ground around Point 197 at la Croix sans Tête. At the time of the Connaught's arrival at the farm there had been no sign of any Germans in the vicinity. The Connaughts' war diary recounts the arrival of the Grenadier Guards four hours later:

'At about 9.30am a small party of the Guards Brigade under an officer forming the point of their advance guard arrived at the farm, but no more of the brigade arrived until about 11.30am. At about 10:00am a message despatched at 9.25am by motorcyclist was received from HQ 5 Brigade, to whom the movements of the Battalion had been reported, stating that it would be sometime yet before the Guards Brigade could arrive and instructing the OC CRs not to leave his position until they were up and had securely occupied the high ground about La Croix sans Tête. The Battalion was ordered to close on Moussy as soon as that position was secure.'[136]

The Grenadier officer noted in the Connaught war diary was probably 19-year-old Second Lieutenant John Pickersgill-Cuncliffe. With him was Major Gilbert Hamilton commanding No. 1 Company and Captain Cholmeley Symes-Thompson, with half of No. 2 Company, who had been sent out as flank guard on the left where the ground rises steeply above the road.[137] Whether all the Grenadiers remained at the farm or continued uphill is unclear, but Cuncliffe and his platoon certainly were ahead of the main body when the attack began. Nor do we know for sure if it was his warning or that of the Connaught outposts which Major Sarsfield received at about 10.30am alerting him to a large body of German infantry approaching the farm. Sarsfield's response was immediate and the Connaughts were deployed east and west of the farm:

'The attack was supported by artillery fire and pushed forward with great vigour. The enemy endeavoured to turn our right flank by moving through the woods and, against our centre and left he advanced across the open ground in very large numbers. By 10.30am approximately, in spite of his losses which were very heavy, he had almost succeeded in turning our right

flank and, most of our men who were holding the position close to the farm on the west having been killed and wounded, the enemy had succeeded in pushing forward to within 100 yards of the farm.[138]

As the German infantry advanced towards the farm, the Connaught outposts around Point 197 were driven in along with Lieutenant Cuncliffe and his men. During the initial clash with the leading elements of the enemy the young officer was wounded along with several of his men who were taken prisoner, although it appears Cuncliffe was left lying on the battlefield.

At the farm the situation was beginning to get a little desperate on the right flank in the wooded slopes of the Bois de la Bovette. In response Major George 'Ma' Jeffreys, who was in temporary command of the Grenadiers, sent three platoons of No. 4 Company up to support Hamilton whilst Lieutenant Colonel Fielding sent 3/Coldstream up to the farm, supported on the right by the whole of the Irish Guards under Major Herbert Stepney. The first indication that Major Jeffreys had of the Coldstream Guards moving up to the farm was when they passed the Grenadiers' headquarters. Jeffreys then met Lieutenant Arthur Smith the Coldstream adjutant:

> '[He] *told me that Major Matheson,*[139] *their commanding officer, was moving up to Cour de Soupir. I went and met Matheson on the road by the farm. One company of the 3rd Battalion Coldstream had come into action west and northwest of the farm and with our No. 2 had driven back the Germans, who withdrew some hundreds of yards on this side.*'[140]

It was during a later conversation with Matheson that Jeffreys was told of the death of John Cuncliffe who had been shot dead by a German officer as he lay wounded on the ground. The incident was verified by men of his platoon who had been taken prisoner when the Germans advanced and subsequently abandoned when the situation was reversed. Jeffreys in his diary account tells us this German officer was shot immediately by the advancing Coldstream.

But the battle was not yet over. Pressure now came onto the left flank and German infantry was only held off by Nos. 1 and 2 Companies of the 2nd Battalion Coldstream which were sent in support. The 2/Coldstream were, up to this point, being held in brigade reserve but it wasn't long before their companies were sent forward to bolster the right flank defences, leaving a mere two platoons in reserve. The fighting in the wooded area on the right flank was rendered more difficult by the steep edge of the spur which fell away sharply into the

Braye valley below. Bernard Gordon Lennox was sent up to rally the Grenadiers and try to work round the left flank:

> 'I found two platoons of my own company under 'Goose'[141] all right, then we went further off to the right to see if we couldn't get round the enemy's left. We were pulled up by a steep ravine, and we had to go some way round to get over it: a steep climb brought us onto the other side of the valley and here we found the Irish Guards and some Coldstream and Nos. 3 and 4 Companies Grenadier Guards all mixed up. It was here that the Irish Guards and Coldstream Guards paid a heavy toll in officers. There were some damnable snipers up in the trees and kept on sniping the officers. Poor Guernsey and Arthur Hay were killed at almost the same spot, and several others wounded: Dick Welby slightly in the shoulder, 'Goose' had also been wounded in the right hand, but these two stuck to it manfully. Sally Walker[142] and Harcourt-Vernon[143] also had wounds.'[144]

Although this action cleared the ridge to the right of the firing line there was no further appreciable advance made here but at least contact was made with Major Edward Armitage and the men of A and D Companies of the KRRC.

Any artillery support from XXXVI Brigade was hampered by the early morning mist, but as Arthur Griffith pointed out, 'the dense woods up to and over the horizon line, permitted only a very limited view being obtained from the valley bottom'. The brigade's guns were in place north and east of Soupir and as the mist cleared the German observers on the heights above were able to direct fire onto any movement – particularly onto the British batteries. However, the appearance of a section of 18-pounder guns from 71/Battery during the late afternoon did much to improve the situation on the right and assisted in repelling a counter attack just before dusk. Noticeably these guns were practically the only artillery support 4 Brigade had all day. The guns were under the command of Lieutenant Griffith:

> 'I was unable to get any view [of the enemy] from the farm buildings, so went out and found our firing line holding a low bank a short way in front of the farm and west of it. These were chiefly Coldstreams, with some other guards oddments. I was standing up looking through my glasses, and had just been shown the Germans lining a not very distant hedge, when I was hit through the arm. A sergeant tied me up and I went back to find a position for my guns.'[145]

Griffith was soon joined by Captain William Cree[146] who took command and decided to bring the guns into the open in order to bring a more effective fire on the enemy:

> '*As soon as we left the cover of the road and trees, we were promptly shelled by our own artillery, who put over about 20–30 rounds of shrapnel before we were able to stop them with vigorous signalling rearwards. Fortunately their shooting was not accurate and we sustained no casualties. Subsequent investigation proved it was the remaining four guns of our own 71st Battery which had mistaken us for German guns retiring!*'[147]

With Cree observing from a forward position, Griffith remained with the guns some 200 yards behind the infantry firing line. Almost as soon as they opened fire the infantry, 'for some unknown reason now retired through us'. Griffith and his battery were now left completely isolated:

> '*As we were now left between the opposing lines, and the hostile shelling had become more intense, and moreover German infantry could be seen beginning to advance, the teams were ordered up, while the guns continued firing until the last possible moment … As soon as we stopped firing the German infantry advanced at the double, firing as they came, and it now became a race as to whether we should reach the cover of the trees and our lines before they reached us. However our infantry eventually grasped our predicament and their fire on our pursuers finally settled matters in our favour.*'[148]

It had been a close run thing and the battery only just avoided being overrun by the German infantry. Griffith's diary demonstrates a remarkable generosity towards the Guards whose late intervention came not a moment too soon! For his coolness under fire and bravery in getting the guns limbered up and out of action, Griffith was awarded the DSO. Discretion being the better part of valour, the battery was moved back under cover of the trees and came into action again shortly afterwards but not before Griffith and two men who had been wounded in the action were sent down to Soupir.

At noon, encouraged by their success in holding off the enemy, Matheson and Jeffreys felt the time had arrived to take the offensive. The German line was static in the turnip fields north of the farm and a spirited charge might just dislodge the enemy. But even before the Guardsmen had time to fix their bayonets and move forward, the Germans in the front line stood up and with white flags waving began to run forward with their hands up in surrender. George Jeffreys witnessed the event:

'*Unfortunately men of all units – Grenadiers, Coldstream, Connaught Rangers and Irish Guards – rushed forward to seize prisoners, and though both Matheson and I shouted to them to stand fast, we could not stop them and a confused mass of British and German soldiers was the result. On this mass the German soldiers in the rear at once opened fire, causing a number of casualties.*'[149]

Bernard Gordon Lennox watched aghast as both German and British soldiers fell, 'it was here most of the casualties occurred. The men learnt a lesson and there will not be much more notice taken of the white flag'. Jeffreys was sure there was never any premeditated treachery intended by the Germans, the leading line, he felt, had had enough and was very low in ammunition; the support line behind them, however, had no intention of surrendering and opened fire when the British troops ran forward.

The confusion which followed was the prelude to another attack, this time from the direction of Ostel. It was met with the customary Guards resolve in the form of the 3/Coldstream machine-gun section and the Grenadiers who lined the road north of the farm. The enemy attack soon withered away but any thoughts of a further advance that afternoon seemed to be out of the question. The muddle which surrounded the fighting on the 4 Brigade front was exacerbated by the news that the 3rd Division was in trouble at Vailly. Initial reports reaching I Corps HQ at noon of a general retirement of 3rd Division units was fortunately corrected and by 2.00pm a more realistic appraisal of the situation was in front of Sir Douglas Haig. Realizing his left flank was under threat if the 3rd Division was pushed back to the river, he took steps to fill the gap between Chavonne and Vailly with 1 and 2 Cavalry Brigades which were ordered to Soupir. Haig's own assessment of the situation is contained in the I Corps war diary:

'*A little later, an officer of the 15th Hussars rode in and reported that he had seen signs of our 3rd Division having been beaten back. The situation was critical. An advance by the enemy through Chavonne on Soupir would have cut the communications of the Corps; the last battalion of my reserve brigade had been drawn into the fight near Chivy, and I had no infantry that I could detach. The only men immediately at hand were a troop of the 15 Hussars and a squadron of the South Irish Horse. These I despatched at once to the threatened flank, and I also called upon the 2nd Cavalry Brigade to move to Soupir.'*[150]

Captain Arthur Osburn was in reserve with 4/Dragoon Guards and remembered thinking that had the Germans counter attacked that afternoon things would have become very nasty. At about 4.00pm the brigade was halted in the woods to the northwest of Soupir:

> 'Our General and some of his staff suddenly appeared. He evidently thought the situation, especially the position of the infantry who had crossed over behind us, precarious. He made us a speech … "You must stay here at all costs! Everything may depend on you! Don't give an inch of ground. You may have to sustain seventy or eighty per cent casualties! Remain and die like gentlemen!" We looked at each other. Like Gentlemen – how else do people usually die?'[151]

Brigadier General de Lisle's speech certainly put, 'the wind up' Osburn who then, 'made quite elaborate and feverish' medical arrangements for what he expected to be an, 'enormous battle'. The men of 1 Cavalry Brigade had evidently received a similar pep talk from Brigadier General Charles Briggs as the 11/Hussars war diary betrays the urgency with which the regiment was ordered to Soupir:

> 'We received an order to go to the left of the 1st Army [I Corps], Sir Douglas Haig is anxious about his left. The 2nd Army [II Corps] are not joined up with the first, and their right is being driven back over the river. We arrive at Soupir and take up a dismounted position on the left of our infantry [2/Ox and Bucks], also succeed in getting in touch with the right of the 2nd Army. The gap is a biggish one and a nasty bit of country. As we arrive, we see streams of wounded being brought down the track, the Guards have been having a bad time of it.'[152]

The remainder of 1 Cavalry Brigade was deployed in a second line at Chavonne which enabled 11/Hussars to be withdrawn. Shortly afterwards 2/Ox and Bucks were moved to Soupir at which point Arthur Osburn felt it was almost an anticlimax that no German counter attack actually took place and the Dragoon Guards retired to Soupir Château with the Hussars.

Back at Cour de Soupir the day was drawing in but the German batteries continued to shell the British positions as they had for most of the day. Two companies of 2/Coldstream were sent down to Chavonne where they spent a wet night with the cavalry and a further two were pushed across to the right to where the Irish Guards were digging in. Artillery support we now know was practically non-existent-apart from the 71/Battery appearance at Cour de Soupir – XLI Brigade crossed at Bourg and then retired to Veil-Arcy firing only twelve rounds all day – although Sergeant Reeve with 16/Battery was adamant that the battery, 'stayed in action all day and night', but conceding that they only, 'blazed off a bit'. At least 35/Heavy Battery managed to fire thirty-four rounds which was more than 44/(Howitzer) Battery managed at Verneuil.

* * *

The Connaught Rangers were ordered back to Soupir as soon as it was dark. As a battalion they were clearly viewed with some disdain by the Guards. Major Jeffreys remarked in his diary that they had been, 'notorious for straggling in the retreat' whilst Bernard Gordon Lennox dismissed them as the rabble which, 'occupied', rather than, 'held' Cour de Soupir Farm and writes in his diary that they, 'did not remain long before making a "strategic movement to the rear"'. Not only is this allegation plainly false but even more slighting is the lack of acknowledgement by the Grenadiers themselves as to the part played by the Connaughts in the fight for Cour de Soupir Farm. Though to be fair, according to Sergeant John McIlwain, a Connaught reservist serving in D Company, Colonel Fielding, in his temporary role in commanding 4 Brigade, did send a, 'message of congratulation ... for the manner in which we had held the position after the severe counter attack by the Germans'. The final accolade as to the fighting ability of the Connaughts came from Major Henry Dillon, a company commander with the Ox and Bucks Light Infantry. Writing in a letter home on 23 September, he mentions the fight for La Cour de Soupir Farm: 'An Irish regiment were the first to get to the top and they fought like nothing on earth'.

It has to be said that Major Sarsfield's early occupation of the farm on 14 September was carried out with the same spirit of initiative which drove Hunter-Weston's advance with 11 Brigade at Vénizel. Sadly it had the same outcome. What is difficult to understand is that at 5.30am the Connaughts were already halfway to the brigade objective, yet the first of the Guards battalions did not cross the river until 8.30am, despite the evidence from the Connaughts' war diary – and that of 5 Brigade – both of which confirm that brigade headquarters were aware of the Connaughts' position at Cour de Soupir Farm.

John McIlwain's diary – although inaccurate in places and often quite damning of some of his officers – places him on the right flank at Cour de Soupir and describes the death of his platoon officer, 21-year-old Second Lieutenant Victor Lentaigne:[153]

> *'He was the younger son of Sir John Lentaigne, the well known surgeon of Merrion Square, Dublin. He was a modest, quiet lad who could have been severe with me many times ... He was over eager to get into action. His orders yesterday were to hold his platoon in reserve till called upon ... He fixed his sword in the ground to mark the point of advance, went forward alone and was not seen again.'*[154]

Victor Lentaigne was one of three Connaught officers killed with a further five wounded. In the ranks 18 men were killed, 102 wounded and 97 declared missing. The Grenadiers' losses were comparable: two officers – John Cuncliffe and Frederick des Voeux – killed and six others wounded in addition to seventeen other ranks killed, sixty-seven wounded and seventy-seven missing.[155] The Coldstream casualties amounted to two killed – including Second Lieutenant Richard Lockwood – and sixty-three wounded in the 2nd Battalion and twenty-five killed and 153 wounded in the 3rd Battalion.[156] The dead included the 26-year-old Lieutenant Percy 'Perf' Lyulph Wyndham who had inherited the magnificent Clouds estate at East Knoyle two years previously on the death of his father, the Rt Hon George Wyndham MP.[157] 'Perf' had been married for less than two years to the Hon Diana Lister and was a cousin of the 17-year-old Edward 'Bim' Tennant who himself would be killed serving with the Grenadier Guards in 1916.[158] Tom Bridges – a family friend – was at Soupir Château with 4/Dragoon Guards when he heard of Wyndham's death: 'the evening was marred by the death of a friend, Percy Wyndham, close by, and the opening of a heavy battery on our billet later in the night'.

After dark Matheson and Jeffreys reorganized their respective battalions from the 'proper mix-up' which the day's fighting had produced. It was agreed between the two battalion commanders that the Grenadiers would hold a line from the wood east of the farm as far as the Chavonne road, the 3/Coldstream along the Chavonne road to link up with the 2/Coldstream at Chavonne. On the right of the Grenadiers the Irish Guards were in contact with the KRRC of 6 Brigade. Thus the 2nd Division found itself digging in from the southern edge of the Beaulne spur, across the Braye valley north of La Metz Farm to Cour de Soupir Farm and down to Chavonne.

Darkness was also the opportunity for recovering the wounded, some of whom had been lying out in front of the lines since the engagement began. Jeffreys had seen a, 'considerable number', of both British and German wounded as well as, 'a very large number of dead Germans'. There were also those who had been lying doggo and had been waiting for darkness to give themselves up. The sheer numbers of wounded men threatened to overwhelm the battalion medical teams which had been working feverishly for most of the day. The farmhouse was already full and the wounded now overflowed into the farm enclosure buildings, yet even though as many wounded men as possible were taken away that night by the few horse drawn ambulance wagons that could be spared, many were not taken down to Soupir until 16 September. Inevitably there were many wounded men in the woods on the right flank who were not found and died as a result.

The medical facilities for the 2nd Division were initially overwhelmed with the sheer numbers of wounded. Two advanced dressing stations were established at Moussy and in some caves near Chivy with the main dressing stations at the château at Verneuil and the rather ostentatious château at Soupir. At Verneuil conditions were made more difficult by the nearby artillery batteries which ensured the building was frequently shelled as German batteries searched for the British guns. 5/Field Ambulance took over the château at Verneuil around lunch time on 14 September and by the end of the day the building itself and the surrounding stables and outbuildings were filled with wounded. Major Frederick Brereton estimates some 9 officers, 166 other ranks and 54 Germans were admitted during the day, a number which included 48-year-old Lieutenant Colonel Charles Dalton[159], the 2nd Division ADMS.[160] Dalton was severely wounded by a shell splinter as he was assisting with the carrying of casualties into the château. 6/Field Ambulance arrived on the night of 14 September to assist in bringing in the wounded and over the course of the next twenty-four hours another seven officers and eighty-five other ranks were admitted.

But Verneuil had become too much of a shell trap to continue in its role as a divisional collecting station, it was becoming very exposed and three days later it received a direct hit which prompted the move to Viel-Arcy on the 20th . Brereton, in his account of the RAMC on the Aisne, writes of the moment when the direct hit on the château took place:

'It smashed through the château, shrieked across the operation room, and plunged through the mirror hanging over the salon fireplace. Orderlies still hovered around. Instruments were lifted carefully from the sterilizer. The anaesthetist looked round at the mirror and dripped chloroform. He lifted up the eyelid of the unconscious patient, grunted his satisfaction and again bent to listen to his breathing. The operating surgeon had not even raised his head. His busy fingers played about the wound, one hand grasped the scalpel ... finally as the patient was lifted from the table he turned and examined the mirror. "Broken it eh?" he observed; "that's bad luck for the Germans!".'[161]

The château at Soupir did not take on the role of a main dressing station until 17 September when 4/Field Ambulance moved into the building. Prior to that, No. 3/Cavalry Field Ambulance had occupied the building along with 1 and 2 Cavalry Brigades which, readers will recall, had been sent to reinforce the left flank after the 3rd Division had got into difficulties. 3/Cavalry Field Ambulance had already been severely mauled by shell fire on the night of 15 September when a large shell fell amongst a group of horses and men at the château. Five men were killed, and a further eight were wounded. The bombardment continued, forcing the ambulance to move south of the river but even as they crossed the river they attracted further salvos which followed them across the flat, open ground all the way to Viel-Arcy.

The château building and its grounds were situated close to the church at Soupir. A construction of pretentious proportions, its grand architectural design even encompassed the stable block, a magnificent building some two storeys high and so ornate it was sometimes mistaken for the main building. Surrounded by elaborately designed gardens and boasting a large lake to the southwest, the château was the home of Maria Boursin, the alleged mistress of Gaston Calmette the editor of the Paris newspaper *Le Figaro*.[162] A diary account of an 11/Hussars officer speaks of the 'great scramble' in the château kitchen when the regiment arrived on 14 September:

'We make soup and heat up bully beef. No bread, biscuits soaked in soup. The house servants produce wine from the cellars, real good claret, they gave it to us wholesale. About 11.00pm having given orders and made all the arrangements for an early start get Purser to pull off my boots and prepare to bed down in one of the bedrooms.'[163]

Sergeant John McIlwain had cause to visit the château with several of his platoon of Connaught Rangers and one gets the distinct impression they were on the look-out for 'souvenirs':

'This château was a magnificent building inside. When I, with two or three more, entered to find the big kitchen occupied by a party of the 15th Hussars who declared they were in possession by order of their CO. Ladies boudoirs and the bedrooms were littered with empty jewel and plate cases, their contents removed probably by the owners. In chests of drawers were dainty but stoutly woven linen handkerchiefs, which was all there was worth our attention, apart from a barrel of good quality bitter wine on tap by the back door. Very welcome after a march on a hot day.'[164]

All this was to change on 17 September, within days the three story building was catering for the seemingly continual stream of wounded who were being brought in from the surrounding area. Under the command of Major Percy Falkner the château was taking in an average of fifty casualties per day on top of the German casualties being treated in the nearby church. Soupir Château remained in the hands of 4/Field Ambulance until it finally left on 12 October, by which time the building had suffered severely from German artillery and the ravages of war. Maria Boursin also owned property in Paris to which she hastily retired when war reached the Aisne. By November 1918 – after the war had run its course and three battles had been fought on the Aisne – the building lay in ruins and Maria Boursin never returned to Soupir to rebuild her home.

Chapter 9

On the Chemin des Dames – 1st Division

*It's only when you press yourself flat into the earth that
the bullets cease to sing their song of death around you.*

Lieutenant Alan Hanbury-Sparrow – *The Land Locked Lake*

Douglas Haig's orders for 13 September were for his two
divisions to continue the advance and cross the Aisne. The
ground facing him was similar to that further west: a series of
high spurs running down from the Chemin des Dames ridge towards
the valley bottom and the river. Running east to west are the Pargnan
and Bourg spurs with the village of Moulins at the head of the valley
between them; next is the shorter Troyon spur running down from
Cerny-en-Laonnois which has Vendresse to the east of it and Beaulne
to the west.

Once the aqueduct at Bourg had been secured by the cavalry,
Brigadier General Ivor Maxse's 1 (Guards) Brigade and Herman
Landon's 3 Infantry Brigade followed on and advanced northeast
towards Paissy where they took up a position to the left of 2 Cavalry
Brigade. At 4.00pm Edward Bulfin's 2 Infantry Brigade was across the
river and gathered west of Paissy in and around Moulins, releasing 2
Cavalry Brigade which withdrew to Bourg. By 6.00pm on 13 September
the last man of the 1st Division was on the north bank of the Aisne.

The crossing of several thousand infantrymen and innumerable
wheeled transports over the aqueduct made life quite difficult for the
sappers of 23/Field Company. Charged with maintaining the integrity
of the canal towpath, Lieutenant Richard Bond was relieved to find it
was wide enough but realizing it was not possible to leave the path for
another mile – until the Bourg-Vailly road crossed the canal – he began
supervising the construction of a corduroy road to enable the traffic to
leave the towpath:

'The towpath was hard put to it to stand the strain of the traffic, and the Company was fully employed in keeping the surface in condition, rapidly filling up holes with whatever material was handy, in intervals, between units, and suffering the objurgations of gunners temporarily held up by more than usually extensive repairs, whilst from time to time a long-distance shrapnel shell from the Chemin des Dames would fall with a sizzle into the water.'[165]

Second Lieutenant Jock Marden and the 9/Lancers had crossed the river further upstream and advanced ahead of the main body towards Paissy where they eventually formed up behind a battery of XXV Brigade's guns:

'We then climb a hill and form up in mass behind a battery in action – our usual procedure. Naturally we receive several hostile overshoots aimed at the battery. We hastily pack up our lunch and having mounted, retire in open order at a walk for 300 yards. Six horses of my troop wounded, Lucas killed, two men wounded. The General thinks it a brave thing to do to sit down behind a battery in action in close formation. Anyhow, he's thrown away his best squadron leader – feel very depressed as I was very fond of Lucas.'[166]

Marden's diary, written from a junior subaltern's perspective of the battle, is in places quite critical of the regiment's deployment and of the brigade staff, offering, as it does, a refreshing insight into the daily toil of a cavalry officer on the front line. He felt particularly sad at the death of his squadron commander, 33-year-old Captain Douglas Lucas-Tooth who was hit by a shell splinter.[167] His thinly veiled sarcasm of Brigadier General De Lisle's wisdom in deploying cavalry in close proximity to artillery units in action possibly stemmed from the disastrous cavalry charge in which Marden took part at Audregnies on 24 August when 2 Cavalry Brigade suffered very heavily against the guns of the German IV Corps.[168]

That night the 1st Division and 2 Cavalry Brigade occupied a line from Paissy through Moulins, Oeuilly and Bourg and Briggs' 1 Cavalry Brigade was sent back across the river. All-in-all the prospects for the next day looked good. Haig – as we know – was still working on intelligence which suggested the enemy in front of him was thinly deployed, he had little, if any idea, of the movement of the German VII Reserve Corps which had already arrived on the Chemin des Dames. The local movement of German rearguards appeared to suggest the German Army was still in retreat, a belief which was repeated in the

The aqueduct over the Aisne at Bourg. It was the towpath on the right which was used by units of the 1st Division to cross the river on 13 September 1914. Once across the Aisne the modern day D925 was accessed via a corduroy road built by the sappers of 23/Field Company.

A British 18-pounder field gun in action. In 1914 British troops had not been issued with steel helmets.

The modern day road bridge at Vénizel. The photograph was taken from the site of the original bridge crossed by 11 Brigade on the night of 12 September.

Bucy-le-Long and the high ground above which was occupied by 11 Brigade. La Montagne Farm is beyond the tree line to the left of the private house.

Second Lieutenant Jock Marden 9/Lancers. *'Gave the ferry boy a Franc for courage.'*

Corporal John Lucy, 2/Royal Irish Rifles, taken after he was commissioned. *'The line staggered under the ferocious smash of machine gun fire.'*

Lieutenant William Read, 3 Squadron RFC. *'The air all round us was thick with shell bursts.'*

Lieutenant Kenlis Perceval Atkinson, 4 Squadron RFC. *'Funny noise those shells make when they burst, not a loud bang, sort of a 'plop'.'*

Lieutenant Baron 'Bron' Trevenen James, 4 Squadron RFC. Described by John Mowbray as '*an exceptional man*'.

Lieutenant Donald Swain Lewis of 4 Squadron, who with Baron James, pioneered air-to-ground radio communication which was first used over the Aisne Valley in 1914.

The Royal Aircraft Factory BE2a. '*When one considers that this revolution in artillery observation had taken place with just two BE2a aircraft from the Wireless Flight, the magnitude of the achievement can be appreciated.*'

General Hans von Zwehl. Despite his age he was still a formidable commander, ably demonstrated in his defence of the Chemin des Dames.

General Alexander von Kluck. His maverick style of command was in direct contrast to that of General Klaus von Bülow.

Sir Douglas Haig, commanding I Corps on the Aisne.

Sir Horace Smith-Dorrien, who stood his ground at Le Cateau and commanded II Corps on the Aisne.

Lieutenant Colonel John Longley who was in command of 1/East Surrey Regiment. He was soon promoted and eventually commanded the 10th Division.

Lieutenant Colonel Ernest Montresor was killed in action on 14 September whilst in command of 2/Royal Sussex Regiment.

Lieutenant Colonel Francis Towsey, commanding 1/West Yorkshire Regiment. Douglas Haig was furious after hearing of the West Yorkshires' retirement.

Captain Harry Sherwood Ranken, the medical officer attached to 1/KRRC. He was awarded a posthumous Victoria Cross.

Soupir Château was the home of Madame Maria Boursin before the war.

The château was used as a dressing station in 1914 and badly damaged. By 1917 it was totally destroyed.

All that remains today of the once magnificent building is a stone archway constructed on the original site of the château. Close by is Soupir Churchyard Cemetery where so many of the casualties treated at the château are buried.

Above: La Metz Farm used as a battalion HQ by 1/Battalion Royal Berkshire Regiment.

Left: Lieutenant Alan Hanbury-Sparrow who fought with the Berkshires as a platoon commander.

Men of 1/Leicestershire Regiment near La Rouge Maison Farm.

The three dispatch riders who served with 1/Signal Company, Royal Engineers. Left to right: Corporal J N Perks, Corporal T Daish and Corporal H Hodder, All three NCOs were commissioned soon after and survived the war.

1/Leicestershire Regiment in action. A machine-gun team – probably in the La Rouge Maison Farm area – firing from a concealed position.

Brigadier General Aylmer Hunter-Weston.
'*Reckless courage combined with technical skill and great coolness in emergency.*'

Brigadier General Beauvoir De Lisle commanding 2 Cavalry Brigade. Jock Marden held him responsible for the death of Captain Douglas Lucas-Tooth.

Brigadier General Count Edward Gleichen who commanded 15 Infantry Brigade on the Chivres spur.

Brigadier General Aylmer Haldane. He commanded 10 Infantry Brigade at Bucy-le-Long.

Private Ross Tollerton, the Cameron Highlander VC who carried his company officer to safety.

Private Frederick Dobson VC, the Coldstream Guardsman who brought in a wounded man near Cour de Soupir Farm.

The demolished bridge at Pont Arcy in the background with the pontoon bridge constructed by the Sappers of 5/Field Company in the foreground.

Above: Lance Corporal Charles Fuller, 2/Welsh Regiment. He won his Victoria Cross for rescuing Captain Mark Haggard who was wounded during an attack near Chivy.

Major Bernard Gordon Lennox who commanded Number 2 Company, 2/Grenadier Guards. He was killed near Bodmin Copse during the First Battle of Ypres in November 1914.

Captain Robert Dolbey, the medical officer attached to 2/KOSB.

Lieutenant Alexander Johnston who was on the staff of 7 Brigade. '*I expect that we shall find that the enemy have been able to retire more or less unmolested on to a strong fortified position.*'

The headquarters cave of Lieutenant Colonel Pearce-Serecold, commanding 2/King's Royal Rifle Corps. Serecold is standing third from left.

Cave art in a cave above Bucy-le-Long. The regimental badge of the Hampshire Regiment is amongst French and German regimental insignia.

The sucrerie at Cerny taken before the war. This building was the focus of the British attack on the Chemin des Dames on 14 September.

Left: The Loyal North Lancs memorial at Cerny cross-roads close to the site of the sucrerie.

Insert: Regimental badge detail on the column.

The château at La Fère-en-Tardenois occupied by Sir John French during the BEF campaign on the Aisne in 1914. GHQ was situated in a similar building a short walk away in the town square. In 1914 the château had a second floor which was badly damaged along with the roof during the Second World War.

Sir John Denton Pinkstone French, Commander-in-Chief of the BEF on the Aisne. French appeared to have little control over the battle which added to the growing conviction that he was very much out of his depth.

Caves at Paissy village, some of which were used by Captain Arthur Osburn to shelter and treat French North African casualties.

Mont de Soissons Farm which was used as a casualty clearing station and where Captain Jim Pennyman was taken after being wounded at Missy.

GHQ Operational Order No. 24 issued at 6.00pm on 13 September with the optimistic order to, 'continue the pursuit tomorrow at 6.00am and act vigorously against the retreating enemy'.

For Edward Bulfin, a vigorous advance over potentially difficult ground without prior reconnaissance grated harshly on his professionalism and with this foremost in mind, he instructed Lieutenant Colonel Eric Pearce-Serocold, commanding 2/KRRC, to send an officer's patrol forward under the cover of darkness to gather as much intelligence as possible. Accordingly, Second Lieutenant Oswald Balfour and eight riflemen managed to evade German pickets and established the presence of the enemy on the ridge:

> 'The patrol moved straight up the road on to the high ground north of Troyon and succeeded in locating a German picquet at the point where the road turns northwest immediately north of Troyon. Five Germans were seen, and apparently they heard the approach of the patrol, owing to a man slipping down the bank, which caused his mess tin to rattle. Some of the enemy followed down the road, but the patrol got away on the grass siding.'[169]

Balfour and his men were safely back in British lines by 2.30am in time to report to the general and rejoin their battalion before the brigade moved off. No doubt the report would have indicated the road from Vendresse up to the Chemin des Dames was well sheltered from enemy view until it turned sharply to the left and continued along a sunken road to the junction at Cerny-en-Laonnois. Had the patrol not alerted the German picquet they would have found a small cluster of buildings at the junction where the abandoned sucrerie building with its conspicuously tall brick chimney was located, just yards from the Chemin des Dames. In reality Balfour's patrol provided little intelligence of use, the sucrerie and its surroundings would all too soon become a familiar feature to all the 2 Brigade battalions.

The plan for 2 Brigade's attack was simple enough: under the immediate command of Lieutenant Colonel Pearce-Serocold, both the KRRC and 2/Royal Sussex would move quickly to occupy the high ground above the hamlet of Troyon. Pearce-Serocold would then move to take the crossroads at Cerny whilst Lieutenant Colonel Ernest Montresor remained in support with 2/Royal Sussex at Vendresse until required. The 1/Northamptons under the command of Lieutenant Colonel Edward Osborne Smith were under orders to climb the spur above Moulins and attack the ridge on the left of the 1st Battalion Queen's Royal West Surrey Regiment (1/Queen's) from 3 Brigade, detailed as flank guard on the extreme right.

The early start was the beginning of a day which would become forever etched into the memory of Sergeant Bradlaugh Sanderson. Apart from the 2.30am start in heavy mist and rain, he recalled, 'we had no overcoat only a waterproof sheet'. A reservist who had been mobilized at the start of hostilities in August 1914, Sanderson had been with 2/KRRC at Mons and all through the retreat and his greatcoat – and those of the rest of the battalion – had been left at Landrecies on 25 August after their encounter with the German 7th Division. He was now advancing with D Company and feeling the cold:

> 'We moved out of Paissy at 2.30am past the outposts and crept silently up the hill with fixed bayonets. We were told that we were going to surprise an outpost in front, that's all … We went gingerly through a village – Troyon – and up the slope of a big spur in front. We got to the top, reformed and were going through a cutting in the hillside nearly at the top, marching on either side of the road in single file. Suddenly a squad of cavalry came dashing through which was upsetting the whole show.'[170]

The squadron of cavalry included Jock Marden who had earlier found himself leading the advanced troop and being, 'not at all ready', having had no breakfast! On the way up to Troyon he had great difficulty reading the map in the dark, every time he stopped to strike a match in order to get some idea as to where he was, he received an irate command from the rear to hurry up:

> 'Thoroughly exasperated, I go on without being able to use the map through our own infantry in Troyon and up a valley past rows of Germans asleep in trenches. Ably supported by the squadron we retire in a hurry, as they wake up when we get to the far end. A regular steeplechase back over sunken roads and wire fences. Luckily it is too dark for accurate shooting.'[171]

Whether the Germans were all asleep or not, Sanderson was of the opinion that the cavalry's blunder into the German line proved their salvation alerting Sergeant Bradlaugh Sanderson's company of KRRC to the German presence. The German line was positioned astride the sunken road at the point where a track which ran down from the Chemin des Dames cut across the road. Duly roused, the men of the German picquet began firing straight down the road and although Marden reckoned it was too dark for accurate shooting, one round did hit Lieutenant Riversdale Grenfell who was killed immediately before the Lancers turned and galloped back down the road.[172]

D Company of the KRRC stood its ground. The company commander, Captain Augustus Cathcart, sent Lieutenant Seymour Mellor back to report to Colonel Pearce-Serocold, who was sheltering under the lee of the hillside near Troyon with A Company.[173] Cathcart's men were being fired on from three sides but refused to give way. Following his platoon commander, Second Lieutenant Stuart Davison, Sergeant Sanderson heard Cathcart shouting, 'extend over the ridge right and left':

'The day was just breaking when we got into position. We had two killed in a few seconds. Then the Germans turned two machine guns on to us from a haystack, not thirty yards to our front. My officer seized hold of a man's rifle, at the same time shouting, "There are hundreds of Germans behind that haystack." Then he stood up and deliberately fired, standing. I shouted, "Get down sir." He was shot through the eye immediately and died a few minutes after. Before he did that however, he said, "Hold on to this position as it is on the flank. Don't retire until you get orders."'[174]

Out on the right flank, Sanderson and his company were soon reinforced by A Company at about 5.45am which is more or less the time B Company appeared on the left flank. The battalion was now astride the sunken road, dawn had broken and fortunately the mist was still clinging to the hillside masking the British positions a little from the German guns which were in position some 600 yards in front. But from the weight of fire being directed onto the KRRC it was obvious this was no German rearguard but a substantial body of troops and British reinforcements were needed urgently. Pearce-Serocold responded quickly and dispatched a runner to Colonel Montresor requesting that the Royal Sussex reinforce the firing line.

The unmistakable noise of battle on the heights above had already alerted the Royal Sussex and sensing he would soon be needed, Montresor had already moved the battalion up from Vendresse in anticipation. By 6.30am the battalion was deployed on the left and right of the KRRC. The arrival of the Sussex lengthened the firing line and enabled A and B Companies of the Sussex to outflank the German position on the left; the Sussex war diary notes with some satisfaction that 'fire was opened and continued for some minutes when it was seen that a large number of Germans were putting up their hands to surrender'. Sanderson was one of the many witnesses to the events which followed, 'I heard a lot of shouting and everybody was standing up. The Germans had put up a white flag and were coming in by hundreds to surrender'. As the Sussex men rose to their feet to bring in the prisoners the Germans in the trenches behind them opened fire on both their own men and the British. The deadly crossfire created by that of their own men who had not thrown in the towel and the rapid fire being returned by the British riflemen cut down many of the hapless German infantrymen in the act of surrendering. Nevertheless, some 300 Germans were taken prisoner. It was a similar occurrence to that witnessed by Major Jeffreys at Cour de Soupir which had been the prelude to a number of so-called 'white flag' incidents all of which were anathema to the British notion of 'fair play'.

A similar incident involving the Royal Sussex occurred a short time later on the right of the line when the Germans were again outflanked and surrendered. On this occasion the surrendering Germans were fired on by two of the guns from a German battery near the sucrerie building. We are told that practically all these men were shot down by their own side. Whether Sanderson was confusing the two surrender episodes is unclear from his account but he does express his shock when the German gunners deliberately opened fire on their own. 'I had a sneaking fancy all wasn't right', he wrote, 'then they deliberately opened fire at short range'.

With two battalions now fully committed, Bulfin, realizing he needed to reinforce the firing line, ordered 1/Loyals to move up the hill from Vendresse where the battalion had been placed in reserve earlier in the morning. On their way up to Troyon the Loyals passed German prisoners being escorted down towards the river and Second Lieutenant James Hyndson, marching with B Company, noticed the enemy soldiers, 'were in tears'. Hyndson was the officer commanding Number 8 Platoon:

> *'On approaching the crest of hill we come on signs of conflict. Helmets lying all over the place and also rifles. A good deal of blood, and several wounded and dead lying about. We reach the crest and halt just under it. The bullets now seem to be coming from all directions. After a short rest we are ordered to attack factory.'*[175]

Bulfin's orders from division were not to push on beyond the Chemin des Dames, but as yet the strongpoint ahead of him – consisting of the sucrerie and the adjoining farmhouse – was preventing his brigade from reaching its objective. This sector of the line was defended by three battalions of the German 27 Reserve Regiment and the guns of 14 Reserve Field Artillery Regiment, and it was against these that the Loyals advanced. Facing the barrage of fire, which was being directed at them, Hyndson described his platoon's advance into what appeared to be certain death as beyond comprehension:

'I extend my platoon after Loomes (he is far in front of his platoon waving them on; this is the last I saw of him). Loomes is on my right and Goldie on my left.[176] *Had only gone a hundred yards under a perfect hail of bullets when I heard a singing sound on my right. Two eight-inch shells had pitched 20 yards to my left and blew sky high a few of my platoon. The shells emitted a tall cloud of black dust and smoke. Truly terrible missiles. We go forward, but as yet I can see nothing. At last we reach the firing line. How anyone reached it is beyond comprehending. And such a line. All manner of regiments are there, and the dead and wounded are lying around in scores. We carry the factory and hold on like grim death. Allason is a little to my right and Goldie landed up to me. He shortly afterwards moved off to the left by rolling on his side, and that was the last I saw of him.'*[177]

The Loyals carried the attack to the sucrerie factory building as ordered with B and D Companies advancing across a quarter of a mile of open ground. Their casualties – which were alarmingly heavy – included the commanding officer, Major Walter Lloyd and his adjutant, Captain Richard Howard-Vyse who were reported to have been killed in the first rush.[178] But their advance provided the catalyst and with the Loyals now in possession of the sucrerie buildings, Lieutenant Vere Dashwood and his machine-gun section from the Royal Sussex brought up their two Vickers guns and into a position from which they could bring a heavy fire onto the German batteries to the east. Dashwood's men effectively prevented any attempts by the German gunners to withdraw their guns, each time horses and limbers were brought up they were shot down by the fire from the sucrerie building, 'the guns of both batteries became derelict', exclaimed the Sussex war diary. The Loyals' war diary suggests the factory building was occupied sometime after 11.00am but by 12.30pm they were running short of ammunition. Lieutenant Hyndson again:

'The German machine guns were very nasty; they keep traversing up and down our line. A great increase in the noise of cracking whips overhead always heralded their return. Many men were hit and the casualties became truly appalling. We get no reinforcements or ammunition and soon exhaust our supply. Germans heavily counter attack.'[179]

By this stage, Sergeant Sanderson of the KRRC had lost nearly half his men and was also running short of ammunition. He sent an urgent request for both and remarked that, 'I got the ammunition but no reinforcements'. The situation was becoming desperate, even more so since the German line was being strengthened by units of the German

X Corps from the Second Army and a Horse Artillery *Abteilung* from the 9th Cavalry Division.

* * *

Let us leave 2 Brigade lodged precariously around the sucrerie for the moment in order to consider the movements of Brigadier General Maxse's 1 (Guards) Brigade. Maxse's brigade had suffered heavily during the retreat from Mons when 2/Munster Fusiliers under the command of Major Paul Charrier, had fought a desperate rearguard action at Etreux on 27 August.[180] The battalion had been detailed as rearguard to the brigade but Charrier did not receive orders to retire until it was too late. Cut off just before they entered the town of Etreux, the final engagement was fought in an orchard before the surviving 256 men and 3 officers who were left standing, surrendered. Maxse was quite rightly criticised by Haig for his handling of the affair and it was not until 5 September that the 1st Battalion Queen's Own Cameron Highlanders (1/Camerons) joined the brigade to bring it up to strength.

Leaving their bivouacs at Paissy, the 1/Coldstream was detailed as advance guard to the brigade and moved at 6.45am through Moussy and Vendresse. Avoiding the sunken road – where the initial engagement had begun earlier that morning – the battalion climbed the wooded slopes above Vendresse in single file to reach the high ground of the Troyon spur in order to approach Cerny from the southwest. Extending across the flat top of the plateau and guided by the tall chimney of the sucrerie, which they could just make out through the mist and driving rain, the battalion, led by Lieutenant Colonel John Ponsonby, soon came under heavy rifle and shell fire, Ponsonby noting with some pride that, 'the men advanced splendidly, no man hesitated, although many were falling on all sides'.

Meanwhile the Camerons and 1/Black Watch discovered one of the numerous tracks which ran up onto the spur from the southwest and had already arrived on the top near the quarries on Mount Faucon. Extending into skirmishing lines they moved between two of the quarries for some 500 yards and lay down with the Black Watch on the right. At 7.00am the advance began again, this time towards the distant finger of the factory chimney, but as soon as they left the cover of the wooded area they came under attack from the front and the right. Whilst A Company bore the brunt of this attack, the remaining companies continued extending their lines with one company of the Black Watch on the right and the elements of the Scots Guards on the left. It must have been a magnificent sight and one which the Germans on the Chemin des Dames had cause to remember as the highlanders swept through the enemy trenches and took up a firing line some 80 yards beyond the road.

With two half companies across the road the remainder of the battalion moved up the small Blanc Mont spur where they were able to bring fire to bear on the Chemin des Dames ridge. The Camerons now occupied an 'S'- shaped firing line which was attacked at 8.00am along its whole length. The weight of enemy infantry eventually forced the right flank to fall back behind the bank of the Chivy road.

Attacks on the battalion continued throughout the morning, during which time Lieutenant Colonel McLachlan was wounded whilst on the left of the line C Company were introduced to the white flag ruse:

> 'No 11 Platoon of C Company on the left (2/Lt Smith-Sligo) had 13 men killed altogether owing to the fact a body of Germans advanced waving their rifles above their heads and apparently wishing to surrender. On the platoon going forward they were decimated by the fire of another German line behind, and the line apparently wishing to surrender lay down and probably fired also.'[181]

Although this 'white flag' incident may have been the same one as described by Sergeant Sanderson, it is possible it was an entirely separate event, bearing in mind the Camerons were west of the sucrerie and the men of 11 Platoon went forward to receive the surrendering Germans. Nevertheless, it appears that this time it was a deliberate ploy by the Germans to lure the unsuspecting British infantry out of cover.

In the intervening time – whilst the Camerons and Black Watch were dealing with the left flank – John Ponsonby and the Coldstream Guards reached the brick wall which surrounded the sucrerie at about the time the factory chimney was brought down by enemy shell fire. Thus it was sometime around 9.30am when Ponsonby, with a mixed party of men from all regiments, and Number 2 Company of the Coldstream pushed on over the road itself:

> 'We made rushes by sections and got to the sunken road and pressed on forward to a village, Cerny by name. At this time I suppose we were about 100 to 150 strong, but under the circumstances it was impossible to estimate numbers, we could only hope the remainder of the battalion would come on ... Charlie Grant took 50 men down one side of the village, Aldam, Paget and myself keeping down the centre of the village with the

remainder. In the village I found a large German ambulance corps; a German colonel came out of one of the houses. I saw he had about 20 medical officers with him and there appeared to be a whole medical arrangement and appliances in the house.'[182]

On the far side of the village they stumbled across German troops. At first Ponsonby thought they were British or even French troops but quickly realized they were in fact the enemy who, after a brief but sharp firefight, vanished into the gloom. At the northern edge of the village the party were discovered and John Ponsonby was hit in the ankle. Surrounded, they remained in the wood until dark when they managed to evade the enemy during a rainstorm:

'We passed German troops within 50 yards, but by keeping as quiet as possible and with the aid of the storm of wind and rain, we passed through them unobserved. We could only go at the rate of about one mile an hour, as I could not be carried any faster ... At 5.00am we got onto a main road and walked in to one of our field ambulances at the village of Vendresse.'[183]

John Ponsonby's advance over the Chemin des Dames was not the only one that morning. A mile further east along the ridge the Queen's, together with the 1/Northamptons, had also advanced over the road, meeting little opposition until the ground fell away from them by La Bovelle Farm. Here the battalions found themselves looking down into the valley of the Ailette which separated them from the German 8-inch artillery batteries on the far rim. Nothing was done to capitalize on this advance but the Queen's did wreak considerable havoc with their machine guns on German troops who were unfortunate enough to be moving to the east. It is almost heartbreaking to ponder on the fact that at two separate points along the Chemin des Dames, barely a mile apart, the German line had been infiltrated with very little difficulty by a substantial number of British troops who were then forced to withdraw in the absence of any support.

The Northamptons' advance was graphically described by Lieutenant Evelyn Needham who advanced with the battalion up the Moulins spur and was in sight of the Chemin des Dames at 11.30am. Needham, known to his friends as 'Jack', could see the ridge to his front and had a grandstand view of the battle around the sucrerie:

'It was still very wet and misty and we could only just make out the ridge opposite with its telegraph poles running along the Chemin des Dames, its haystacks and its factory chimney. But we could see the 1st and 2nd

Brigades attacking the terraces to our left front, and a wonderful sight it was – just like watching a field day on the Fox Hills or Salisbury Plain, except there were continuous puffs of smoke about, both on the ground and in the air, and that one saw little figures collapse and lie still! The noise of gun fire, machine guns and rifles was incessant, but only an occasional spent bullet came over us on our hill, or a very occasional shrapnel burst. Why the Germans did not plaster our hill-top with shrapnel I cannot imagine.'[184]

Ordered to advance in extended order, C and B Companies moved up to take a position on the left of the Queen's. Needham and his platoon were part of C Company and were initially masked from enemy observation by the mist and a shallow depression in the ground. Intent on maintaining pace and focused very much on staying alive, Needham did not notice his passge over the first line of German trenches as they topped the rise and halted on the road itself. After straightening up their line with the Queen's they went on:

'About a hundred and fifty yards beyond the road the gradient begins to flatten out, and it was soon pretty evident that we had been seen! 'Everything seemed to open on us at once – rifles, machine-guns, artillery, etc. The noise was deafening, the rifle and machine gun bullets made a noise like a stock whip being cracked in one's ear as they passed … It never seemed to stop. Nothing seemed to stop. Men were falling now right and left. We were advancing in two lines, and my platoon was in the second line … on we went – it seemed like miles that we had advanced, whereas it was only about three hundred yards. Men continued to fall, the noise continued deafening, but we could see no shells bursting over the enemy, and we were cursing them accordingly.'[185]

As their advance ground to a halt Needham recalled lying flat on the ground for about twenty minutes, 'being utterly unable to find out what was happening elsewhere'. There were no orders and they lay there not knowing whether to advance, retire or maintain their positions. 'Then the rain stopped and the mist began to clear, and presently to our joy shrapnel started to burst about twenty to thirty yards in front of us, right over the German trenches'.

The clearing mist had enabled Lieutenant Colonel John Geddes' XXV Brigade RFA to finally bring their guns into action. Up to this point in the battle the British brigades fighting along the Chemin des Dames had been without artillery support. Bringing guns to bear on the enemy positions was impossible in the misty conditions, as without clear observation there was every possibility the gunners would be firing on British troops. Here the Germans had a clear advantage over the British gunners; their guns had been in position well before the attack began and they knew the dispositions of their troops; but at least the mist provided some cover under which the gunners of 116/Battery could manhandle their guns up above Troyon. They were now in action just behind the firing line. Although this single battery could hardly be termed 'substantial' artillery support, it did fire some 1,200 rounds and was kept supplied with ammunition entirely by hand – and it at least managed to redress the balance of firepower a little. The welcome shrapnel which Needham saw bursting over the German trenches was most likely from 114/Battery which was firing from a field just east of Troyon, 'their fire caused the enemy's rifle and machine-gun fire to lessen a bit, which was a real blessing'.

Lying pressed to the ground north of the Chemin des Dames, the Northamptons were finally ordered to retire by Lieutenant Colonel Osborne-Smith which they did under the cover of shrapnel fire from 114/Battery. The Queen's were also forced to pull back after the French Colonial Division had failed to make headway on their right, digging in along the line of the Chemin des Dames around 4.30pm with the Northamptons. One gets the distinct impression that once the Northamptons had advanced over the Chemin des Dames they were rather at a loss as what to do next. Needham and his platoon, 'slithered down the slope backwards on our hands and knees for about fifty yards', until they were out of sight of the enemy and retired to the Chemin des Dames where they dug in using the roadside ditch. 'It was now 1.00pm and all hands set to, to dig like badgers. The men had only their entrenching tools, of course, we officers had nothing but our hands and swords, for what they were worth!'

* * *

Although the clearing mist had enabled the British gunners to get to work, it also precipitated a series of renewed German attacks on the British positions, particularly on the sucrerie. At 1.00pm an attack, launched at the entire frontage of 1 Guards Brigade and 2 Brigade, pushed the British out of the buildings – which at the same time exposed the Camerons' right flank – forcing their eventual retirement back towards the Chivy valley. By this time it had also become obvious that the 2nd Division on the left had not made progress and their hoped for appearance on the Chemin des Dames was not going to materalise. The order to withdraw from the sucrerie were prompted by shell fire from the German batteries on the far side of the Ailette valley, James Hyndson was told to get his men out by Captain Lionel Allason. There were not many left:

> '*Allason*[186] *orders me to retire and I do so with two Loyal North Lancs, three Black Watch, two Cameron Highlanders. We move back at a fast double, and coming to a Donga, take shelter there. We are subjected to a terrific bombardment and it is death to show a hand. The shells seem to come right in and sweep the hole out. We lie there for some time and then move a little further back. I strike the Gloucester Regiment ... they have come up to support us and have had no casualties. They are all very eager to go on.*'[187]

Sergeant Sanderson of the KRRC gave the order himself to what was left of his platoon:

> '*I gave the order to retire, calling one after the other, those remaining to keep up a rapid fire so as to render the retirement effective. But the hounds got a Maxim onto us. The chap next to me got hit in the leg and arm and he said, "Don't leave me Sergeant." Another chap and I got to him and dragged him along, crawling until we got him to a coal-box hole. The fates were unkind for the other chap got hit so I left my water bottle and scooted ... I got back with four men out of sixteen.*'[188]

The German counter attack at 1.00pm brought the 1st Battalion Gloucestershire Regiment (1/Gloucesters) from 3 Brigade into the fight on the ridge, although 3 Brigade had been instrumental in breaking up a German counter attack on the left flank earlier in the morning, B and C Companies were now sent up to help stabilize the line at Cerny. It was Number 7 Platoon of B Company – the advanced platoon of the Gloucesters commanded by Lieutenant Arthur Harding, which James Hyndson met up with as he retired.[189] Hyndson's account really does highlight the confusion which existed along the Chemin des Dames during the afternoon of 14 September. The Coldstream historian likened it to the Battle of Inkermann where groups of men from all regiments became mixed together in the misty conditions and were led by whoever happened to be available.[190] Sixty years later the British infantrymen on the Chemin des Dames were still displaying that same stubborn obstinacy, clinging to positions that had been gained at so great a cost and maintaining a firing line from whatever cover could be found.

Having lost his regiment Hyndson bravely decided to remain with the Gloucesters. This equates to a time of around 5.00pm which corresponds to the late-in-the-afternoon order sent out earlier by

Douglas Haig for a general advance of both the 2nd and 1st Divisions
– a last ditch attempt to push the Germans off the Chemin des Dames–
and for both divisions to establish themselves securely on the ridge:

> *'Towards darkness the Gloucesters are ordered to attempt to advance on the*
> *factory ... They ask me to come and I do so, there being no chance of finding*
> *my unit. We move off and have several escapes from "Jack Johnsons" and*
> *move up the road. Reach top of road when half battalion in front get*
> *panicky. The General's escort bolted and the half battalion of Welch opened*
> *fire on us. Luckily they fired high, so no damage was done. The Gloucester*
> *Regiment's leading company had scattered, and it seemed as if we were in*
> *for another fight, for we did not know who was firing at us.'[191]*

The 2nd Battalion Welch Regiment, mistaking the Gloucesters for the
enemy, then charged and two of the Gloucesters were bayoneted. To
add insult to injury, they then opened fire on the unfortunate
Gloucesters again! Presumably after apologies all round the advance
continued up towards the Chemin des Dames but failed to make any
ground, Hyndson's only comment being, 'after a good deal of not
knowing what to do, we got orders to retire'. The general referred to
could only have been Herman Landon who was commanding 3
Brigade at the time. Thus the young Second Lieutenant had taken part
in two attacks on the Chemin des Dames, been fired upon by both the
Germans and his own side and remarkably, remained unscathed.
Readers will not be at all surprised to hear that he ended the war intact
and with the ribbon of the Military Cross on his chest. That night
Hyndson sheltered under a waterproof sheet with Arthur Harding,
'having supped off biscuits and jam'.

Darkness saw the hard-pressed units of the 1st Division digging in
along a line which ran along the Chemin des Dames from a point juat
under two miles east of the Cerny crossroads, with its right flank in
touch with the French Moroccan Division of XVIII Corps. It then
skirted south of the sucrerie and headed southwest to a point where it
crossed the high ground north of Mont Faucon and on into the Chivy
valley. Here it linked up with the line held by units of the 2nd Division
at the southern end of the Beaulne spur.

After a heavy bombardment the sucrerie had been reoccupied by the
Germans and the abandoned guns – rendered unusable by the British
– had been limbered up and removed. As dusk fell 3 Infantry Brigade
pressed forward in the gap between Haking's 5 Brigade, Lieutenant
Charles Paterson reporting that B and C Companies of the South Wales
Borderers had reached the ridge but after being fired upon by outposts,
had retired after losing the two remaining companies in the dark!

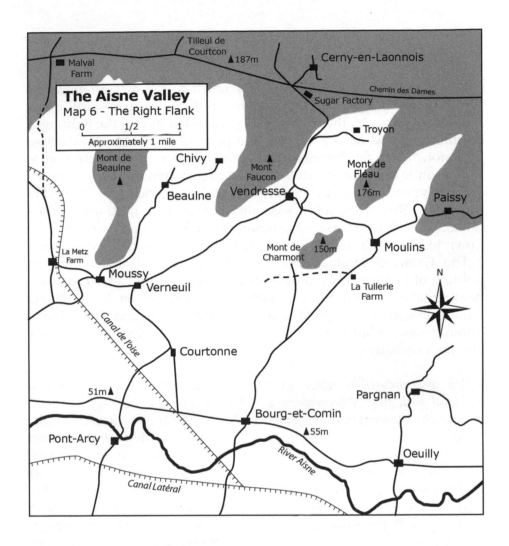

Haking, we know, retired after his advance with 5 Brigade and Colonel Northy's half battalion of 1/KRRC, after stumbling around in the dark looking for 3 Brigade, did likewise.

*　*　*

We must now return to the plight of the Cameron Highlanders and the Black Watch and the German counter attack on the left flank. As 1 Brigade fell back from the factory the Camerons and Black Watch fought a desperate fighting withdrawal until they reached the shelter of the woods north of Vendresse whilst smaller parties worked their way down the Chivy valley. But one party of some sixty Camerons under the command of Major Hon Alfred Maitland, stubbornly hung onto the ground they had taken at Blank Mont.[192] Seriously short of ammunition they resorted to collecting rounds from the dead and wounded before they were forced to withdraw leaving Maitland dead behind them.

Devotion to duty was clearly very much to the fore amongst the ranks of the Cameron Highlanders on that shrapnel-torn ridge. Lieutenant James Matheson was badly wounded during the fighting in the morning and he was carried to a place of safety by Private Ross Tollerton. After the battalion had retired Tollerton had returned to Matheson to take him down to the dressing station but found himself and his wounded officer effectively cut off by advancing Germans. For three days Ross Tollerton – wounded in the head, back and hand – remained with the stricken Matheson before he was able to carry him down to Chivy. His award of the Victoria Cross was richly deserved.

The Cameron Highlanders had been all but decimated in the fighting of 14 September, only 6 officers and 200 men answered their names that evening at roll call. Writing to his father on 24 September whilst aboard the hospital ship SS *Asturias*, Captain Lord James Thomas Stewart Murray reflected on the Cameron Highlander's attack and their casualties:

> 'We were ordered to attack across an open plateau, exposed to the most awful shell fire. My company was the leading one, and suffered most severely. We went into action with 5 officers and 221 men, the roll call after the battle showed no officers and 86 men, I fear Mackintosh, Alastair Murray (Polmaise) and Hector Cameron[193] are all gone, Iain Maxwell (Lovett's nephew) was severely wounded, and I myself slightly. My Company Sergeant Major was killed. I felt his loss very much, as we had done 10 years' service together continuously in the same company. Part of the Black Watch (who were on the right) and most of my company got almost as far as a sugar factory held by the enemy, only to be beaten back with tremendous losses.'[194]

As the fighting around Cerny ebbed and flowed, von Zwehl, the German VII Reserve Corps commander, ordered a counter attack on the British left flank to divert some of the pressure away from the hard pressed 27 Reserve Brigade. Three battalions and two machine-gun companies from 25 Reserve Brigade launched their attack at 10.00am with the intention of driving a wedge between Haig's two divisions. This attack was met by 1/SWB and the 2/Welch with assistance from 113/ and 46/Batteries and from all accounts the German attack appears to have been stopped very effectively by the two 3 Brigade battalions.

Von Zwehl in his account of the engagement admitted to heavy casualties:

'One battalion had to retire with heavy losses. The remains of it assembled under the steep slope, south of Courtecon. The other two battalions were compelled to give up their positions, as the companies had got thoroughly mixed up ... They assembled on the reverse slope between Malval Farm and Courtecon. The brigade commander was mortally wounded.'[195]

It was during this engagement that Lance Corporal William Fuller of 2/Welch won the second Victoria Cross of the day for carrying a wounded officer, Captain Mark Haggard, a nephew of the novelist Henry Rider Haggard, to safety. Sadly Haggard died from his wounds the next day.[196] As had happened elsewhere, once the mist cleared the British gunners were able to bring down a substantial bombardment on the Chemin des Dames. Watching from the relative safety of a wood, Charles Paterson, the South Wales Borderers' adjutant, felt the Germans were not getting it all their own way as he watched, 'swarms of Germans on the ridge, rather massed. Our guns open on them at 1,800 yards, and one can see a nasty sight through one's glasses. Bunches of Germans blown to pieces'.

There was a more sombre attitude amongst the men of the Cameron Highlanders and the Black Watch. 1st Division casualties from the fighting on 14 September amounted to over 3,500 officers and men and many of these were from the two highland regiments. The Cameron Highlanders alone lost some 600 officers and men and amongst the casualties suffered by the 1/Black Watch was their commanding officer, 44-year-old Adrian Grant-Duff, Major Lord Stewart Murray and Lieutenants Cumming, Don and Boyd.[197] Six other Black Watch officers were wounded along with 40 other ranks killed, 112 wounded and 35 missing.

Lieutenant Hon Gerard Freeman-Thomas, was the only officer killed in the 1/Coldstream but ten others, including John Ponsonby, were wounded along with 343 other ranks, many of whom were posted as missing.[198] Edward Bulfin reported 41 officers and 926 NCOs and men killed, wounded or missing from 2 Brigade, of these the Royal Sussex lost five officers killed, including the commanding officer, Ernest Montresor and four other officers wounded. Eleven other ranks were killed; seventy-nine wounded and 114 were still missing by nightfall, many of whom were wounded and still lying out on the battlefield. Amongst the Sussex dead was 25-year-old Sergeant George Hutson of

B Company.[199] Hutson competed for Great Britain in the 1912 Stockholm Olympics winning a bronze medal in the 5,000 metres and a team bronze in the 3,000 metre-race.

The Loyals suffered badly in their advance to the sucrerie and reported 78 other ranks and 12 officers killed, wounded or missing.[200] Included amongst the dead was their commanding officer, Major Walter Lloyd, who was only in his third day of command after the death of Colonel Guy Knight at Priez on 11 September.[201] There is no accurate figure for the number of men wounded or missing from the battalion but from the war diary we know casualties were, 'very heavy indeed'. The officer casualties in 2/KRRC were eight killed and missing – of which only two were recovered for burial – and seven wounded, which together with the 306 other ranks killed wounded or missing, represented a sizeable proportion of the battalion.

Initially the wounded were brought down to dressing stations which had been established in the Mairie at Vendresse and at the crossroads south of Vendresse near La Mal Bâtie Farm. But these two aid points were completely overwhelmed early on in the morning by the sheer numbers of wounded men flooding down from the fighting on the Chemin des Dames. Consequently Vendresse Château, belonging to the Comte de la Maisonneuve, was taken over by 3/Field Ambulance and a little further south at Moulins, 1/Field Ambulance established itself in a cluster of buildings which were sheltered from shell fire by the high ground above. 2/Field Ambulance originally set up its dressing station in a farm near Oeuilly but shell fire soon encouraged a rapid move south of the river to Villers, where they established themselves in the château and local Mairie. It was not long before the relatively secure Villers became the divisional collecting station. Close to the firing line the advanced dressing stations – which in many cases were combined with regimental aid posts – were at Beaulne, Troyon, Chivy and Paissy.

2/Field Ambulance originally set up its dressing station in a farm near Oeuilly but shell fire soon encouraged a rapid move south of the river to Villers, where they found a more secure base in the château and local Mairie. It was not long before the relatively sheltered Villers became the divisional collecting station but a crisis point was reached on 15 September when the numbers of wounded pouring into Villers were getting beyond the available resources of the field ambulance staff. An appeal to the French for assistance resulted in twenty motor ambulances and drivers arriving the next day to move wounded to Fère-en-Tardenois and Bazoches. This was the first instance in which British wounded had been transported by motor ambulance – as

Brereton said of the occasion, 'It was not quite a red letter day for the RAMC which was to come on the 20th when motor ambulances were first issued to all field medical units'.

Reflecting on the day's events, Lieutenant Charles Paterson was thankful that he and his friends in the battalion had, 'not yet taken a knock', but with 220 casualties sustained in one day's fighting and the German Army entrenched in front of him, he knew, 'there was lots more to come'.

Chapter 10

Trench Warfare

The shrapnel we don't care a damn about, but this other brute
seems to forge its way through anything making a deafening
explosion with a sort of black yellow cloud.

Major Bernard Gordon Lennox – describing the
effects of a 'Jack Johnson'

The heavy British casualties sustained on 14 September 1914 may
be regarded as the brutal backwash to the wave of optimism
which had been expressed in GHQ Operational Order No.24 the
previous day. On 15 September Douglas Haig and William Pulteney
were ordered to consolidate their positions but Smith-Dorrien was
instructed to continue the attack with his II Corps. In reality the two
divisions of II Corps were in no position to maintain their attack on 15
September, particularly in light of the lack of effective artillery support
which had been a feature of the previous day's offensive; in fact it
wasn't until 19 September that any replacements for the 18-pounder
artillery pieces lost at Le Cateau began to arrive. On 14 September the
3rd Division had only just managed to stem a German counter attack
and Fergusson's 5th Division had made very little headway on the
Chivres spur. The complete lack of progress by Fergusson's division on
15 September together with the withering barrage of shell fire which
descended on the whole BEF frontage, finally convinced a wavering Sir
John French that the German retreat was over. Operational Order
No.26, issued by GHQ at 8.30pm on 15 September, effectively signalled
the beginning of positional warfare on the Aisne.

On either flank of the BEF the French armies has reached similar
conclusions. German reinforcements had successfully seen off any
ambitions the French armies may have had of breaking through. On 14
September the French XVIII Corps under General de Mas-Latrie had

lost Craonne and Craonnelle and to the west Boëlle's IV Corps had
failed to turn the flank of von Kluck's First Army at Nampcel. Whilst
deadlock looked almost certain it was vital to hold the Germans on the
Aisne if the possibility of turning their flank west of the Oise was to
become reality. As one might expect, such a move had not by-passed
German thinking at OHL. Eric von Falkenhayn, who had succeeded
von Moltke on 15 September 1914 as Chief of the German General Staff,
was only too aware that the German right flank was, 'in the air' and
without any appreciable reserves behind it. With a strategy that, to a
certain extent, mirrored that of the French and British, he ordered a
series of strong counter attacks along the Aisne front to the west and
east of Reims in order to hold the Allied armies and to allow German
units to be moved to the west. These attacks fell largely on the British
sector.

It should be said, however, that the perception of 'permanence'
which characterized the trench warfare of later years was far from
present in the minds of the men who now hastily dug their trenches on
the Aisne. For those serving along the British line the prospect of an
advance to victory was always at the back of their minds, as was the
possibility of the war being over by Christmas; the tragedy being that
a large proportion of those harbouring such optimism would be dead
or wounded by Christmas, and not as they hoped, back in England. A
prophecy of what was to come can be found in the pages of the *Official
History* of 1914 – albeit written in retrospect – when Sir James Edmonds
offered the 'recipe' for trench warfare which evolved on the Aisne and
which would become familiar to the soldiers on both sides of the front
line for the next three and a half years:

'*Artillery fire, though intermittent, never ceased for long. By day, sniping
made it impossible to move about or to work except under cover; constant
vigilance was required to detect enemy infantry attacks in good time. Night
was livelier even than day, and was made almost as bright at times by the
enemy's flares and light balls; but during darkness working parties and
supplies came up and reliefs were carried out.*'[202]

Trenches were hardly a new phenomenon in warfare, Brigadier
General Aylmer Haldane had, 'a good deal of experience of a
campaign of this nature', when he had been attached to the Japanese
Army as an observer in Manchuria in 1904. Haldane felt that trench
warfare was bound to have been visited sooner or later on Europe,
given, 'the huge forces placed in the field by both sides and the limited
frontage for deployment'. The French were so opposed to trenches and

all that they stood for, that during the Battle of Charleroi, when General Charles Lanrezac had ordered his corps to entrench along the Sambre, many chose to ignore the order. Trenches contravened the spirit of *élan* which underwrote the French military doctrine of *avance*, no better expressed than by a young French officer in the 33rd Infantry Regiment called Charles de Gaulle:

> 'Everywhere, always, one should have a single idea: to advance. As soon as the fighting begins everybody in the French Army, the general in command, the officers and the troops have only one thing in their heads – advancing, advancing to the attack, reaching for the Germans. And running them through or making them run away.'[203]

Naturally the Germans did not expect a situation to arise where positional warfare would be necessary since the Schlieffen Plan envisaged a complete victory in the west within forty days. They had, however, taken into consideration the material requirement for dealing with the French and Belgian forts. Unwittingly their arsenal of heavy siege batteries, searchlights, grenades and periscopes, all designed for the reduction of fortress defences, had in fact equipped them for trench warfare and they diverted these resources to the Aisne with some alacrity. On 14 September, the first trainload of heavy batteries and equipment arrived on the Aisne from Maubeuge.

Thus, when the Germans stood their ground on the Aisne and dug themselves in along the high ground, the French and British had little option but to begin their own parallel line of defences, resulting in the birth of what was to become known as the Western Front; a line of fortifications which would eventually stretch from the Swiss border to Nieuwpoort on the Belgian coast. Protection against the heavy calibre, high explosive shell fire, forced the British to dig ever deeper trenches and enter what became known as the 'Augustan Period' of field fortifications: narrow trenches with vertical sides, rarely continuous, 18 inches to 2 feet wide and often without traverses. Compared to the more elaborate defences which began to appear in late 1914, these holes in the ground were positively amateur. Barbed wire was soon introduced, although the feeble single strand in front of the South Wales Borderers' trenches was dismissed as, 'ridiculous' by Captain Guy Ward. Needless to say both sides soon adapted to living below ground. Lieutenant Arthur Mills, a special reserve officer serving with 1/DCLI, arrived on the front line in October when the ferocity of the early days of the battle had all but died down:

'We passed the morning sitting in the dug-out, reading a few old papers and
smoking and talking. By eleven the sun was high enough to peep in over
the top of the parapet and warm us, and it all seemed to me a very pleasant,
lazy sort of existence. There was no firing except for an occasional "ping"
from a sniper the [company commander] kept posted at the corner of the
trench, and an answering shot or two from the German side. Rifle fire
seemed a matter of tacit arrangement. When our sniper was joined by a
friend, or fired two or three times in a minute instead of once every three
or four, the German fire grew brisker and life in the trench less tranquil.
Our sniper was thereupon reproved by the [company commander] and
was silent, whereupon the German fire died down.'[204]

Some brigade commanders took the opportunity to ensure all officers
were fully versed in the building of trench defences. Whether Hunter-
Weston had a notion as to what the future would bring or not, his
directive to the 11 Brigade battalions on 30 September instructed
commanding officers to go round the whole of their defences with their
officers, 'pointing out for instructional purposes good and bad points
of various works'. It was on the Aisne that the hated working parties –
drawn largely from men serving in the infantry battalions – were first
used to construct new trench lines, the Somersets' war diary records
fatigue parties digging new trenches on 28 September, using, one
hopes, tools more suited to the job than the 1908 Pattern Entrenching
Tool. The British infantryman's entrenching tool was quickly found to
be totally unsuitable for the task and it was only when the area was
scoured for shovels which were distributed to the front line units and
consignments of tools were brought up by the engineers that British
casualties from the heavy German shelling began to decline. The spade
was becoming a weapon of war.

Trench raids – that feature of later trench warfare which so often
resulted in heavy casualties – were first practised on the slopes above
the Aisne. Edmund Meade-Waldo, the machine-gun officer with 17
Brigade, wrote of a raid carried out by the 3rd Battalion of the Rifle
Brigade on 25 September 1914:

'The 3RB tried to capture by surprise a German advanced trench opposite
their centre. The attack was a failure, Boden[205] and Mackenzie being killed
and Kennedy wounded and many ORs killed and wounded. The attack took
place an hour before dawn when the Germans were naturally standing
to!'[206]

Meade-Waldo's rather sardonic comments did not reflect the feeling amongst senior officers who were convinced of the value of maintaining morale amongst the troops by offensive action. A note in the II Corps diary suggests that morale is best kept by, 'small local attacks and enterprises, even with the knowledge that they must entail loss of men on missions of minor importance'. Offensive spirit was always regarded by senior officers as important in maintaining discipline and morale. Later in the war battalions would endeavour to maintain an aggressive dominance of no-man's land by constant reconnaissance and fighting patrols. Trench raids could be carried out by small parties of men or, on occasion, by entire companies or even battalions and were generally deployed to gather intelligence on enemy forces or to destroy a particular enemy installation. In truth they were an unpopular but necessary facet of trench warfare.

Trenches were of course not a complete protection from shelling and the profusion of caves and quarries in the area offered what appeared to be a more substantial shelter from the often fatal attentions of high explosive. Sadly this was not always the case. During a bombardment on the Guards' positions at Cour de Soupir Farm on 16 September, one 8-inch shell narrowly missed the farm buildings and landed in a nearby quarry where it exploded, killing and wounding over 100 men of the Guards and Ox and Bucks Light Infantry. Major Bernard Gordon Lennox was in the quarry at the time standing with Major Jeffreys and Captain Eben Pike:

> 'In addition this same shell killed three officers of the Oxfords, and a medical officer. How it missed Jeffreys, George Powell, Eben Pike and self will forever remain a mystery. It killed and wounded people who were more under cover than we were, sitting all together. It killed and wounded people to our rear, front and left, but for some unknown reason we all escaped untouched.'[207]

Lieutenant James Huggan's death in the quarry was one of many which befell RAMC doctors attached to infantry battalions.[208] The 25-year-old was a well-known Scottish international rugby player and was killed the day after another Scottish international, Lieutenant Ronald Simson, was killed in action serving with 16/Battery.[209] Serving as medical officer with 1/KRRC, Captain Harry Ranken was the only serving soldier of the RAMC to win a Victoria Cross on the Aisne.[210] On 19 September one of his legs was shattered by shell fire but despite his wounds, Ranken continued to tend to the wounded, ultimately sacrificing his own life. Having borne the shock of amputation he died of his wounds on 25 September 1914. His death was followed by that of Lieutenant William Ball who was killed in action with the South Staffordshires six days later.[211]

The need to provide some sort of shelter from shell fire became a priority amongst the battalions manning the front line positions. On the Chemin des Dames, Lieutenant Evelyn Needham spent the evening of 14 September digging after what he described as a, 'very unsatisfactory' day:

> 'We had attacked, but in vain, without artillery support and with no sort of knowledge as to where we were going, and what we were bumping up against. We had lost five officers (two killed) and over one hundred other ranks ... we all got busy after supper, digging holes for ourselves to form some sort of shelter in the high bank of the terrace which, while giving marvellous protection from hostile shell fire, gave none against the rain.'[212]

They spent the 15th improving their shelters and constructing a large dug-out in the hillside for an officers' mess to the tune of 'hundreds' of 'Black Marias' and 'Coal Boxes' landing with deafening explosions in the valley below. Black Marias were something which Lieutenant Geoffrey Prideaux serving with the Somersets was very familiar with. His diary account of an artillery bombardment at Bucy-le-Long on the 17th has one almost running for cover. He must have wondered if the German gunners were actually aiming at him, bearing in mind this was the second occasion in two days on which he had been caught in such a barrage in the very same village:

> 'About 11.00am the Germans started to bombard Bucy village with their 8.2-inch howitzers, which throw a shell of 290lbs, filled with high explosive. This bombardment lasted for 1 hour and 10 minutes, and was the severest we had undergone ...To show the force of explosion of these shells, one shell fell into a yard and blew to bits seven horses and six men, smashed in the back wall of the house in front and, blew two men who were in the house, into the street. They were not hurt, only shaken, but they were quite black from the smoke.'[213]

Bernard Gordon Lennox was less descriptive, commenting only that the Black Maria 'makes a hole in the ground big enough to bury 3 or 4 horses in'. However he did confess to getting a bad headache when one burst too close! Apart from being dubbed Coal Boxes and Black Marias by the troops they were often referred to as 'Jack Johnsons' after a popular black American heavyweight boxer. Corporal Cuthbert Avis serving with the Queen's was introduced to Jack Johnsons on the Chemin des Dames and thought the, 'noise of the explosion was very nerve wracking and the blast powerful and dangerous', the shell making, 'a deep, wide circumference crater'.

But for Jack Needham and his company of Northamptons up above Troyon, most of the shells tended to land below them in the allotment gardens of the village. It was whilst he was idly watching the allotments under fire on 17 September that the Germans launched an attack on their line in the pouring rain and, 'in considerable strength'. His company was in reserve but was hastily summoned to the firing line where the battalion was ordered to counter attack:

> 'We reached the road (Chemin des Dames) and lay down there for a few minutes to get our breath. Then Payker gave the order to fix bayonets and a few minutes later to charge. Over the low bank we went, Payker shouting, "Come on, the Cobblers!" and the men cheering like hell. I ran as hard as best I could over the roots with my drawn sword in one hand and my revolver in the other, stumbling and cursing over the roots and expecting every minute to be tripped up by my sword scabbard! We charged through heavy rifle and machine-gun fire and men were dropping off in every direction. We got to about thirty yards from the trench we had passed over on Monday and which was now strongly held. By now everyone was pretty well blown, and I was thankful when I saw the whole line throwing themselves down flat.'[214]

With a firing line established, the Northamptons and the KRRC on their right kept up a continuous fire on the Germans in front of them. After, 'what seemed like hours later', Needham was informed by a messenger that his company commander, Captain Robert Parker – or Payker to the company officers – had been killed and he was now in command.[215] Not only that, said the messenger, but the company of KRRC on his right had all their officers killed or wounded and he was now in command of those as well! Sending a runner back to ask for orders, the message arrived back from Osborne-Smith telling Needham to hold on where he was and keep up as much fire as possible on the German trench:

> 'Then suddenly I heard the men shouting, "They're surrendering!" and looking up I saw a line of white flags (or rather white handkerchiefs or something of the kind tied to the muzzles of rifles) held up all along the German trench ... I shouted to the men to cease fire and stop where they were.'[216]

Needham watched as several hundred German infantrymen left their trenches and began moving towards A Company where they stood apparently talking to Captain John Savage and Lieutenant John Dimmer of the KRRC.[217] After a few minutes Dimmer and Savage turned and began walking back to the British line – the white flags were still in evidence said Needham:

'To our horror, after they had got about halfway to us, the Germans opened fire on them and we saw Savage pitch forward dead, shot in the back, while Dimmer threw himself down and started to crawl back to us, eventually reaching our line all right.'[218]

Horrified and unable to take his eyes off the carnage which was unfolding in front of him was 20-year-old Second Lieutenant Cosmo Gordon, a grandson of General Gordon of Khartoum fame.[219] Gordon had been gazetted into the battalion in January and was described by Needham as, 'a typical cheery, plucky boy straight from Sandhurst'. Needham later wrote that he only realized young Gordon had been hit when, 'he pitched forward on his face and yelled out, "Oh my God, I'm hit!" He writhed about on the ground in agony and I tried to keep him quiet, while at the same time trying to watch Dimmer and what was going on down the line'.

Corporal John Stennett was witness to the events from the C Company line where the men had stood up to receive the prisoners:

'All of a sudden the front line of Germans fell flat and a second line opened a rapid fire with machine guns and rifles cutting us down like mowing corn. Of 187 that started 8 of us came out, 6 being wounded and two without a scratch, and if it had not been for the Queen's Royal West Surreys we should have been prisoners or perhaps done in, but they took them in hand and cut them up in all directions. Then they had the sauce to show the white flag again but the Queen's ignored it.'[220]

Stennets's account was written in England after he had been evacuated with wounds received during the white flag encounter. But although he confuses his dates, he is correct about the second white flag incident during which he is quite sure the Queen's ignored the enemy's signs of surrender and opened fire. On this occasion, a short time after the first, another party of Germans approached the Northamptons' lines with their hands up. This time there was no discussion and the second group were mown down almost to a man by the Queen's machine guns. Whether this group did genuinely wish to surrender or not will forever remain a mystery but this and other similar incidents did have serious repercussions for some prisoners of war whose experiences are described later. The encounter concluded with the British occupying the trenches evacuated by the Germans, Needham finding the trench, 'full of dead and dying Germans', which they proceeded to fill in, 'burying the dead, all of us furious and embittered at having seen Savage and Gordon killed under the white flag like that'. All in all it had been a bad day for the Northamptons.

It had not been a good day for the Queen's either. Apart from the German counter attack on the Chemin des Dames and the dreadful white flag episode, Cuthbert Avis was aware that earlier in the morning the Moroccans on the left of the battalion had been pushed back by the German 28th Infantry Division and units of XII Corps which left the Queen's flank unprotected until it was hastily filled by reserves from the British 2 Brigade. But to make matters worse, the subsequent French artillery barrage also plastered the Queen's trenches causing some casualties. Then, wrote Avis, 'the commanding officer, Colonel Warren met his death by a sniper's bullet and the adjutant, Captain Charles Wilson was killed at regimental headquarters near a haystack'.[221] Avis ends his diary on 18 September having been wounded by a shell splinter and evacuated.

* * *

Whether a conscious decision to concentrate infantry attacks on the right of the BEF's line had been made by the Germans or not, after 19 September it certainly looked as though this was the case. On the left flank, Vailly, Missy and Bucy-le-Long were heavily shelled on a regular basis but no infantry attacks were forthcoming apart from that made on the 3rd Division on 20 September. The assault began with a diversionary attack on 9 Brigade which was southwest of Rouge Maison Farm and was dealt with swiftly by the Royal Fusiliers. Any discussion the Germans may have had about counter attacking was probably interrupted by some very accurate shelling by two howitzers from XXX Brigade. The Fusiliers then drove the enemy snipers from the woods to their front and by 1.00pm peace had once again descended on the line. A similar artillery bombardment had been directed at the 7 Infantry Brigade positions between 8.00 and 9.00am that morning and it soon became apparent that the attack on 9 Brigade had been a feint to draw reserves away from the main focus of attack.

In the 7 Brigade firing lines were 2/Royal Irish Rifles and 1/Wiltshires with the 3/Worcesters in reserve. Leading the attack were two German infantry Regiments, IR56 and IR64. The first Alexander Johnston at 7 Brigade HQ heard of the attack was a message from the Irish Rifles stating that they were under heavy attack. Brigade HQ was situated at the time close to the minor road running northeast from Croix Bury on the D925. The events which followed were chronicled in Johnstone's diary account which levels a degree of criticism at his brigade commander's use of reserves:

> *'The General* [McCracken] *therefore promptly sent up one company of the 2nd South Lancs to their support. This was a mistake. I thought so at the time and still do: the 2nd Irish Rifles though heavily attacked had not asked for help yet and were pretty well holding their own. The result was that our reserve of one weak battalion was already diminished by one quarter. Soon after there seemed to be fairly heavy musketry fire in the 1st Wilts lines and the General promptly sent up another company of the 2nd South Lancs. Here again we had merely heard heavy firing so far, and like the 2nd Irish Rifles the 1st Wilts still had a company of the 3rd Worcesters as a local reserve.'*[222]

With only two companies of the South Lancs left in reserve Johnstone bit his tongue and awaited developments. In the meantime German infantry, screened by dense undergrowth, had pushed through a gap in the line between the Worcesters and the Wiltshires and were firing across in enfilade at the Irish and Worcester lines. John Lucy remembered the South Lancs arriving in support and the shot which first indicated they were being fired on from behind:

> *'An officer from an English regiment came up offering reinforcements, saying he had a company close behind us in the woods. This had been sent forward to support us by strengthening our weakening line, but he was told he was not wanted. He was shot down with a bullet through his head, as he was delivering his message.'*[223]

A second officer from the same company was also shot down and a short time later Johnstone witnessed a company of 2/South Lancs which, 'came bolting in on us: there was perfect pandemonium while we stopped these fellows and tried to get them to go on again'. There is no indication that this was the same company, but for a short while it looked as if the Germans had finally managed to achieve what they failed to do a week earlier – break through and split II Corps from Haig's I Corps divisions on the right.

> 'The Germans had obviously got through our line somehow and one did not
> know what had happened to the 1st Wilts in front. We called up the last
> company of the 2nd South Lancs, who were in the cutting just below us,
> but had great difficulty in getting them to go forward ... the situation
> indeed seemed serious, the Germans were right in our position now, the
> wood within 150 yards of Brigade HQ was full of German snipers picking
> off our men as they showed themselves, they had got a maxim there too
> which was doing a lot of damage.'[224]

Whilst this was taking place, the three companies of Wiltshires – in the
centre of the line – were holding the enemy at bay but, like the Irish
Rifles, were under a heavy artillery attack. Second Lieutenant Clive
Gaskell, a Special Reserve officer who had only been with the battalion
for twenty-four hours, recalled his baptism of fire vividly:

> 'We were lying along the edge of the road and by this time the rifle fire was
> very heavy and also the Germans were putting over lots of big HE shells –
> several of these burst along our road and just above us in the stubble. We
> were smothered in earth and stones and the man next to me (Private
> Stagg)[225] and several more of my thirty [men] were killed and also Captain
> Reynolds who was in the trench.'[226]

From Clive Gaskell's evidence it seems that there was yet another
white flag incident opposite the Wiltshire lines that morning. There
had already been a successful ruse employed earlier by the Germans
who had taken one section of trench after shouting across to the
Wiltshires from the woods that they were firing upon their own men.
Gaskell then watched fascinated as a large number of Germans stood
up without their rifles and with their hands above their heads:

> 'They looked immense men. Then one of their officers walked boldly out
> towards me and said, "Come and take us." I thought this a very happy turn
> of events as hitherto I thought we were certainly getting the worst of things
> and I was about to go forward towards him when I heard, "don't you show
> yourself there," and turning round I saw a subaltern of the 2nd South
> Lancs – Sutton by name – who had crept up to me along the road. "Oh,"
> he said, "if you had been out from the beginning you wouldn't be taken in
> so easily. It's only a trick. They have got a machine gun hidden there and
> when you and your men get up they shoot you down".'[227]

Fortunately before Gaskell could react, someone loosed off a round
and the Germans ran for cover.

Events turned in favour of the British when a company of 2/South Staffords from the 2nd Division began working their way up the valley on the enemy's left flank and a gun from XXIII Brigade RFA opened fire on the gathering German infantry. 'They got the range first shot', wrote a relieved Johnstone, 'and had to risk putting a shell into our own fellows: however as it happened it was the turning point of the day'. Clive Gaskell thought the first shell, 'had laid out the whole lot', with its, 'terrific explosion and volume of bright green smoke'. Johnston was right about it being the turning point, at around 4.00pm an advance by the Wiltshires, Irish Rifles and Worcesters finally pushed the enemy back to their own lines, leaving, the *Official History* tells us, 'the ground behind littered with his killed and wounded'. Johnstone stood by his criticism of McCracken:

> *'I am convinced that had we been more careful with our reserves until we had some idea of the situation, and then given a unit a definite task such as to clear the wood just N of Brigade HQ, we should have done much better. As it was we were at one time in rather a tight corner with only a platoon in reserve and the Germans within a few yards of Brigade HQ.'*[228]

The day's fighting had cost 7 Brigade some 400 casualties, most of which were from 2/South Lancs. The Wiltshires' casualties, although comparatively light, did include the commanding officer, Lieutenant Colonel Arthur W. Hasted. Hasted was the second commanding officer in 7 Brigade to be wounded in the space of two days, joining Colonel Wilkinson Bird of the Irish Rifles who was badly wounded on 19 September.

* * *

The attacks on the 2nd Division on the morning of 20 September began at dawn and fell on the King's Liverpool Regiment's front, east of the canal and on the Connaught Rangers, positioned on the ridge further to the east on the Beaulne spur. Lieutenant William Synge of the King's found dawn of 20 September to be wet and misty when he was, 'rudely disturbed by the rattle of machine gun'. Hurriedly moving his men under cover, he spotted the tell-tale cloud of steam which issues from the water jacket of the Maxim machine gun betraying its position in the strip of wood which ran down to the lock keeper's house. 'We knew the range, and that machine gun was finished off in half a minute'. Watching from his company trenches – which were a little above those of C and D Companies – Synge and his men were able to catch the

German attack in a deadly crossfire, 'it was exactly like ferreting for rabbits, and I do not think many of those who came out of the wood got back into it again'.

At about 9.00am the German infantry made a second, more determined attack:

'The attack had now veered round to our right, and we could catch glimpses of the enemy running about on the high ground above. As they were also firing down onto us through the wood, things were by no means pleasant. At this time I was sent back by the Colonel with a message to the second-in-command, who was back on the hill top above Moussy, finding a position onto which we might fall back if the worst came to the worst ... on getting back to the Colonel, who was in the same place. Namely where the pathway entered the wood, I found that matters were going very badly indeed'.[229]

The Connaughts by this time had been shelled out of their trenches, the German artillery getting the exact range of the forward trenches which, in the words of the war diary, 'made them untenable'. The King's right flank was now dangerously exposed and enemy infantry began firing down on the King's from above, 'for a moment or two we all thought that they were through and that very soon we should be surrounded'. But Synge's qualms were soon dispelled by the arrival of reinforcements in the form of two platoons from B Company of the Highland Light Infantry and six from 2/Worcesters. The consequent counter attack captured the first line German trench beyond the Connaughts' positions but elation turned to anguish when the relieving force was ambushed in the woods. There was momentary chaos as the British fell back on A Company of the King's:

'The Colonel, however, refused to retire, and sent me up with a message to the commander of A Company, which was holding the trenches in the wood, to the effect that he must hold out, and there were no more reinforcements. This captain, owing to the thickness of the wood was very much in the dark as to what was going on, swung his line round slightly so it was facing the crest, and ordered his men to fire rapid fire until further orders into the trees towards the hill-top ... this move, I think, saved the situation, for the Germans began to withdraw.'[230]

It had been another close call. Synge was of the opinion that, 'had the country been more open, and had they been able to see what they were doing', the Germans would have got right through the British lines and into Moussy where they would have captured the guns and, 'also probably the Brigadier and his staff'. The *Official History* felt the day belonged to the King's as their casualties did not exceed fifty, but far in excess of that figure was the casualty return from the Highland Light Infantry. After leaving Verneuil to support the Worcesters – under attack on the Beaulne spur – every man from B Company who took part in the counter attack was either killed or wounded. Lieutenant William Lilburn, who led the two platoons of Highlanders, only managed to get back himself after dark with a few of the survivors. The day's fighting cost the Highland Light Infantry three officers killed and two others wounded, they also lost Lieutenant John O'Connell, the battalion's medical officer who was killed tending the wounded. In the ranks twenty men were killed, seventy wounded and twenty-five missing.[231]

Other casualties of the day included Major William Sarsfield, the commanding officer of the Connaughts who had led the battalion since late August. The shell fire which drove the battalion out of its trenches killed Sarsfield and 22-year-old Second Lieutenant Robert de Stacpoole, the fourth son of the Duke of Stacpoole. Three other officers were also killed along with thirty-five other ranks killed and wounded.[232]

John McIlwain was less than complimentary in his diary about Robert de Stacpoole's brother, George, who was serving in the battalion. Commenting on the day's events, MacIlwain was not pleased at the prospect of having Lieutenant de Stacpoole as his company officer, 'who is hardly in a fit state to take charge of anyone. His nerves are all to rags'. Although not corroborated by the war diary, MacIlwain does give us an indication of the strength of the battalion – despite being reinforced by about 200 officers and men from the special reserve a week earlier – he estimated the battalion was less than 400 strong at roll call on 21 September.

Up at Cour de Soupir Farm the Grenadiers were under shell fire for most of the day on 20 September but were not under any direct infantry attack on the scale of the attacks launched against the two brigades on their left. Major Bernard Gordon Lennox and his company relieved Number 3 Company at dawn and were busy improving the trench when a Jack Johnson exploded just above him:

'The man in the pit next door was badly hit by a shell, and has since had his arm off. My coat had the right arm nearly taken off at the shoulder and the left sleeve cut to bits, and it was only a yard off me, but I am thankful to say I was not inside the coat at the time. After that they left us pretty well

alone till the afternoon. The battery that is plastering us like this is so close that one has no warning of the shell coming along: the only thing one hears is the burst and woe betide you if you aren't down in the bottom [of the trench].*'233*

After dark there was a half-hearted attack which failed to materialize on the Guards' frontage but did have the effect of ensuring every other man was standing at arms in expectation. Gordon Lennox was of the opinion that the German infantry were reluctant to face the Guards in their entrenched positions, adding, 'I think they are very wise'.

Chapter 11

The 6th Division

*It seems a favourite trick to shoot one's finger off when one is
cleansing one's rifle, two men were admitted to hospital today
having blown off their fingers cleansing their rifles today.*

Lieutenant Neville Woodroffe – 1/Irish Guards

Although the 6th Infantry Division was mobilized on 4 August
1914, it remained in the Cambridge area until 7 September.
Concerns at home that England might possibly be invaded by
the Germans prevented the full six divisions from being transported to
France in early August. Amongst the officers and men of the division
there was a real fear that they would arrive too late to join the fight.
They had been following the fortunes of the BEF over the retreat from
Mons and the advance from the Marne to the Aisne and it was with
some relief that orders were received to proceed to Southampton. The
West and East Yorkshire Regiments were packed aboard the SS *Caudor
Castle* which docked at St Nazaire at 9.00pm on 9 September. The 1st
Battalion the Leicestershire Regiment (1/Leicesters) arrived aboard the
SS *Braemar Castle* at 8.00am the next morning. On board was Captain
Robert Hawes who was still technically a newly-wed, having married
Eleanorah Rydon a matter of months before mobilization. Hawes had
been a gentleman cadet at Sandhurst in 1902 with the author's
grandfather, Howard Murland. The two young men formed a firm
friendship whilst in E Company and even though they went their
separate ways on being commissioned, their friendship was rekindled
when they met up again in India. In 1911 Robert Hawes returned to
England to take up his appointment as adjutant of the 3rd Battalion, he
was not to see his old friend again.

The division was initially delayed by the decision on 29 August to
move the British seaboard base at Le Havre to St Nazaire, some 250

miles further south. This huge transfer of stores was completed in a week – a testament to the Royal Navy's dominance of the channel and its surrounding waters – and placed the 6th Division southwest of Paris and even further from the Aisne valley. Strangely there was little urgency noticeable in getting the three brigades of Major General John Kier's division into line with the BEF, which at the time was crossing the Marne on its way north. If the experience of the 1st Battalion East Yorkshire Regiment (1/East Yorks) is anything to go by, it was a fairly leisurely introduction to war. After disembarking at 9.20pm on 9 September, the East Yorks took some ten days to make the journey to the Aisne crossing at Bourg. The first twenty-eight hours were spent courtesy of the French railways which took them to Coulommiers. From there the battalion marched to Doue where it arrived at 3.00pm on 12 September, remaining stationary – apart from a route march – for the next two days, drawing supplies and waiting for 18 Brigade HQ to catch up. When the battalion did resume its move north on 15 September, the war diary reports that it was held up by brigade supply trains and ammunition columns. The battalion finally crossed the Aisne at 6.00am on Sunday 19 September.

Exactly what news had filtered through to Kier's brigades as they marched north is imprecise but on 16 September Lieutenant Billy Congreve with the 3rd Rifle Brigade was still under the impression that the Germans were retiring.[234] It must have come as some surprise then, to hear that the advance had stalled and instead of joining III Corps as originally planned, the newcomers were now to be put into general reserve. For once Sir John French had made a strategically sensible decision; there was little point in deploying the division on the left flank with the 4th Division which is presumably where they were destined. Nevertheless, there had been some discussion at GHQ as to the deployment of Kier's division before it was decided to use the fresh troops as reinforcements for what was now a very tired and depleted BEF; only the divisional artillery brigades would take up their allotted place in III Corps. Consequently 16 Brigade was sent to relieve 7 and 9 Brigades above Vailly, 17 Brigade was placed in corps reserve and 18 Brigade went to relieve the hard-pressed 1 and 2 Brigades on the furthest extremity of the BEF's right flank.

18 Brigade, under the command of Brigadier General Walter Congreve VC – the father of Billy Congreve – began the relief of the 1st Division units after dark. The 1/West Yorkshires would have been a welcome sight to the Coldstream Guards in the trenches at Troyon, their casualties over the previous few days had been comparatively light but had included two officers from No.1 Company killed and

Captain Alfred Egerton who was wounded after serving only one day with the battalion. After completing the handover with Major Leslie Hamilton, the Coldstream Commanding Officer, Lieutenant Colonel Francis Towsey deployed his A and B Companies under Major Alexander Ingles into the firing line and his remaining two companies into the support trenches along with the HQ staff. The troop movements during the relief must have alerted the Germans as they were fired on shortly after 9.00pm which did little more than hone the vigilance of the men in the firing line. But much more was to follow at daybreak.

On the right of the West Yorkshires the Moroccan troops of the French XVIII Corps were in position on the extreme left flank of the French Fifth Army. Arthur Osburn was quite distressed by the wretched sight of these North African troops who were not equipped for the cold and rain of a European autumn on the battle-strewn slopes above the Aisne:

'Drenched with rain, without food or medical aid, they squatted in the mud on the hillside around Paissy. Huddled up together like wounded animals supporting shattered limbs or badly mutilated faces, they were as pathetic a sight as the German wounded had been outside Braine. Those sodden hillsides, strewn with dead horses and dead men, must have been in gruesome contrast to ...the whispering palm groves of Ghardais and Side Okba.'[235]

Osburn could see no sign of any French medical services or any ambulance transport to move them from the firing line. Taking it upon himself to tend to their wounded he and his small medical team established a dressing station in the caves at Paissy. 'Like the prophets of old, we hid them by tens and fifties in the caves of Paissy where, in their saturated cotton clothing, they huddled close together for warmth'.

20 September was another cold day with heavy showers of hail and rain and it was on the poorly-equipped French colonial troops that the first onslaught of the morning fell. Commanding the German Seventh Army on the Aisne, Josias von Heeringen must have been only too aware of the fragile nature of the French line at this point and began softening up the French lines early that morning. The West Yorkshires on their left reporting heavy shell fire from about 4.00am onwards and at 4.14am some Moroccan troops began leaving their positions. Although they were encouraged to return, the West Yorkshires' right flank was immediately put under pressure and became increasingly

vulnerable in the face of the wavering Moroccan troops. With this in mind, Colonel Towsey sent an officer's patrol under Lieutenant Thomas Meautys out to his right in order to get a fuller picture of what exactly was taking place.[236] Meautys and his men confirmed Towsey's worst fears; the Moroccan troops on his right flank were in no position to contain a resolute German attack and appeared still to be in some disorder. Towsey had no choice but to deploy one company to protect the right of his battalion's position. Private Charles Rainbird was with D Company:

> '*As dawn was breaking this morning, there occurred one of those hellish mistakes which occur in every war. We saw through the half light a large body of men evidently retiring on our right. Our Colonel ordered my Company 'D' to swing round so as to cover their retirement if they should prove to be allies. After advancing about 200 yards we saw that they were allies (Zouaves) when, to our horror they suddenly turned and opened fire on us. Oh God, it was awful, every one of us exposed to a raking fire and no cover; they had evidently mistaken us for the enemy. My mates were falling all over the place and there was 37 killed in less than two minutes. Naturally our boys opened fire on them, in spite of the CO's shout of "Don't fire!" I dropped one fellow as he was in the act of firing, then we received the order to retire.*'[237]

In the confusion of the early morning a party of Moroccan troops had opened fire on the West Yorkshires as they moved into position, an incident which underlined the delicate nature of the French positions and the nervousness of the men holding them. After this the line appeared to settle down and there was a pause before the second German attack was made sometime after 10.00am. This time the West Yorkshires were ready for anything and easily checked the attacking enemy infantry and for a while it appeared as if the Moroccan infantry had regained their composure. But this attack was only a precursor to another more determined assault.

Meanwhile Jock Marden had been turned out of his billet at 4.30am with the 9/Lancers to provide support for the infantry. Detailed with eight men to act as, 'intercommunication between English right and French left', he established himself on the ridge to await developments:

> '*Dig ourselves a little trench for protection from splinters. Leave 2 men with the OC West Yorkshire Regiment on the ridge and remain below with the rest. Note the OC West Yorkshires is sitting eating in the support trenches*

... Am shown remains of last intercommunication patrol – officer killed[238]
– 3 horses – 4 men! This, I suppose, is to cheer me up!'[239]

Marden's light-hearted rendering cloaked the seriousness of the situation the BEF faced that morning. Colonel Towsey may well have been snatching a bite to eat but it was probably the last chance he had before the next German attack began at about 12.30pm under the cover of a violent rainstorm. The Moroccans were thrown back yet again and Towsey and Lieutenant Meautys both went forward to the firing line to see what was happening – returning a few minutes later with Meautys mortally wounded. According to Captain P H Lowe who was with D Company, the advanced line of the West Yorkshires was on the forward slope of the hill and composed of a succession of rifle pits without any form of communication trenches:

'The trench here was very badly sited, there being dead ground to the front, though the field of fire to the flanks was good. There was no room in the trench for a number of my men, but there were in many places craters made from shell fire ... we beat off comparatively easily two attacks. Then the Germans massed in the dead ground in front. From here they tried to advance by rushes in small bodies. This was more difficult to stop. In the meantime our casualties had been heavy and particularly from machine guns and shrapnel, which was continually traversing our trenches. Near midday two catastrophes took place. The French went, leaving our flank exposed and a short heavy storm of rain turned the ground into a quagmire. Ammunition was being collected from the wounded with the result that all the rifles began to jam.'[240]

Lowe describes how there were only four serviceable rifles in his particular pit and the bayonets on each had been smashed by enemy fire whilst the bolts on two of the weapons were only able to be operated with the aid of an entrenching tool:

'It appeared to me that the final German effort could only be met with a counter-attack. To be prepared, I endeavoured to find out the officers and NCOs who were still effective. On the right it was reported there were none. The men began to get somewhat disheartened. It was impossible to send any message to the rear. At the very moment the Germans were about to advance, a man about 40 yards on my right began to waver. As soon as I got up to deal with the situation I was hit.'[241]

Realizing the need for support Towsey sent a runner to Brigade HQ at Paissy to ask for assistance. But the gap left by the retreating French infantry had given the Germans the opportunity they needed and as the forward companies were overwhelmed, the German infantry took possession of the British firing line, the *Official History* tells us that they charged and, 'swept the front companies into captivity', but in truth, as there were few survivors, only those who were taken captive knew the exact circumstances of what actually happened.

The first Colonel Towsey knew of the disaster that had befallen his battalion was at 1.30pm when a runner from the front line brought the news that the companies had been captured and that the Germans were advancing. Gathering together the remnants of West Yorkshires in the support trenches, Towsey advanced at the head of his men into a hail of fire from his front and right flank. The war diary recorded the inevitable outcome:

'C Company and HQ Company at once advanced towards the front trenches in order, if possible, to save the companies in the firing line; they fixed bayonets and advanced at the double but were met with a heavy fire from the front and right flank. Fire was opened to the front and two platoons turned to the right. The order was then given to retire back to the trench and the original line was again occupied. Owing to this position offering a poor field of fire the CO decided to retire on to Paissy Hill and connect up with the cavalry on our right.'[242]

Jock Marden was alerted to the demise of the West Yorkshires by one of his men:

'He tears down in a great hurry to say that the Yorkshires have bolted and that the Germans are on the ridge – [I] see Zouaves to our right bolting too! This is cheerful – I may be captured. Run up hill and see no Germans – but the Yorkshires have left their wounded behind and bolted – even the reserves. Get my horse and head them off down the valley, and try and stop them. Up comes old De Lisle: "Take 'em back to the firing line; shoot anyone who won't go." Blow! I thought an intercommunication patrol stayed in the reserve trenches – he said, "firing line." Over the ridge we go – back to the forward trenches.'[243]

The retirement of the Yorkshires had peeled open the British line and now the Durham Light Infantry – holding the line to the left of the West Yorkshires – came under a heavy enfilade fire. Their situation was not eased until the arrival of the 2nd Battalion Nottinghamshire and Derbyshire Regiment (2/Sherwood Foresters). The Foresters were in reserve to the north of Troyon, sheltered in the steep-sided valley which ran down to Vendresse. As they moved across the head of the valley a German column was seen escorting the West Yorkshire prisoners – including Private Charles Rainbird – who had survived the morning's fighting. Perhaps those British prisoners were witness to what must have been a demonstration of the, British infantry battalion circa 1914 at its very best, as the Foresters advanced into a storm of machine-gun and rifle fire from their front and left flanks. Crossing ground devoid of cover and with men dropping left, right and centre, the battalion stormed the trenches so recently held by the West Yorkshires and drove out the German infantry at the point of the bayonet

In the meantime 2 Cavalry Brigade was arriving in force with a company of the Royal Sussex. 4/Dragoon Guards, led by Major Tom Bridges, dismounted below the ridge and Bridges – never one to avoid getting into action – was soon running ahead of his men:

> 'I got on ahead and jumping off my horse, told my trumpeter to wait for the squadron and tell Hornby to dismount and look for my signals. I ran on up to the crown of the hill which was bare stubble, and seemed quite deserted until I saw a German officer's helmeted head coming up the other side. I saw him wave to his men, and I did the same to mine, giving the signal to double. We met the Picklehaubers almost face to face and standing up poured rapid fire into them which put them to flight. A second squadron came up on our right and we occupied some shallow rifle pits previously dug by the infantry.'[244]

When the Dragoon Guards went into dismounted action, Trooper Ben Clouting's job was to stay with the horses, but on this occasion, 'the older troopers were quite happy to let the likes of me go instead'. Clouting was soon running up the slope after Tom Bridges:

> 'We dropped into small scoops made by some recently departed infantry... the Germans came on, packed together, hundreds of them, marching four deep and at a distance of some eleven hundred yards. They were coming down the far slope of a valley, marching through agricultural fields, as we opened up with our fifteen-rounds-a-minute fire. The vision was perfect. I could see Germans toppling over as the rest came relentlessly on, but with our artillery pounding away, the Germans could only take so much. All of a sudden they turned and bolted back up the valley.'[245]

With the remnants of the West Yorkshires and the Moroccan infantry, 'in their blue and silver jackets and red trousers', now rallied and advancing uphill, the cavalrymen's charge and rapid fire had successfully turned the approaching German infantry. By 4.30pm all the West Yorkshires' trenches had been retaken and Jock Marden and the 9/Lancers – sent to entrench a position to the rear of the Moroccans – were firmly in place to, 'dissuade them from bolting', again.

Jock Marden, who like most cavalrymen, refers to the infantry as 'feet', felt the, 'run forward was a most dangerous show as everyone fired as they ran, in any direction'. Back in the trenches he recounts how, 'a silly fool', hit him in the head, presumably a stray shot which could literally have come from anywhere – German, British or indeed French! However, flushed with the excitement of the action around him, the young cavalryman was not ready to leave his post. Tying up his wound with a handkerchief he remained where he was until his relief arrived.

With the 'feet' now back in the trenches and a degree of normality restored, the cavalry retired to Paissy. The West Yorkshire war diarist is ,'certain that the Germans advanced under the cover of a white flag', on the right flank, a view which is not supported by Captain Lowe's account of the action – which was completed two years later in 1917 after he was repatriated to Switzerland. In his evidence he makes no mention of a white flag incident taking place – which is not to say it did not occur. Lowe's account tells us the line was already beginning to waver before he was hit, and in the absence of officers and NCOs to hold the line steady, perhaps the West Yorkshires did indeed do as Jock Marden has suggested and, 'bolted'. In the Yorkshiremen's defence, however, although they were regulars they were unseasoned troops who had been put into the front line without the benefit of more experienced men alongside them, and if indeed a white flag ruse was used against them, one can understand how they may have been taken in by it. Later in the war newly-arrived battalions would spend a period of 'probation' in the trenches along with more experienced troops to enable them to acclimatize to the local conditions and practices.

What is not in doubt is the scale of the calamity which had overtaken the West Yorkshires on their introduction to front line duty. As to who saved the day on 20 September that is still a subject of some debate. The men of 2 Cavalry Brigade claim their counter attack was responsible for rallying the French and British infantry – which indeed it did – but full credit must go to the magnificent attack by the Sherwood Foresters which took the front line trenches, albeit at a terrible cost. The battalion lost four officers killed and eight wounded together with forty other ranks killed and 140 wounded.

Yet it was the West Yorkshires who suffered most heavily. At roll call on 21 September it became apparent that apart from eight officers killed and two others wounded – including the commanding officer – seven other officers were missing. Amongst the ranks seventy-one were known to have been killed and 110 wounded but 436 were posted as missing, many of which had been taken prisoner. It had been a very severe baptism of fire for the battalion in what was their first day of action. At Troyon – after less than three weeks since landing at St Nazaire – Major Godfrey Lang took command of what was left of the battalion – five officers and 250 men.[246] When the Loyal North Lancs took over the West Yorkshires' trenches, Lieutenant James Hyndson was very conscious that they were, 'still full of their dead, and it was almost impossible to dig in places without coming on dead bodies'. It was a scenario which would become all too common in the grinding years of trench warfare which lay ahead.

Douglas Haig was particularly critical of the West Yorkshires and of Colonel Towsey himself. According to his diary account, Haig tells us he was informed by Brigadier General de Lisle that, 'the West Yorkshires left their trenches and ran back to Paizy [sic] village headed apparently by the colonel of the battalion'. Not only that, but he went on to say:

> 'This is the worst incident of which I have heard during this campaign. I do not know Lt. Col Towsey but in view of the high character which he holds it may be well to give him another chance, but I recommend that he and his battalion be strongly rebuked and that they are told that it rests with them to regain the good name and reputation which our infantry holds, and which they may have by their conduct on the 20th forfeited.'[247]

There is, however, a final footnote to the West Yorkshire disaster, Frederick Coleman recounts being on the Tour de Paissy just before the final attack on the West Yorkshires' trenches:

> 'By General Allenby's haystack on the Tour de Paissy was a big telescope mounted on a tripod. It was in disgrace. It served the divisional staff soberly and well until the very moment of the German attack on the West Yorks trenches. Seeing men coming over the ridge, Colonel Home, General Allenby's GSO1, declared his field glasses made him think them Germans. To make sure, the big telescope was turned on the ridge. For the first time in its history a moist film formed over the inner lens. A line of grey

smudges was all that could be made out through its formally far-seeing eye. When later events proved that Home was right, and the men in sight were Germans, moments ever precious to the guns were forever lost'.[248]

* * *

The pandemonium on the right flank of the BEF may have influenced von Heeringen's decision to press home another attack the next morning, a decision which led to a personal protest from the commanding general of the VII Reserve Corps, Hans von Zwehl. 'The daily repetition of attack orders', he felt, could not achieve any success without reinforcements. According to von Zwehl at least another division was required, if not a whole corps, with artillery support.[249] His protest seems to have had the desired effect as 21 and 22 September were relatively quiet. The French Fifth Army made some progress on the Chemin des Dames capturing the Ferme d'Hurtebise and the opportunity was taken for the British to carry out some much needed reliefs. 17 Infantry Brigade took over the positions occupied by 5 Brigade who were withdrawn into corps reserve and 2 Brigade once again found itself on the Chemin des Dames on the extreme right of the BEF.

* * *

On 21 September the 1/Leicesters crossed the Aisne late in the evening and relieved the Worcesters and the Royal Irish Rifles at 11.00pm. The trenches were to the right of La Rouge Maison Farm and – at this point in the campaign – were subjected only to regular shell and sniper fire; nevertheless this daily hail of metal soon began to make an impact. Over the course of the next twenty days that the battalion spent in the front line, five men were killed and sixteen wounded. Three officers, including the battalion adjutant, Captain Edmund Tidswell and Captain Robert Hawes were wounded and tragically Hawes died of his wounds on 23 September after being taken down to Vailly.[250] The author's grandfather received news of his death ten days later whilst in India, 'poor old Hawes has been killed', he wrote in his diary, 'one of my best friends, we spent such a long time together at Sandhurst and then at Belgaum'. It was to be the beginning of a long list of deceased friends which Howard Murland would record in his diary over the next four years.

There were several half-hearted attacks on 2 Brigade and against the left of the French XVIII Corps during the morning of 26 September which were quite easily beaten off but it was against the frontage occupied by 1/SWB on the Mont Faucon spur that the most serious attack occurred. The battalion held a line running across the spur with a large quarry situated almost at its mid-point. The steep sides of the spur which fell down towards Vendresse on the right were thickly wooded. At dawn a large force of some 1,200 German infantry from the 21st and 25th Divisions of XVIII Army Corps attacked the battalion. Lieutenant Charles Paterson thought it to be, 'the most ghastly day', of his life:

> 'At 4.15am the Germans attacked. Main attack apparently against my regiment, which is on the left of our line. D and A Companies in the trenches. B and C hustled up in support, and soon the whole place was alive with bullets. News comes that they [Germans] are trying to work their way round our left.'[251]

Captain Guy Ward, commanding C Company, remembered getting word that D Company had retired to the shelter of the quarry:

> 'This allows the Germans to get into the wood and so bring the lot of us under fire. We form up on a bank and prepare to hold it. Leaving Stewart [Lieutenant Charles Stewart] in charge I go back to the battalion and on the way ask the Welch, who were in reserve for help, they send a platoon to Stewart ... News comes which Welby [Major Glynne Welby, OC D Company] is killed and Prichard [Lieutenant William Prichard] is wounded. Curgenven [Captain Victor Curgenven] is sent to take command of D Company.'[252]

D Company was clearly taking the brunt of the attack. Charles Paterson was with HQ Company when he heard the news that the Germans had broken through the line and apparently got into D Company's lines in the quarry which formed the nub of the battalion's defences. For a while there was confusion, compounded by Major Anthony Reddie, the battalion's second-in-command, who brought in the disturbing news that C and D Companies had surrendered which, if true, would precipitate a general retirement back towards Vendresse. Guy Ward was sent up by Lieutenant Colonel Bertram Collier to find out exactly what was happening and report back:

> 'As far as I could make out what happened was D Company had a line of trenches in front of the quarry and by night several sentries in advance of the trenches. Their custom was to withdraw as soon as it was light enough for the sentries in the trenches to see. As soon as the sentries fell back this morning, the Germans, who evidently had been assembling during the

night, followed close behind them and got their machine guns and snipers in position before those in the trenches realized that there were more than just the sentries moving in front of them. The men in the trenches must have been quickly wiped out and the Germans advanced to the quarry. I can't make out if they actually entered the quarry, I think not as C Company appeared on the scene with fixed bayonets at which the Germans fell back. Curgenven told me they advanced at the charge but did not get into them. There were no German dead in the quarry.[253]

For the remainder of the morning the Borderers held their own, not needing to call on the 18 Brigade reinforcements which were on stand-by. At 11.30am the German infantry – realizing their attack had failed – began to withdraw under the cover of their artillery batteries on the Chemin des Dames. It was the moment the British gunners had been waiting for, as the German infantry became visible in the upper Chivy valley the gunners opened fire inflicting heavy casualties on the hapless Germans. The guns of 115/ and 116/Batteries fired over 1,100 shrapnel and high explosive rounds per battery while the XLIII Brigade guns recorded 307 shrapnel and 235 high explosive shells being fired after their batteries came into action. We have no definite indication of the damage inflicted on the Germans during their retirement but the *Official History* suggests that the number of enemy killed 'must have exceeded the total casualties of the British'.

The British casualties recorded in the I Corps War Diary amounted to six officers and 423 other ranks killed, 6 officers and 91 other ranks wounded and 110 missing, the vast majority of whom were subsequently found to have been killed. By far the largest number of dead and wounded came from the South Wales Borderers. The battalion had lost 4 officers killed and 3 wounded with 86 other ranks killed and 95 wounded.[254] Twelve men from D Company surrendered during the initial engagement at the quarry, an episode which incensed Charles Paterson who considered surrender to be cowardice. In his diary he refers to the regiment by its old numeric, the 24th of Foot:

'May they be spared to reach England again and be tried by Court Martial and get what they deserve. Never has the 24th surrendered yet, and in spite of the casualties the rest of the Regiment stuck to it and fought like Englishmen and 24th men could fight. We are now left with three officers each in three companies, and only two in the fourth, instead of six in each, a sad sad business.'

Harsh words indeed and a sentiment which would have been far from the mind of Captain Guy Ward who was detailed to recover the bodies of the dead:

'It fell to our lot to do the melancholy job of burying D Company's men. Poor old Welby, Sills and Simonds and 27 men, also 14 Germans, but there were many further out. They were Saxons I think, great big men. We put our officers and men in the communication trench leading from the quarry to the front trench: as the front trench is no longer to be used.'[255]

* * *

If 26 September was the 'most ghastly day' of Charles Paterson's life, for the 1/Cameron Highlanders, the previous day had been 'one of sudden and crippling disaster'. The German shell fire which greeted that dawn began falling on the Cameron Highlanders' positions on the Beaulne spur at around 6.00am. The battalion's trenches were a series of unconnected shallow rifle pits, each capable of holding a section of six or seven men. Directly behind D Company's forward trenches was a large cave which was being used as Battalion HQ – another similar cave nearby was sheltering some of the officers and men of C Company. In command of the battalion was Captain Douglas Miers. The reader will recall that the battalion had suffered serious losses on 14 September which included Colonel McLachan amongst the wounded and had reduced the battalion to 6 officers and 200 other ranks.

Some thirty minutes after the bombardment began Douglas Miers was wounded by a shell splinter and returned to the HQ cave to have his wounds attended to by Lieutenant John Crocket, the battalion medical officer. Sending word to Captain Allan Cameron – the next senior officer in the battalion – to take command, Miers waited in the cave to hand-over to Cameron officially. His departure for the dressing station at Verneuil was delayed by another salvo of German shells and it was whilst he remained in the shelter of the cave that two large shells scored direct hits, one on top and the other at the entrance. The whole structure was brought down entombing the twenty-nine occupants.

This was another serious blow to the battalion. Not only had Miers and Allan Cameron been killed in the falling rubble but three other officers, John Crocket, Lieutenant Napier Cameron and the battalion adjutant, Lieutenant Kenneth Meiklejohn were also killed along with the Regimental Sergeant Major, George Burt.[256] There were four survivors including Bandsmen Rosser and Ursell who escaped unscathed and Corporal Mitchell who was pulled out alive but badly crushed. Command of the battalion fell to Captain Ewen Brodie who was one of only two officers left alive.[257] Three days later the new draft of officers and men – sent out to replace the losses of 14 September – arrived with the new commanding officer, Lieutenant Colonel Douglas McEwen.

With McEwen's arrival on the Aisne on 28 September the British positions were almost exactly the same as they had been at nightfall on 14 September. The morning had begun with the usual mist, which, on the 2/Coldstream frontage, allowed a small patrol of three men to approach the forward German trenches unseen. Suddenly the mist lifted placing the three men in range of enemy rifle fire, two were shot down and the third escaped with only a graze to return to the safety of the Coldstream front line. Not waiting for darkness to bring in the two wounded men. Private Frederick Dobson crawled out under heavy fire across the exposed ground to find one of the men dead and the other badly wounded but alive. Having applied first aid he returned to his company trenches to collect a stretcher. Accompanied by Corporal Brown the two men successfully brought the wounded man back to safety. Dobson was awarded the Victoria Cross and Brown the Distinguished Conduct Medal for their selfless acts.

Dobson's VC was the second which had been awarded to men of the Coldstream Guards since war had been declared and the seventh and last to be won on the Aisne in 1914. By early October both sides were exhausted; frontal attacks – no matter how gallantly led or undertaken – had proved ineffectual and the two sides appeared content for the time being to throw high explosive at each other. But unbeknown to the Germans, plans were afoot for the BEF to move to Flanders.

Chapter 12

Ubique

In the afternoon the Rev. Blackburn conducted a short divine service close to our bivouac and amongst the trees. He asked if it was safe as it was exposed, but everywhere was exposed. The enemy opened fire where we were paraded and rounds fell about 100 yards off, the chaplain ducked his head and excused himself.

Major G B MacKenzie – 2/Siege Battery

The artilleryman on the Aisne in 1914 either fought with the Royal Field Artillery, (RFA) the Royal Horse Artillery (RHA) or the Royal Garrison Artillery (RGA) which manned the heavy and siege batteries. The RHA was an integral part of the Cavalry Division and with its lighter 13-pounder guns provided artillery support to the cavalry brigades. Unlike infantry regiments, the artillery has no regimental colours; its colours are the guns themselves and are treated with the same reverence. Neither does the artillery have specific battle honours, their battle honours are encompassed in the word 'everywhere' or *Ubique*, an honour unique to the gunners. *Ubique* is a declaration that wherever there is battle there are gunners. + WRONG

When war was declared the artillery went to war with three principle weapons in its armoury. The 18-pounder field gun, which initially only fired shrapnel, the field howitzer firing a 35-pound shrapnel or high explosive (HE) round and the 60-pounder gun – or 'cow guns' as they were sometimes called – which could throw a 60-pound HE or shrapnel shell. The 18-pounder was adopted for service on Christmas Eve 1904 and despite the early difficulties with the recoil function, the gun proved to be an enormous success; versions of the Mark II were still in service during the Second World War. Successful trials during 1914 with HE rounds saw the gun adapted to fire shrapnel, HE, smoke and gas shells throughout the war, its range was 6,525 yards or 5.9

kilometres. The 60-pounder Mark I field gun entered service a year later in 1905 replacing the older 4.7-inch gun. Weighing in at some 4.5 tons it was at the limit of what could be drawn by horses but its range was significantly longer at 10,300 yards or 9.4 kilometres. The Mark II version of this gun saw service in the Western Desert during the Second World War. Finally in 1908, the 4.5-inch field howitzer – designed by the Coventry Ordnance Works – was taken into service. Weighing 1 ton it had a range of 7,300 yards or 6.6 kilometres.

Whilst gunners referred to all their weapons as 'guns' there were essential differences between the field gun and the howitzer which lay in the length and elevation of their barrels. Howitzers had a short barrel and a relatively low muzzle velocity and in order to increase its range the barrel was depressed from its starting point of 45 degrees; the field gun, on the other hand had a longer barrel with a higher muzzle velocity and its barrel was raised from the horizontal to increase its range.

This mix of guns was similar to that of the Germans, although the German High Command had introduced heavy mortars and howitzers in anticipation of reducing the heavily reinforced walls of the bastions which were the French and Belgian forts. Their arsenal of 105mm (4-inch) and 150mm (5.9-inch) howitzers together with the formidable 210mm (8.2-inch) howitzer, which were used to such great effect on British and French troops on the Aisne, settled once and for all the question of which arm would conquer the battlefield during the next four years.

In what must be regarded as a very short-sighted move, the French rejected howitzers almost entirely from their weaponry, opting instead for the quick firing 75mm field gun – the *soixante-quinze*. In line with their doctrine of *L'offensive à outrance*, the French High Command saw a mobile artillery corps making such good use of ground that a long-range gun would not be required to get within effective range of an enemy. Howitzers, on the other hand were weapons which suggested concealed positions, accurate and calculated map shoots and deliberate counter-battery firing and accordingly, were largely excluded from French military thinking. Not every French artilleryman agreed with this principle, some continued to warn that the high rate of fire of the French '75s' made it the ideal gun for neutralizing the enemy's fire but completely useless in knocking out the heavy batteries deployed against it. Charles Deedes, a British staff officer with GHQ thought the French guns, 'looked like toy cannon when compared with our splendidly horsed and heavier 18-pounders'. Fortunately the French hadn't discarded all their heavy guns, there were still some 300 in service and some of these were soon in action on the Aisne and elsewhere.

The control of British artillery on the battlefield was, in theory, the responsibility of the divisional Commanders Royal Artillery (CRA), but in effect they had little actual control over their guns. Supported by a small staff and a brigade major, some CRAs were used by divisional commanders purely as administrators whilst others were used more as a channel of control putting into effect divisional orders for the deployment of guns. In 1914, artillery was still seen as an accessory to the tactics employed by the infantry, there was no conception of the CRA being a partner in the planning of operations. Moreover, there was no centralized control of artillery in early 1914 beyond that of the divisional structure; the artillery fire plan, which was to become such a crucial element in future battles, was not part of the planning process. Whilst this rather blinkered control of a division's guns may have worked well in the past when gunners were in close proximity to the infantry, on the Aisne the shortcomings created by poor communication with the infantry, particularly by batteries which were forced to come into action some distance from their targets, were quick to surface.

Even during the advance from the Marne the lack of co-ordination between infantry and artillery had, on numerous occasions, resulted in 'friendly fire' episodes which unfortunately continued to bedevil the British on the Aisne. On 13 September, for example, the 4th Division war diary records a complaint from 11 Brigade – timed at 11.42am – that the Rifle Brigade was being fired upon by the division's guns and the next day Lieutenant Arthur Griffith and his section of 71/Battery guns at La Cour de Soupir Farm was fired on by his own battery! Friendly fire was a phenomenon which even Jock Marden complained about in his diary on 18 September: 'Why don't gunners have telescopes or field glasses?' he asked, 'then perhaps they wouldn't shell their own side so much!' Despite Jock Marden's sarcasm, however, which was undoubtedly shared by many infantrymen, the gunners were learning quickly and by the concluding weeks of the campaign there was more evidence of the allocation of artillery zones being used in an effort to tie each brigade of guns to a specific frontage. This development went some way to reducing the incidents of 'friendly fire' and introducing a fire plan discipline.

The decentralization of control over artillery was but one of a number of features which was reflected in the British artillery manual – *Field Artillery Training 1914* – a volume which had numerous failings within its pages, not least of which was its attempt to reflect the dual purpose of the British Army of 1914 – that of Imperial police force and potential European partner in a continental war. This inability to completely define the form of warfare in which it envisaged the artillery to be engaged was not apparent in the French and German tactical manuals. In both cases the tactical doctrine was clearly defined – there was little doubt in the minds of French and German military planners where the next war would be fought, or indeed against whom! But here again there were differences between the two. Whereas the German Drill Regulations for the Field Artillery recommended concealed positions and the use of indirect fire control by observers, the French – as we know – were in favour of a more direct method of fire control by placing their batteries out in the open and close to their infantry where the targets could be identified by the gun teams themselves.

The lack of a clear tactical doctrine in the British manual and its vague references to 'positional warfare' and the 'war of movement' did little to educate artillery officers and merely drew attention to the great debate on the employment of artillery on the battlefield taking place in military circles in Britain at the time. In general, the spirit of the 1914 regulations leant towards the French belief that batteries should take up their firing positions in the open so as to give continuous direct fire to the infantry. Unfortunately on the Aisne the opportunities where this was possible were few and far between and where battery commanders were able to get their guns forward, casualties amongst the gunners tended to be high. It was not uncommon for a battery to cross the river and be unable to find a suitable position from which to come into action and subsequently to retire. All too frequently guns were withdrawn from exposed positions having not fired a single round.

A case in point was XL Brigade which reached the pontoon bridge at Vailly at dawn on 14 September and crossed over to the village to wait for the infantry to clear the high ground. Finding the steep hillsides thickly wooded the XL Brigade batteries could not locate any suitable gun positions or observation points:

'We hunted everywhere for targets and positions and although we were under intermittent rifle and gun fire, it all seemed to come out of the blue. Later on in the morning the Infantry Brigadier told the colonel that the enemy were getting round to our left and we must clear out back across the river and try and find positions to support the infantry from there.'[258]

It was very much the case in 1914 that the three arms – cavalry, infantry and artillery – each saw their role in isolation of the other and the principle of co-ordination between the three elements was not one which was generally considered to be of importance. Consequently any interaction between fire and movement was lost in the failure to formulate an agreed doctrine of strategic and tactical ideology. All this was to come later.

Without doubt the campaign on the Aisne produced a new set of difficulties for the gunners who found themselves ascending a steep learning curve of development. Not only were the 18-pounder field guns found to be woefully short of range but even after the crossing of the river had been successfully negotiated and the infantry were dug in on the slopes of the spurs, the guns were still struggling to reach the German positions. Alexander Johnston's diary records his frustrations on this subject:

> 'The German observation posts are extraordinarily good: directly there is any movement anywhere they shell the place at once ... one can see them building redoubts and trenches about 1,000 yards away. But they are pretty well out of range of our artillery who therefore cannot stop them, while if we endeavour to do so we get shelled to blazes at once.'[259]

A few days later on 19 September Johnston was again watching the Germans, this time moving across his front towards 4 Brigade. 'We could do nothing ourselves but as the Germans were very conspicuous on the hill I should have thought our gunners could have done something, however, they did not'. Unfortunately for Johnstone and 7 Brigade, beyond the river on his frontage there were few suitable sites where batteries could be brought into action as these were generally overlooked and under direct observation. It was only the 60-pounder heavy batteries which could reach the enemy guns from the southern heights above the river. The 48/Heavy Battery guns could reach the traffic running along the Chemin des Dames, 'sometimes we got a shot off at enemy ammunition wagons on the move, or traffic on the long road running east and west; at about 10,000 yards range we stopped the traffic'.

The 3rd Division artillery brigades in particular were handicapped by the width of the Aisne valley opposite Vailly which, together with the lack of cable and telephones for forward observation, made artillery support a logistic nightmare, a factor perhaps not always fully appreciated by the infantryman under enemy shell fire. However, where the guns were able to be brought forward they were often very effective in supporting the infantry. Battery commanders such as Wilfred Ellershaw of 113/Battery did not shy away from carrying out their duties according to *Field Artillery Training 1914*. He would have been very much aware of the infantry's expectation that batteries should be positioned well forward, an expectation which dated back to the deployment of guns in the South African War. Indeed, the only gunner Victoria Cross of the campaign was won by Bombardier Ernest Horlock of 113/Battery. On 14 September the battery was under the orders of 3 Infantry Brigade and had unlimbered with 46/Battery in a quarry south west of Vendresse near Chivy. The morning was misty and the fighting confused as the infantry struggled to climb the spurs towards the Chemin des Dames. On being ordered uphill, the battery commander, Major Wilfred Ellershaw, observed a German attack developing and engaged it with shrapnel fire at a range of some 900 yards. The battery at once came under heavy counter-fire from German gunners, and despite being twice severely wounded, Horlock continued to aim his gun and remained at his post.

There had already been a classic but very costly example of this tactic at Le Cateau just over two weeks previously. At Le Cateau on 26 August the 5th Division batteries were positioned within battalion lines and while the support they gave the infantry with their direct fire was effective, they were eventually overrun and over thirty guns were lost. Bravery there might have been that day – four gunner Victoria Crosses were won on Suffolk Hill – but the losses in guns and men had severe repercussions for the 5th Division infantry attack on the Aisne. In contrast 108/Heavy Battery was positioned east of Reumont out of sight of the main battle on the reverse slope of the hill and had its fire directed by an observer placed further forward on the Montay spur.

As one might have expected after the first two days of fighting on the Aisne, when the two sides began to dig defensive lines, artillery commanders tended to switch their tactics to indirect fire from more concealed positions which demanded the use of Forward Observation Officers (FOO) – linked to the battery by telephone communication where possible. Some divisions were better placed than others to establish telephone lines. The 3rd Division telephone equipment was in such a bad state of repair when it arrived on the Aisne that most batteries had to fire in the open unavoidably placing the guns under direct observation. Paul Maze, a French interpreter attached to Gough's cavalry, came across the results of such folly on his way to Vailly:

'Immediately beyond the village of Chassemy the shattered remains of one of our batteries stood in front of a wood under full observation from the *enemy, holding the heights on the north bank of the river. Every gun and limber had been pulverized by their fire, and judging by the number of men lying about, few of our gunners had escaped.'*[260]

Where batteries were forced to seek concealed positions without the benefit of telephone connection to an observation point, lines of gunners were used to pass messages to the batteries and it was only by 18 September that enough cable was found for one 3rd Division battery to establish a telephone link to its FOO.

Lessons were certainly being learned quickly – even amongst the French gunners. Jack Hay's diary described an occasion when he was at a French '75' battery observation post near Lassigny in the Sixth Army sector:

'We found ourselves in the fire control or observation post of the battery, and naturally in a very advanced position. The idea is that the battery fires from a concealed spot such as behind a ridge and an observer, often two miles away, directs their fire by telephone or otherwise, all fire being what they call indirect, ie you can't see what you are firing at. Of course the observer has to be able to see everything, and so we naturally did well, and watched the French shells exploding over a German battery about 4 miles away.'[261]

Yet British gunners had great difficulty in finding suitable observation points. The Chemin des Dames, being the highest point in the area, completely masked the position of German batteries beyond it. Direct observation on these gun positions was impossible except by co-operation with the RFC observers, of which more in the following chapter. Where batteries were successfully brought into action on the north side of the valley observers made use of a variety of locations from which to report on the accuracy of their battery's shooting. Likely buildings were soon targeted by the German gunners as were haystacks and trenches. Movement to and from observation points was kept to a minimum and absolute immobility of movement was strictly enforced when German aircraft were overhead.

The frequent references to spies directing German shell fire which appear time and time again in personal accounts and war diaries did have some truth in them, although the 'spy fever' which often seemed to seize the battlefield was frequently generated by inaccurate and false suspicions. Aylmer Haldane recounted an occasion when a dynamo in a local cottage was reported as being used to transmit wireless signals to the enemy, a search revealing nothing but a weaving machine and a startled occupant. On another occasion a 'heliograph' was observed by troops flashing signals which appeared to be directing the shell fire of German batteries and convinced them that this was the work of a spy. It turned out to be a discarded sardine tin caught in the branches of a bush!

However, there were several documented cases of German artillery observers actually being discovered in British lines with telephone lines connecting them to German batteries. Gunner Myatt of 109/Battery wrote of an officer and two men being discovered in a wood with a telephone directing German fire onto British batteries. There was no doubt in Myatt's mind that, 'they were pretty brave men'. Another example quoted in the *Official History* described a German with a week's supply of food being discovered inside a haystack and another disguised as a farmer in a house between the lines. The I Corps Diary made reference to the use by the Germans of motor cars for reconnaissance with the, 'occupants dressed as French or English officers who drive boldly through our lines at great pace'. There is only one, 'safe rule in dealing with Germans', remarks the diarist, and that was to, 'treat them as capable of any treacherous trick'.

* * *

On 23 September four siege batteries armed with the old pattern 6-inch 30 cwt (breech loading) howitzers arrived on the Aisne. These guns, when fired from their travelling carriages as heavy howitzers, had a range of 5,200 yards but mounted on a siege platform, the range increased dramatically to 7,000 yards. Ancient they may have been – they had seen service in South Africa at the turn of the century – but they were the only siege artillery pieces available for use in September 1914. The batteries were brought into position just in time to play their part in what may have been one of the very first organised artillery fire plans used in the Great War.[262] On 18 September Haig entrusted Brigadier General Henry Horne – his Corps Artillery Adviser – with the organization of artillery fire and liaison with the RFC. Horne still lacked the legal authority as a commander of artillery and had to bow to the chain of command by passing suggestions to the relevant CRAs, but it was a beginning. The I Corps Special Artillery Group – which acted under the direct command of Haig himself – made even further inroads into centralizing divisional artillery. On 25 September, for example, the combined fire power of the 1st and 2nd Divisions was brought to bear on the Germans in the Chivy valley. Placed under the orders of Haig, guns from XV and XVII Brigade, a battery of VIII

Brigade howitzers, 3/Siege Battery and a section of 35/Heavy Battery, brought the attacking German infantry divisions to a standstill as fire was swung across the corps frontage, an action we know was very successful. This was a great improvement but Major John Mowbray, brigade major of the 2nd Divisional Artillery, still expressed his frustration at the continuing lack of effective communication:

> '*It is quite clear that divisional artillery require much more effective communication arrangements than we have. There should be a signal company or a section of a signal company allocated for this purpose and able to provide at least four stations with several miles of wire. The CRA would then be able to communicate directly with his brigades and fire could be rapidly controlled. Present arrangement of communications through infantry brigades is most unsatisfactory, many delays, often entirely nullifying the value of messages.*'[263]

We can only ponder as to whether Mowbray himself speculated on what might have been if a concentration of fire power been used on the I Corps front during their attack of 14 September.

Nonetheless, in mitigation it has to be said that GHQ's Operational Orders for the 14 September directed the BEF to 'pursue' a retreating German Army, not to attack entrenched positions. Had the orders from Sir John French been less ambiguous in content the tactics employed on that crucial first day may perhaps have been different. In any case the heavier 6-inch guns were not on the Aisne on 14 September and these would undoubtedly have been a vital component in any such attack.

By their very nature the siege batteries demanded a forward observation station from where the battery's fire could be controlled. 2/Siege Battery under the command of Major G S MacKenzie, was in place by 5.00pm on 24 September amongst the trees to the right of the modern day D967 just southwest of La Tuilerie Farm. The forward observation post was on the high ground of Mont de Charmont, some 200 yards in front of the battery and manned from dawn to dusk. The guns were capable of firing a 100lb HE shell as well as a similar round containing shrapnel, but old stocks of obsolescent ammunition were dangerous and prone to premature detonation as was demonstrated on 25 September when such an explosion killed 22-year-old Gunner Thomas Lacey. Another similar accidental explosion occurred in 1/Siege Battery on the same day, this time killing Gunners Smith and Fuller,[264] while a third premature on 1 October wounded the battery commander, Major C N Ewart, and six men.[265] John Mowbray commented in his diary that the shells were too old and not really safe enough to be used, but added, 'Ewart neglected to order all ranks to take cover while firing'. Major E L Hardcastle arrived to take over command of Ewart's battery on 9 October.

As obsolete as the guns were they were at least able to begin to answer the questions posed by the powerful German guns and also began working closely with the infantry. On 2 October 2/Siege Battery fired four high explosive rounds into the Ostel valley after the Irish Guards reported a German band playing at about 4.30am. John Mowbray was delighted with the results:

'Siege HQ had a telephone message last night from the Irish Guards that the enemy had a band playing and concert in progress in front of them. Without leaving the table he [the CRA] telephoned the battery who fired three rounds from the Guards directions. Message then received, band stopped. Concert ended. Assembly dispersed. Good night!'[266]

A few days later on 6 October the Coldstream Guards directed fire from 1/Siege Battery onto a German trench just in front of their positions. The battery observation post was right up amongst the Guards' forward trenches. Major Bernard Gordon Lennox and the Grenadiers were on the receiving end of the German retaliation at Chavonne:

'Singularly quiet day up to 3.00pm. From then for about 1½ hours the Dutchmen subjected us to a terrific bombardment in the village: shrapnel and high explosive. It was quite like old times at Soupir and we couldn't make out what had woke the beggars up, they simply plastered the village and some came so close that we got orders to be ready to move out of the village at once. This luckily was not necessary and the entertainment closed with net result of three transport horses killed and a lot of tiles and roofs not looking their best. Strolled up to the Coldstream Guards' billets at about 6.30 and saw Tony who told me the reason of their peevishness. The Dutchmen have apparently a big trench about 500 yards in front of the Coldstream with a lot of men in it. The Coldstream got a RA officer to look at it. He telephones down to the big howitzers and they planted their very first shot right into the middle of the trench. Tony tells me he never heard such a squealing and squawking and howling and moaning which went on for the best part of an hour. Our howitzers went pumping on and the result was the Dutchmen became very peevish and let us have it for all they were worth.'[267]

Gordon–Lennox's rather blasé attitude to the shelling at Chavonne was also a feature of George Jeffrey's diary. On another occasion he describes Prince Arthur of Connaught – the colonel of the regiment – paying them a visit: 'He sat for some time and had tea. The 6-inch battery was firing, and every time a shell went off he jumped nearly out of his skin, so fear he didn't enjoy his visit'.

On 7 October 2/Siege Battery turned its guns on the German strongpoint at Fort Condé this time using the RFC to guide its shooting. Their first round fell within the confines of the fort and over the next few days from their position on the southern bank of the river near the Château Bois Morin, north of Chassemy, the battery fired over 100 rounds at targets on the Chivy spur registering several direct hits.

Another gun brought back into service on the Aisne was the anti-aircraft gun. Another relic of the South African War it was largely ineffective. 11/Pom-Pom Section arrived on 22 September and Brigadier General Haldane had one of their guns, which he thought to be 'a considerable novelty', attached to 10 Brigade under the command of a Captain Hudson, 'whose refreshing optimism as to the number of "birds" he brought down or wounded was a source of much amusement to myself and staff'. There is no record of any German aircraft being brought down by one of these guns. Accompanying the unit was Sergeant Major Victor Laws from 3 Squadron RFC. Laws' task was to identify friend from foe in an effort to ensure the pom-pom guns did not shoot down any British aircraft, something which even Laws himself considered unlikely, although he admits that, '[we] may have killed quite a few troops in the front line where the percussion capped shells fell after firing'. John Mowbray was not impressed either:

> 'Converted Pom-Poms sent out for anti-aircraft work, which arrived a day or two ago, already clearly useless. It is slow, the shells do not readily burst and the tracers only work up to 2–3,000 feet. As the planes generally reconnoitre at 5–6,000 feet this is of little use. Perhaps it does keep the hostile planes a little higher.'[268]

The I Corps War Diary shared Mowbray's opinion, declaring the Pom-Poms, 'have been quite useless'.

On 27 September a memorandum on British and German tactics employed on the Aisne was circulated by GHQ, which set the tone for future fighting on the Western Front. Unsurprisingly the future control of artillery was high on the agenda. The section on defence opened with a statement which heralded the birth of the new form of warfare, 'before this war it was thought that artillery bombardment unaccompanied by an infantry attack was ineffective'. The memorandum went on to underline the need for artillery to occupy fully covered and concealed positions using observation stations to direct fire. The Germans had already made good use of observation balloons on the Chemin des Dames for artillery spotting observation and the memorandum conceded that the enemy appeared to be superior to us both in ingenuity and science:

> *We must learn from their methods particularly in terms of aircraft observation ...Their co-operation between the artillery and aeroplane also appears thorough, aeroplanes indicate the direction of targets by throwing out lights or smoke balls which are easily distinguishable at a distance, then they return to the batteries for which they are observing and shortly afterwards (presumably when the aeroplane had had time to give further data) fire is opened with great accuracy.*[269]

In what would become a feature of the next four years of fighting, the memorandum drew attention to the German artillery's habit of systematically searching for targets using map lines, giving the example of German fire on crossroads and supply routes where, 'searching fire is frequently kept up at night'. Arthur Osburn was on the receiving end at Paissy when the German gunners began one of their 'searching bombardments':

> *'Then came the Coal Boxes rumbling roar, as if a thousand clumsy housemaids had fallen down a thousand flights of stairs with loaded coal-scuttles, the ground quivering, the rocky escarpments of the Aisne echoing and re-echoing for miles. These Coal Boxes and Black Marias would come over in salvos of twos and threes; then methodically the German gunners would search for us, ranging from end to end of each valley in huge diagonals, creeping ever nearer towards the brown mass of tightly packed men and horses which cowered away from them under the shelter of the hill; searching until whole valleys were pock-marked with smoking craters ten feet wide.'*[270]

The shelling which Osburn described so graphically was typically fired from batteries concealed in wooded areas. The memorandum hardly needed to point out that German gunners were well concealed and, 'quick in picking up targets and in opening effective fire' – the British troops on the ground already knew that!

The lessons were unquestionably being learned but the material cost of answering the Germans' apparently inexhaustible supply of shells was having repercussions at home. On 17 September Sir John French in a communiqué to the War Office indicated that shell stocks were becoming critically low. The BEF had only 270 rounds for each of its howitzers and 180 rounds for each field gun; the reply from the War Office to the effect that shell shortages were not just the preserve of the BEF was not what Sir John wanted to hear. The guns in Edward Bulfin's 2 Brigade alone were firing an average of twenty rounds per day per gun and daily quotas were inevitably exceeded. A further 300 rounds per gun were shipped across the channel by early October but the shell shortage would raise its head again in late October when the BEF was fighting for survival at Ypres.

By the time the last battery of British guns had left the Aisne, there had been a sea change in tactics and thinking; the artillery was fast becoming the dominant force on the battlefield and over the course of the next four years the RFA would grow from 45 to 173 field brigades whilst the heavy and siege artillery of the RGA would undergo a similar expansion from 32 heavy and 6 siege batteries to 117 heavy and 401 siege batteries. The gunners had come of age.

Chapter 13

Those Magnificent Men in Their Flying Machines

About 50 shells burst all round us, the farthest from us being about 200 feet and some quite close. God knows how we were not hit. Funny noise those shells make when they burst, not a loud bang, sort of a 'plop' noise.

Lieutenant Kenlis Atkinson, 4 Squadron RFC -
describing anti-aircraft fire

On 13 April 1912 the RFC was constituted by Royal Warrant, it consisted of a Military Wing and a Naval Wing, the Naval Wing becoming the Royal Naval Air Service on 1 July 1914. Nine days after the declaration of war on 4 August 1914 the vanguard – consisting of the aircraft of 2, 3 and 4 squadrons flew across the channel on 13 August to land at Amiens. The first to arrive at 8.20am was the 2 Squadron pilot Lieutenant Hubert Harvey-Kelly in his BE2a and by the evening of 15 August they had been joined by 5 Squadron and over fifty aircraft of all shapes and sizes were parked at the Amiens airstrip waiting to fly to the forward airbase at Maubeuge the next day.[271]

The four squadrons of the RFC were very much in evidence during first weeks of the Great War. They reported the German movements north of Mons, they observed the movements of German units before and after Le Cateau and detected von Kluck's swing to the southeast which culminated in the Battle of the Marne. The eventual German retirement from the Marne towards the Aisne was confirmed by Captains Robert Boger and Robin Grey of 5 Squadron who watched the Germans cross the Marne. When one considers all this was carried out from the back of a collection of commercial lorries – some still sporting the company logos – and assorted other vehicles, and all reconnaissance flights were unaccompanied by other aircraft, the performance of the fledgling air service was impressive to say the least. But this Heath Robinson approach to war was soon to change.

Aerial co-operation with artillery was the subject of a communiqué from GHQ dated 13 September. It drew attention to an artillery action which had taken place in the Thiaucourt area on 8 September where, 'about half the artillery of the 6th German Corps was destroyed by our field artillery'.[272] The German batteries were discovered by aircraft of the French *Aéronautique Militaire* and it was based on their intelligence that an artillery fire plan was hastily put together – the effects of which were observed by French aircraft which continued to fly over the battlefield observing the 'complete destruction' of guns and limbers. GHQ made the point that, 'this success shows the results which can be and must be obtained by co-operation of the artillery and aircraft during an action'. Haig's reply on 14 September demonstrated his firm belief in the advantages of aerial observation:

'The French system of employing aviators in action with artillery is a very sound one. I strongly agree that GHQ take the matter in hand at once and establish a similar system for the British Army area. An adequate number of machines should be permanently attached to each Corps and Corps commanders should be given a free hand to use the machines at their discretion.'[273]

Haig's recommendations were fortunately taken seriously by GHQ and led eventually to the formation of corps squadrons – aircraft which were under the control of corps commanders. Corps aircraft were already in use by the Germans. In August 1914 the German Air Service had some 200 aircraft dedicated to short range reconnaissance and artillery control, considerably in advance of the BEF which was still desperately attempting to redress the balance when it arrived on the Aisne. However, as the lines of trenches along the Aisne valley became fixed, the RFC were soon mapping out the enemy positions and batteries along the German front line and in the rear areas, locating rail heads, aerodromes and supply dumps. There were also some early attempts to photograph enemy trenches as demonstrated on 15 September by Lieutenant George Pretyman, a pilot from 3 Squadron, who took five photographs of enemy positions with his own hand held camera and although of dubious quality, the images demonstrated that aerial photography was possible in a combat environment.[274]

Artillery observation from the air had been given little thought before war was declared. Both aircraft and ammunition were in short supply and the consensus of military thinking on the subject was still the subject of debate. However, two young Royal Engineers officers who had joined the RFC in 1913 had been giving a good deal of thought to air-to-ground communication between artillery batteries and aircraft. Both Lieutenants Baron James and Donald Lewis were firm advocates of the use of wireless telegraphy in transmitting information from aircraft to the ground and had in June 1914 successfully carried out a test flight during which they had maintained radio communication. James McCudden, who had transferred to the RFC in May 1913, had his first flight with Baron James and recalled the specially fitted aircraft which were being used in the wireless experiments:

'About 5.00pm I saw Lieutenant B T James, RE, going up alone on a silver doped BE2a, fitted with the first wireless experimental set ... I asked Mr James if he would take me up. With his usual good nature he said he would, so I had my first flight, about the first week of May 1913.'[275]

McCudden was awarded seven days detention and fourteen days loss of pay for his pains but his flight with James was the beginning of his career as a RFC pilot which began in June 1916 after he had successfully received his aero club certificate in the April of that year. Quite how McCudden squeezed into the observer's cockpit space alongside the wireless equipment is not mentioned!

On the declaration of war the Experimental Wireless Flight which had hosted the experimental trials involving James and Lewis was absorbed into the strength of the four RFC squadrons, the wireless flight, its three pilots and its cumbersome equipment were attached to 4 Squadron and Lewis, James and Second Lieutenant Stephen Smith went to war on 13 August. Baron James was a mathematical scholar who, after graduating from Woolwich, was commissioned into the Royal Engineers in 1909. In June 1912 after only a few days instruction he was awarded his Royal Aero Club Certificate at Hendon and in April 1913 he transferred to the Military Wing of the RFC. He was joined eight months later by Donald Lewis and over the next year the two men developed a professional partnership which pioneered the use of wireless telegraphy culminating in what John Terraine described as, 'a new co-operation with the artillery which began an intimate relationship between the air and the guns'.[276]

Effective indirect artillery fire was dependent on the gunners knowing not only their own position, but the position of the target. Once firing began they would make compensations for variations on wind, temperature, gun barrel wear and the type of shell being fired, thus observation of the fall of each shell became vital. We know that this was initially carried out by observers who reported back to the battery by telephone or other means. Initially artillery officers were taken up by the RFC in order for them to plot the positions of German batteries on the map and divisional CRAs would then allocate targets to their batteries. These flights were not without excitement as Lieutenant William Read of 3 Squadron discovered on 16 September:

'At 2.00pm we got orders to do a reconnaissance between Soissons and Vailly, north of the River Aisne. When we were 4,000 feet over Vailly, the Germans opened fire on us with anti-aircraft guns and they made surprisingly good shooting for the first few shots. The first shell was the nearest, it burst about twenty feet below us and I felt the machine shake and the left wing was boosted up a little. I made rapidly for a thick white cloud on my right and as soon as I came out of it they were at us again, but the shots were wide ... we got back to our landing ground at 4.15pm with our report.'[277]

Once the British batteries had opened fire on their targets it was possible for an aircraft to direct fire by a pre-arranged set of signals using an Aldis lamp or a Very pistol. Lieutenant Kenlis Atkinson of 4 Squadron took off from a field north of Bourg on the morning of 15 September to guide artillery fire onto German batteries near the Chemin des Dames:

'Went out again with Roche [Lieutenant H J Roche] to observe effect of gunfire which they were going to fire in salvos for us and to try and find German heavy batteries which have been giving us hell. Did not see any salvos but found 2 batteries of heavy guns hidden in the corner of a wood and fired two Very lights over them to give our gunners the line.'[278]

On the same day an aircraft piloted by Captain Lionel Charlton from 3 Squadron was instrumental in successfully directing fire on enemy positions using Very lights whilst on 24 September, Lieutenant Damer Allen from 4 Squadron used flash signals – probably from an Aldis lamp – from the air to indicate the fall of artillery fire. It was hazardous work which demanded the aircraft remained aloft directing artillery fire whilst the German gunners below – and indeed any handy infantryman – loosed off in an attempt to bring the aircraft and its crew down.

Captain Henry Jackson, an observer with 3 Squadron, was only too well aware of the dangers of working with the artillery from the air. Writing home to his mother on 27 September he described the work he and the squadron were engaged in:

'Our chief job is locating the position of the German hidden batteries, and correcting the fire of our batteries on them. It is most interesting. They have a fairly good anti-aircraft gun, which fires a shrapnel shell with which they make fairly good practice at us, but they have not actually brought anyone down yet. I had a bit of luck about three weeks ago, a bullet from a rifle went through the back of my seat, through my leather flying coat but was turned off by a steel rib in my Sam Browne belt and I was no more the worse except for a bruised back. There are generally shots through our wings but they do no harm and altogether the Flying Corps has been extraordinarily lucky.'[279]

RFC pilots and observers expected to be shot at by the enemy, after all, wrote Atkinson, 'this was war!'. What did irritate British aircrew was the continual barrage of fire from their own side which greeted their appearance; British and French troops had little idea of aircraft recognition and to them every aircraft was potentially hostile. Even after the RFC took to painting a large union flag on the underside of each wing they were still peppered by the infantry – despite a demand from GHQ that this should stop immediately. The problem was only improved after it was pointed out that only the red cross of the Union Flag was visible when viewed from the ground and the troops were confusing it with the black cross used by the German Air Service. Eventually the British adopted the circular markings in use by the French *Aéronautique Militaire*, preserving national identity by transposing the blue and red to form the roundel which is still in use today.

To an extent one can sympathise with the British Tommies in their confusion. By September 1914 they were only too well aware that aerial observation was being used to great effect by the German Air Service. During the retreat it had been noticed that the appearance of a German aircraft – usually a Rumpler Taube – generally heralded an artillery bombardment. The Taube would indicate the direction of targets with smoke balls or Very lights and some time later German artillery would deliver an alarmingly accurate bombardment. Aylmer Haldane described an occasion at Bucy-le-Long on 17 September when the village came under a heavy bombardment from German howitzers after a visit from an enemy aeroplane:

'For three-quarters of an hour the bombardment went on without interruption, and as it was the first time we had been subjected to the fire of heavy howitzers, it perhaps impressed itself more on our memories than did subsequent displays of a similar nature. Fortunately having had my suspicions of a hostile aeroplane, which the evening before had hovered over us and had seemed to pay special attention to the village which lay some 300 feet lower than the trenches, I had ordered the whole of the transport and the bivouacs of the two reserve battalions to be shifted before breakfast. When, therefore, the German howitzers opened fire, their shells, while causing great damage to the houses, failed to inflict much harm on the troops or transport.'[280]

We have no way of knowing whether the artillery bombardment on Bucy that morning was the work of the guns at Condé or not, but Haldane and the men of 10 Brigade would have been delighted with the results of a 3 Squadron reconnaissance of 24 September which they would have considered to be a justifiable reimbursement for their earlier discomfort. Taking off from Feré en Tardenois at 6.30am with his observer to map the exact locations of the German batteries operating on the Chivres spur, Lieutenant Read and his observer successfully mapped the battery positions and landed at the forward airstrip at Serches to confer with the battery commander:

'On our report it was decided to bombard the fort with four 6-inch howitzers which have just arrived from England. We went up again to observe the effect of our shell fire on the fort. It was deadly accurate, every shell falling inside the fort doing deadly work as far as we could see. The enemy's aircraft guns played on us once but we kept out of range of them. Returned to camp at 6.00pm.'[281]

Read's flight over Condé was also observed by General Smith-Dorrien who extolled the virtues of aerial observation in a telegram to GHQ dated the same day, 'I watched for a long time an aeroplane observing fire for the 6-inch howitzers of 3rd Division. It was at times smothered with hostile anti-aircraft fire but nothing daunted it'. The next day Read was in the air again over Missy directing the fire of a 60-pounder battery:

'We got our battery onto them and our shells were just right, and I think we must have paid them back for the bad time they have been giving our troops in Missy. All the while we were circling about and observing, the enemy plastered us with their anti-aircraft guns until the air all round was thick

with shell bursts. I kept turning, diving and climbing so as to offer as difficult a target as possible but we lost height a good deal, and when we were at 3,500 feet they managed to burst a shell near enough to put a piece of it through our propeller. So having got our battery the range we decided to get away and land.[282]

As Read and others had demonstrated, the use of Very lights and flash signalling could be very effective, but as James and Lewis knew, wireless was far more accurate and much faster. Since their arrival in France new wireless equipment had been obtained in Paris which was much lighter and more powerful than the rather bulky Marconi wireless sets, but even with the smaller Rouzet sets the equipment still weighed around 70lbs and filled the observer's cockpit area. In addition a 250 foot aerial had to be unwound from a reel fitted on the outside of the fuselage alongside the pilot before transmission could begin – a procedure which had to be reversed before the aircraft landed. The communication from air to ground was only a one-way signal using Morse code which was received by a ground station located near the battery. Replies from the ground used a combination of visual signals and flashing lights. However, despite the limitations and size of equipment, by late September wireless-equipped aircraft had established a new norm, and when one considers that this revolution in artillery observation had taken place using just two BE2a aircraft from the Wireless Flight; the magnitude of the achievement can be appreciated. John Mowbray was typical of many artillery officers in his enthusiasm of the potential of wireless observation:

'*Without air reconnaissance, accurate artillery work at long range is not possible. We have had some excellent results with an air observer who controls his machine, observes fire and signals results by wireless alone. An exceptional man is evidently needed for this ... the other day James put a heavy battery on target in three rounds.*'[283]

These small beginnings gave rise to the creation of a separate Headquarters Wireless Telegraphy Unit (HQWTU) on 27 September under the command of Major Herbert Musgrave. Musgrave was another Royal Engineers officer who had begun his career with 7/Field Company in 1896. Realizing the military potential of aviation he had learned to fly at the Bristol School on Salisbury Plain and was awarded his Royal Aero Club Certificate on 12 November 1912, joining the RFC a month later. Never a natural pilot, Musgrave's talents lay in research and development and it is largely through his efforts in solving the myriad of technical difficulties involved in installing wireless equipment in aircraft that wireless observation became so successful.

One of the first series of communications sent down by wireless from an aircraft was recorded on 24 September, it was probably from one of the two BE2a aircraft flown by the pilots of the Wireless Flight, but exactly which pilot is not known:

'4.02pm   *A very little short. Fire Fire.*
4.04pm   *Fire again. Fire again.*
4.12pm   *A little short; line OK.*
4.15pm   *Short. Over. Over and a little left.*
4.20pm   *You were just between two batteries, search 200 yds each side of your last shot. Range OK.*
4.22 pm   *You have them.*
4.26pm   *About 50 yds short and to the right.*
4.37pm   *Your last shot in the middle of three batteries in action; search all round within 300 yds of your last shot and you have them.*
4.42pm   *I am coming home now.'*[284]

The success of wireless observation and the increasing demand for dedicated corps wireless aircraft initially exceeded the RFC's ability to fully satisfy all the army's requirements. The four weeks the RFC spent over the Aisne had opened the door for a new age of artillery observation and had seen the beginning of a flying service which would grow from four squadrons into a significant force of some 300,000 officers and men and over 22,000 aircraft.

Chapter 14

Prisoners of War

At Anor we were placed in a wine factory with French native soldiers, French soldiers and our own. It was so crowded that it was difficult to lie down. The German lieutenant told me that a party of prisoners had been attacked here and that very stern orders had now been issued. The party in question were the unwounded officers and men of my regiment.

Captain P H Lowe, 1/West Yorkshire Regiment - after being captured

Being taken prisoner of war by enemy forces can be a hazardous business and little has changed in this respect since opposing armies first clashed on the field of battle. Remaining alive after surrendering is by no means certain in the heat of battle, enemy infantry who are hell bent on killing their foe may not recognize the intention to surrender or indeed be in a receptive frame of mind to take prisoners. Despite international law which surrounds the protection of soldiers who have laid down their arms, there are countless tales of men who, in the very act of surrendering, have been 'dealt with' instantly by their captors or even summarily executed *en route* to captivity. On the Aisne in 1914 wounded men were certainly killed by the Germans if the evidence of men captured can be taken at face value. Whether the same can be said of the British is difficult to establish but war is a brutal business as witnessed by Private Arthur Burgess of the Cameron Highlanders who, after his capture, was a helpless spectator at the death of one of his battalion officers, Hector Cameron, on the battlefield:

'*2nd Lieut H W L Cameron, severely wounded in shoulder and both legs, was lying on a waterproof sheet and was unable to stand. A German non-commissioned officer shot him dead with a revolver, presumably because he was unable to walk. This occurred about 7 or 8 o'clock pm of the night 14/15th. Corporal Mackae and Private Moffat, both of 1st Cameron Highlanders were witness of this.'*[285]

Prisoners taken on the Aisne in September and October 1914 were subject to the same lottery of life and death which the BEF had experienced since the encounter at Mons on 23 August. Apart from the dreadful episode witnessed by Arthur Burgess, the evidence found in written accounts of surviving prisoners of war suggests that British prisoners were generally treated with a reasonable degree of care on the battlefield. But it was often a different story once prisoners found themselves being herded into captivity. Time and time again the accounts of British soldiers tell of an almost ritual abuse from German soldiers and civilians and an alarming refusal from organizations such as the German Red Cross to provide water and food to men who were clearly in a poor state of physical and mental health. A number of those who were captured on the Aisne had to endure conduct from their captors which can only be described as vindictive and barbaric. Even if we accept that much of this appears to have been the result of the white flag incidents, which both sides depicted as treachery on the part of the other, it still contrasts hugely with the treatment of German prisoners by the British.

Captain Lancelot Robins was captured on the night of 14 September whilst returning to the 2/Welch lines after reconnoitring the enemy outposts in the Chivy valley. Having shot three Germans with his revolver he heard what he thought was a patrol from his own battalion and whilst running towards them he was struck over the head with a rifle. He had run straight into the arms of a German patrol:

'*I was knocked down by the blow which was delivered with the butt end or the barrel of a rifle, and was rendered unconscious for the time. I was afterwards struck across the face, from which I have lost the sight of the right eye and the left eye has been affected. I could easily have been shot, but I think they wished to avoid the noise as I must have been quite close to our own lines.'*[286]

Robins was eventually taken back to the German lines and the next morning, still suffering from concussion, he was marched with a large group of others from the Black Watch and Coldstream Guards to Laon. One Coldstream Guardsman, Private James Napier, remembers seeing Robins:

'Captain Robins was speaking German (I did not then understand it). He wouldn't give way to the Germans. When he walked into the yard the German officer talked to him; he talked back, you could see he was defying him; there were no blows. About 10:00 in the morning 60 (all of us which were there) fell in and they marched us into the road.'[287]

Clearly still concussed, Robins is very hazy about the events which took place on the march, all he recalls is collapsing and being badly treated along the road.

'I was knocked down either by a German or by the rush of the other men behind me, all of whom I heard afterwards were hit or kicked. On getting up, I picked up my water bottle which had fallen over my head, and seeing a German running at me with his rifle held in both hands, I swung my water bottle, which was full, clean into his face. I was then knocked down and struck over the face, and it was this blow I believe destroyed my eye.'[288]

James Napier's evidence accused an unnamed German officer of instigating further brutality by forcing the British prisoners to, 'run the gauntlet', between two lines of German troops:

'After about a kilometre we were stopped by an officer with the badge of a skull and crossbones who spoke very good English and said, "If I had my own way I would shoot every private and hang every officer wearing the king's uniform". He said we had showed the white flag and when they came to take us had opened fire. Also we had used dum-dums that day. He then turned and made a speech to the Germans. After about 60 yards the infantry, who were on the right and the artillery who were on the left closed in on the prisoners from each side using their feet, butts of rifles, whips, sticks and throwing broken bottles. Captain Robins had his head broken at the top and his eye closed up.'[289]

Judging from the apparent *Totenkopf* insignia on the officer's headpiece he may well have been from a Prussian cavalry regiment and he clearly appeared to be incensed by the white flag incidents which had taken place, blaming the British for so doing – the exact opposite of what had actually taken place. He was also angry at the British use of what he termed soft-nosed dum-dum bullets, a story which may have originated from the soft-nosed ammunition used in the British service revolver which some captured officers would have been armed with. Although the dum-dum was a British invention developed for use in India, it had been outlawed at the Hague Convention of 1899.

Another Coldstream guardsman, Private John Cooper, thought the officer sporting the *Totenkopf* insignia was a general or some other high ranking officer and after the order was given for the German troops to line each side of the road, 'the British prisoners had to run between them for 4–500 yards'. Cooper thought Robins had his eye knocked out and said he saw two men, 'of a kilted regiment', knocked down and killed. If this was not enough, the remainder of the march to Laon was punctuated by frequent beatings which finally stopped when the group were herded into cattle trucks for a three-day journey to Sennelager prisoner of war camp. Private Arthur Burgess was also in the party of prisoners with John Cooper and Lancelot Robins, he remembers quite clearly being made to run the gauntlet. Although some details are slightly different, his account concurs with the others:

'Just before we got to Laon we, a party of about 77 English, were made to run the gauntlet along a road between German reserves for about 120 yards. They threw stones, bottles, whips, rifle butts at us; Major Robbins (sic) lost the sight of his eye through this, Private Giles of the Coldstream Guards, also lost the sight of his eye through this...two men, presumably of the Black Watch, were knocked down and as they never reappeared, were presumably killed.'290

A similar account of British prisoners being forced to run between lines was described by Sergeant L Heath of 1/West Yorkshire Regiment. He was captured on 20 September when his battalion was overrun north of Paissy and taken by train to Anor, a small town southeast of Maubeuge. Here the party of prisoners was split up into three groups:

'On the platform there were two lines of Germans at about six paces intervals, through which the first party had to go. This must have all been pre-arranged because the Germans were all armed with sticks, rifles etc and there were also Germans near each truck we had to get in; directly the first party were driven through the small gate so they were attacked by the Germans on the platform. After the first party had gone there was an interval of about a quarter of an hour, and then the second party was marched off and the same was repeated to them. I was with this party.'291

Being unable to walk, Lieutenant Claude Wallis was fortunately not required to suffer the same indignities as Cooper, Burgess and Robins, or indeed Sergeant Heath, but he was subjected to some unnecessarily brutal treatment by his captors. An officer with 1/Loyal North Lancs, he was wounded on 14 September and left in the ruins of a house after the battalion had retired. From his description it would seem likely he was in one of the buildings near the sucrerie close to the Chemin des Dames. He was found by a party of Germans early the next day:

> 'After about a quarter of an hour ... another party of Germans entered and threatened us with bayonets and made signs to us that if we did not get outside we should be bayoneted. I crawled out of the house on hands and knees together with a few men who were able to do this. The remainder – about 10 – stayed in the house, being unable to move, and I do not know what happened to them. Outside two Germans lifted me to my feet while one stood behind me with a bayonet, with which he prodded me and shouted, "March". I took two or three steps forward, but collapsed from weakness and in doing so the bandage and tourniquet round my arm became loose, and the blood commenced to flow very badly. Eventually a stretcher was found.'[292]

On his way to what Wallis describes as a field dressing station, he and the two Cameron Highlanders with him were abused and kicked, one of the highlanders being clubbed with a rifle butt. At the dressing station Wallis finally had his wounds looked at by a German doctor, 'he spoke a little English and was quite good, cleaning and dressing the wound, and also giving me some food and a little wine'. Wallis was then taken to a small cottage where there were about twenty wounded British soldiers lying on the floor:

> 'The men had been mostly wounded the day before, and had had no attention as yet to their wounds. Late in the afternoon the doctor who had dressed my wounds looked into the room and I asked him if he could attend to some of the men. He refused, saying he had no time, but would attend to some tomorrow. No food had been given to any of these men since they had been taken ... during the night one man who had been shot in the head went mad and eventually died in the early morning in delirium. A second, wounded in the stomach, died quietly.'[293]

These accounts were all recorded by men who were taken prisoner on the right flank of the BEF on, or immediately after, the first day of fighting when one of the most notorious white flag incidents took place involving the men of Royal Sussex Regiment. The hostility demonstrated by the Germans – as inexcusable as it was – may well have originated from what they perceived as treachery on the part of the British in shooting down men who were attempting to surrender. Interestingly, accounts from men of the West Yorkshire Regiment who were captured on 20 September are largely – apart from Sergeant Heath's experience - devoid of any instances of such violent behaviour by their German captors.

24-year-old Second Lieutenant Bertram 'Bertie' Ratcliffe had been with 1/West Yorkshires since graduating from Sandhurst in September 1913. He was wounded in the right lung at about 6.15am during the second German attack. After the Moroccan infantry on the right of the West Yorkshires had retired in disarray the two front line companies were surrounded and he was taken prisoner at 2.00pm:

'I was taken to a small village behind the lines where I remained the night. I saw no infractions of the ordinary laws of war. A number of other officers were captured at the same time as myself, but they were taken off the first day, as they were able to walk. The Germans tried to force me to walk, but I could not. I had a British soldier with me, a man of my own regiment, who was very badly wounded in the arm; and on the second day, after resting the night in this small village, when a sentry noticed I could not get along, he allowed me to get on the tailboard of a cart in which there were a number of German soldiers.'[294]

They were in fact lodged for the night in a church which had been prepared for German wounded. Captain P Lowe was one of the officers Ratcliffe mentions as leaving the next morning. Lowe was taken to Laon where he was put in the former French barracks. He was sure that the Germans were overwhelmed by the numbers of their own wounded:

'I am of the opinion that the Germans here could not cope with their own wounded, much less attend to ours. There were English who had been here more than a week and who had never been looked at. The head doctor when we did get to see him was polite, dressed our wounds, and saw to the worst cases of the English rank and file.'[295]

He may well have been correct; Lieutenant Wallis recalled how a mattress which Major Arthur Nicholson of the Cameron Highlanders was using was taken away for use by German wounded.[296] Nicholson also had to complain furiously to the doctor to get him to attend to two or three of the badly wounded British soldiers. Nicholson and Wallis were eventually taken to Laon where they found British wounded who had received no medical attention whatever since being captured. Several men died as a result of neglect. Wallis refers to, 'another man of the Welch Regiment had been shot through the throat', who died three days after his arrival having had no medical treatment, a man whom Wallis says, 'could have been easily saved'. One of the neglected wounded at Laon was Private Lawson of the Royal Scots Fusiliers who was captured on 14 September. He was left lying on the battlefield until the following day when, he says, a German parson took him to a house where he spent the next five days. At Laon he was only seen once by a French doctor before he was sent to Germany. During the three-and-a-half day journey to Kassel in a cattle truck he was given one bowl of soup and two pieces of bread.

Captain Herbert Sutherland was wounded on 14 September just north of Vailly whilst fighting with 1/Northumberland Fusiliers. His subsequent treatment by his German captors was, in his opinion, quite reasonable under the circumstances. Sutherland had been wounded in several places, a bullet through his right thigh, shrapnel wounds in his back and shoulder and a splintered shoulder blade. As the battalion retired he was unable to get back and after being found the next morning he was carried back to a haystack on a waterproof sheet by four German infantrymen. There his wounds were attended by two medical orderlies and the next day he was carried back to a field dressing station where a doctor examined his wounds but, 'did not disturb the dressings'. Taken eventually by an ambulance wagon to a hospital at Filain, his wounds were looked at again by a German doctor:

> '*In the dressing room were four or five English soldiers who were all wounded. I was left in the room with them for about two hours, during which time one of the soldiers died and his body was taken away. I asked the German doctor if he was going to take the man's identity disc and small book or report on the man's death. He replied that he was not going to. I told him that according to the Geneva Convention he should do so, but he said he was not complying with that convention.*'[297]

It was at Filain that Sutherland met Gerard Kempthorne, the medical officer attached to 1/Lincolns. Kempthorne had been captured on 14 September after the Lincolns had retired and remained on the battlefield attending the wounded and recalled that after being relieved of his field glasses and map, how a 'middle-aged subaltern arrived talking perfect English and remarked [that] he had many friends in England and we ought to be fighting on the side of Germany'. Kempthorne had refused to leave the field until all his men had been cared for and it was in the process of doing this that he was wounded in the leg by British shrapnel. Sutherland only learnt afterwards that the Germans had offered to take Kempthorne back out of danger, 'but that he had refused to go until all the wounded had been taken'.

Private Harry Horry was one of the Lincolnshire wounded left on the field. initially wounded in the right thigh he had been wounded a second time in the foot. According to Horry's evidence he was left on the battlefield for five days during which he fed himself on raw swede before being finally picked up and taken to a nearby farm – possibly d'Hameret Farm on the modern day D15 – where he spent another eleven days in the company of other wounded British soldiers. He complains that they were given very little food during this time and although not ill-treated as such, his story is one of neglect by his captors. His account of his journey to No. 3 *Lazarette* at Hamburg in a cattle truck without food or water was typical of many prisoners' experiences and ironically he was fortunate that his wounds, albeit not life threatening, were serious enough for him to be involved in a prisoner exchange in August 1915.

There were a number of quite remarkable escapes recorded by men who were captured on the Aisne in 1914, an activity which was made considerably easier by the relative proximity of neutral Holland. Would be escapees only had to make for the neutral frontier and once successfully negotiated, freedom beckoned. Coldstream Guardsman Private John Cooper was one who made a 'home run' on 30 September 1918 in the company of Sergeant Edward Facer who was captured on 15 April 1917 serving with 21/Australian Machine Gun Company. Imprisoned at Dülmen, southwest of Münster, the two men took three days to reach the Dutch frontier.

There was a great deal of publicity devoted to the escape of Bertie Ratcliffe in 1917 who was captured on 20 September in the West Yorkshire trenches on the Chemin des Dames. He succeeded in escaping from a train with five other British officers:

> *'At about 8.00pm we arrived at a small junction 2 kilometres south of Crefeld; it being dusk we five left the train as it was drawing out of the station, ran a short way along the line until we came to a crossing, where we divided into three groups – Major Hall went one way, Captain Morgan and Lieutenant Ross another, and Squadron Commander Briggs and myself a third. We each had a map and compass with us and some chocolate. I was dressed in full uniform, with a British warm.'*[298]

Ratcliffe's compass had been sent to him by his mother whilst he was a prisoner at Ingolstadt. Concealed in a tin of Harrogate toffee he managed to hide it from the authorities until his escape from the train. His companion, Edward Briggs, was one of the pilots on the famous Royal Naval Air Service raid on the Zepplin sheds at Friedrichshafen in November 1914. Briggs was the only pilot not to return and was brought down after the fuel tank on his Avro 504K had been holed by machine-gun fire. Ratcliffe and Briggs became separated the following morning when they were seen by a sentry:

> 'Before he had time to do anything we turned and fled in a different direction, at the same time separating from one another; he followed me, but I ran for about a quarter of an hour, then lay down in a ditch getting my bearings by my compass … I went into an opening of the forest and across a space of low heather. I was going very quietly along when just on my left, I saw a sentry walking towards me. Looking before me I saw a piece of barbed wire about 6 inches from the ground. I started to run as hard as I could over the frontier, but I had only done about four paces when I caught my foot on a bush and fell. The sentry followed me and when I got up he was standing 2 yards from me.'[299]

It looked very much as if his bid for freedom was over. The sentry walked over to him and asked who he was, Ratcliffe says the resulting conversation lasted half an hour and involved bribing the man with twenty-five marks, after which the sentry pointed out the direction of the frontier. Bertie Ratcliffe crossed the border into Holland at 5.30am where he was taken to Venlo police station and from there to the British Consul at Rotterdam. He was possibly the first British PoW to make his way back to England where he received a hero's welcome and was invited to lunch with George V. Only three of the five men – Ratcliffe, Edward Briggs and Morgan – who had escaped from the train, successfully crossed the frontier into Holland.

Yet in reality the majority of the men captured on the Aisne remained in German hands for the remainder of the war. For some such as Captain Lowe of the West Yorkshires it was a long captivity accompanied by the mental strain of imprisonment in a confined space. Writing after his release in 1918 he recalled the boredom and stress of captivity:

> 'For older officers who, like myself had been prisoners from practically the beginning of the war, the effect of imprisonment is mental. The winter is the time that tells. One's exercise is walking round and round a muddy or snow covered track within a wire fence.'[300]

Perhaps what was more exasperating for him and others like him who were taken in the early months of the war, was the rapid promotion which many of his brother officers who were captured later on in the war had benefitted from. Thus officers who were his junior in September 1914 arrived in captivity as majors and lieutenant colonels. 'I was, of course, unfortunate', he wrote, 'as after 23 years service I am still a captain, thus though one of the oldest of the English officers, I was one of the juniors with a corresponding lack of cubic air space'. Lowe's comments on imprisonment draw attention to the plight of the prisoner of war, whom, like the badly wounded and disabled discharged as unfit for further service, bore their scars quietly and practically unnoticed.

Chapter 15

Epilogue

We understand the whole of the BEF is being relieved on the Aisne by the French, but we do not know our destination although rumours point Flanders way.

Captain James Jack, Scottish Rifles –
on hearing of the move from the Aisne

As the last British units withdrew from the Aisne they left their legacy in the form of hastily dug trench lines. When the French territorials finally arrived to relieve the Grenadier Guards at Soupir on 12 October, Bernard Gordon Lennox remarked in his diary that the French *poilus* were too short to see over the parapet of the Guards trenches but felt that it would only be a temporary occupation before the line moved north again. How erroneous his assumption would prove to be.

The BEF had entered the Great War scarcely prepared for a major European conflict and unable to act as more than a subordinate partner to its French Allies. After the retreat from Mons and the reversal of fortune which was epitomized by the Battle of the Marne, the British arrival on the Aisne marked a distinct change in the nature of the fighting experienced in the western theatre up to that point. The sluggish advance of the BEF towards the Aisne impacted on the advance of the French armies to either side and thus allowed the German Army precious time to reinforce and dig in on the Chemin des Dames. Thus the high ground to the north of the Aisne valley witnessed the beginnings of a trench-based encounter which was largely dictated by the tactical nature of the fighting. On the Chemin des Dames the Germans found a position that they could defend effectively and in order to hold that vital ground they resorted to the spade. In response the Anglo-French armies which were attempting unsuccessfully to evict them with frontal assaults and outflanking movements found themselves digging positions which ran parallel to those of their adversaries. As that process replicated itself time and again in many localised actions, so the still embryonic lines of 'trenches' gradually snaked their way north and west as both sides attempted to get round the open western flank in the hope of ending the war with a final battle. The trench system which came to characterize and then symbolize the Western Front for generations to come was created by the weeks of flanking attacks which were forced upon both sides by the stultifying stalemate on the Aisne. The picturesque rolling hills and valleys of the Aisne had unwittingly given birth to positional warfare that would eventually create a 400 mile livid scar across a good deal of Western Europe.

Although neither side envisaged a war conducted from fixed positions, it was the Germans who had the advantage of a ready supply of equipment suitable for this troglodyte 'trench warfare'. Barbed wire, spades, duckboards and trench mortars were readily available, resources which the British and French armies sadly lacked in sufficient quantities. The German artillery was distinctly more powerful and used to much greater effect than the inadequate artillery support offered by the Allied armies to their infantry units. The intensity and accuracy of the German guns, qualities which had taken the BEF's GHQ by surprise, was undoubtedly another reason behind the issue of Operational Order No. 27 from Sir John French on 16 September, instructing his divisions to dig in and hold their positions against German attacks. Sir John was correct in thinking that trenches enabled both sides to hold ground and protect themselves against shell fire but with no subsequent orders being issued until 1 October – marking the beginning of the BEF's withdrawal from the Aisne – the British were left without direction from their commander-in-chief. It was in those two vital weeks, when the humble spade became the most sought after weapon in the valley, that trench warfare can be said to have become a reality.

If the Aisne gave birth to the Western Front it also marked the ascendancy of heavy artillery as a major weapon of modern warfare. Faced with the demoralizing and destructive capability of the German heavy batteries, the BEF was forced to re-examine its strategic use of artillery. For the first time in the Great War, fire plans which focussed the fire of British batteries on to a single target or area were used on the Aisne, alongside the all important wireless liaison between aircraft and artillery batteries which would become an essential feature of air/artillery co-operation in the years to come.

The reader will recall General Joffre's intention of enveloping the German right flank which was bent back near Noyon south of the Oise River in order to break the deadlock on the Aisne and resume the offensive. These plans were hardly a secret and had certainly not gone unnoticed by the German High Command whose purpose was to carry out the same manoeuvre on the French left flank. This was the so called 'race to the sea', a race which neither side wished to win as victory would constitute a failure to turn the other's flank. On 17 September – with orders to outflank the German right – Maunoury's Sixth Army, which had been reinforced by the French XIII Corps, clashed with the Germans at Carlepont. The attack failed leaving Joffre to try again on the Second Army front north of the River Avre nine days later. This time there was a partial gain as the French left wing reached Péronne but a reinforced German II Corps managed to hold the right of de Castelnau's forces. The hold on Péronne was short-lived as on the 26th de Castelnau was pushed back across the River Somme.

By 25 September the German High Command was becoming impatient and ordered their First, Second and Third Armies to take the offensive to hold the British and French on the Aisne in order to prevent the movement of reinforcements to the Somme, thus enabling the German offensive in the north to reach Amiens and the channel coast – hence the German attacks of 25 September. The 'race' was well and truly on but it is not within the scope of this book to describe the sidestepping scramble of the French and German armies which culminated in the First Battle of Ypres in October and November 1914. Suffice to say that by 9 October the battle lines had been extended from the Aisne to within 30 miles of Dunkirk, by which time the first units of the BEF had already left their positions on the Aisne and were moving towards Flanders where the final battles of 1914 would be fought.

The first units of the BEF to move were from Allenby's cavalry and Smith-Dorrien's II Corps. Joffre had agreed to the transfer of the BEF to Flanders – particularly as the 7th Division and the 3rd Cavalry Division were about to be landed at Ostend. It must be said that the move was carried out extremely well with all movements carefully concealed. Battalions were moved under the cover of darkness and their places taken by French troops, by 9 October II Corps was advancing towards Béthune and III Corps was moving on Armentières and Bailleul. The evacuation was completed by 15 October and four days later Douglas Haig and I Corps arrived at Hazebrouck.

The British battle casualties sustained during the Aisne fighting has been put at approximately 560 officers and 12,000 other ranks, an attrition rate of experienced officers and NCOs the BEF could ill afford to lose.[301] The high proportion of officer casualties had much to do with the great emphasis that was placed on personal bravery. Officers were expected to lead from the front thus setting an example to the men and the alarming numbers of officers who were killed or wounded bears testament to this mindset. However, the lessons learnt in the South African War – where officers were particularly targeted by the Boer snipers – appear to have been either forgotten or ignored. The practice during the South African war of officers and men being indistinguishable through their battlefield dress and armament was not evident on the Aisne. The Northamptonshire subaltern, Lieutenant Jack Needham's attire was typical of officers going into battle; he writes of carrying his sword when leading his men, which – together with his distinctive officer's uniform – would have made him a highly visible target to enemy riflemen. Such practices, combined with undoubted bravery, ultimately led to great swathes being cut through the officer corps and it was a trend which would be maintained after the move north.

As the men who fought on the Aisne moved north with their respective units, very few would have contemplated a future featuring a war that would drag on for another four years. For many of those who were now heading north to Flanders – in the vain hope of finding the open flank – their life expectancy would be measured in days or weeks.

If Sir John French had been concerned by the casualties inflicted on the BEF on the Aisne, what followed at Ypres provided a shocking induction of what was to come as trench warfare became established. Amongst those whose accounts appear in this book and who lost their lives during the savage fighting which has gone down in history as 'First Ypres' was Major Lord Bernard Gordon Lennox of 2/Grenadier Guards, along with his regimental colleague Captain Cholmeley Symes Thompson who were both killed within a week of each other near Zillebeke in November and are buried with their comrades in the tiny Zillebeke Churchyard Cemetery. Charles Paterson, the adjutant of 1/ who was mentioned in despatches in September only survived another month. Promoted to captain in October, he was badly wounded at Geluvnelt and died of his wounds on 1 November 1914 and now rests at Ypres Town Cemetery. Two commanding officers who led their battalions on the Aisne are commemorated on the Menin Gate Memorial: Malcolm Green of the South Lancashire Regiment was killed on 17 November and Hugh Crispin's name is also there inscribed. Crispin – killed on 30 October during the heavy fighting south of the Menin Road near Ypres – had taken command of 2/Royal Sussex after Ernest Montresor was killed on the Chemin des Dames. (Six days after Ernest Montresor's death, his son-in-law, 24-year-old Lieutenant Geoffrey Russell Fenton, was killed in action whilst serving with 2/Connaught Rangers.)

The rate of attrition amongst battalion commanding officers in the first weeks of the Great War was staggeringly high. By the time the BEF arrived on the southern heights above the Aisne Valley in September 1914, six commanding officers had been killed in action or had died of wounds, five had been taken prisoner and one had been wounded. The Aisne campaign saw a further five commanding officers killed in action and six wounded and of the commanding officers who led their battalions to Flanders in October, a further seven would not survive beyond 1914. Lieutenant William Synge's commanding officer, 45-year-old Lieutenant Colonel William Bannatyne was killed near Polygon Wood at Ypres on 24 October. Also killed at Ypres was Lieutenant Colonel Norman McMahon DSO who commanded 4/Royal Fusiliers. He was killed on 11 November the day before he was due to take command of a brigade. He is commemorated on the Ploegsteert Memorial. Lieutenant Colonel Reginald Alexander, 3/Rifle Brigade, died of wounds on 20 December and is buried at Bailleul Communal Cemetery and Major Edward Daniel, who commanded 2/Royal Irish, was killed in action at Le Pilly on 20 October and has his name on the Le Touret Memorial.

1915 saw the death of 23-year-old Lieutenant Robert Flint DSO, the RE officer who worked with Johnston ferrying men across the river at Missy. Mentioned in despatches he was killed near Kemmel on 12 January and is buried at Dranouter Churchyard Cemetery. Major John Leslie Mowbray DSO the Brigade Major to the 2nd Division CRA was killed on 21 July 1916 whilst in command of a battery of XLI Brigade guns. His headstone can be found at Péronne Road Cemetery, Maricourt. Almost a year later Mowbray's nephew, 21-year-old Lieutenant Maurice Mowbray MC was killed on 23 August 1917, serving with 89/Field Company. Major Wilfred Ellershaw, the battery commander of 113/Battery attained the rank of brigadier general before his death on 5 June 1916 aboard HMS *Hampshire*, an occasion which also marked the death of Lord Kitchener. Ellershaw's name is on the Hollybrook Memorial at Southampton as is that of Horatio Herbert Kitchener.

A particularly tragic story is that of the three boys of the Meautys family. Lieutenant Thomas Meautys was killed with the West

Yorkshires on 20 September which must have been heartbreaking for his wife Nora and parents Thomas and Ellen Meautys. His younger brother, 19-year-old Lieutenant Denzil Hatfield Meautys, died of wounds on 7 May 1917 and a month later tragedy struck again in June 1917 when the eldest brother, Captain Paul Dashwood Meautys was killed. Denzil is buries at Etaples Military Cemetery and Paul at London Cemetery, Neuville-Vitasse, near Arras.

Major Charles 'Bertie' Prowse DSO who commanded the Somerset Light Infantry rose to command 11 Brigade in 1916 but was killed on 1 July of that year on the Somme. He was mentioned in despatches four times and is buried at Louvencourt Military Cemetery near Doullens. Lieutenant Geoffrey Prideaux who served with Prowse was promoted to captain soon after leaving the Aisne and was killed on 19 January 1917 having been promoted brigade major to 11 Brigade. He was awarded the Military Cross in 1916 and now rests at Hem Farm Military Cemetery, near Albert on the Somme.

Amongst those who survived the war was George Jeffreys who fought with the 2/Grenadier Guards at Soupir Farm. After realizing his ambition of commanding the battalion he was appointed brigadier general in command of the Guards Brigade in 1917 and by the end of the war he was commanding the 19th Division. After the Armistice he became member of parliament for Petersfield and was created a Baron in 1952. He died, aged 82, in 1960. Captain Guy Ward who fought with the South Wales Borderers ended his war as a lieutenant colonel with a DSO and died in March 1933 aged 58. He is buried at Brookwood Cemetery.

There was an understandable tendency amongst senior officers to promote the careers of those infantry commanders who had demonstrated personal bravery and an offensive spirit. One such commander was Edward Bulfin, the commander of 2 Brigade. Bulfin's attack on 14 September 1914 was pressed home in his usual determined manner and his performance during the First Battle of Ypres followed a similar pattern. His dogged determination and clear qualities of command resulted in his promotion in October. In 1916 he was commanding the 60th Division on the Vimy sector and in 1917 he was promoted to lieutenant general in command of XXI Corps in Palestine. Bulfin retired in 1926 and died at home in Bournemouth in 1939.

John Ponsonby DSO, who was wounded at Cerny, was initially promoted to command 2 Guards Brigade and then the 5th Division which he led until the end of the war. He retired as Major General Sir

John Ponsonby in 1928 and died in 1952. Brigadier Aylmer Haldane went on to command the 3rd Division and in 1916 was appointed to command VI Army Corps. After the war he became General Officer Commanding Mesopotamia and retired in 1925. He died aged 88 in 1950 and is buried at Brookwood Cemetery. Haldane wrote several books, one of which was an account of his escape from captivity during the Boer War in *How We Escaped from Pretoria*. Brigadier General Gleichen continued to command his brigade until March 1915. Subsequently, as a major general, he commanded the 37th Division until October 1916. He was then appointed Director of the Political Intelligence Bureau of the recently established Department of Information, of which his close friend, the author John Buchan, was a deputy director. Gleichen held this post for the rest of the war. He retired from the army in 1919 and died in December 1937.

Lieutenant Colonel Arthur Wolfe-Murray who commanded 2/Highland Light Infantry became a brigadier general and died at home on 7 December 1918. He is buried at Eddlestone parish churchyard in Scotland. John Longley who commanded 1/East Surrey Regiment so ably on the Chivres Spur was appointed a brigadier general in 1915 and shortly afterwards command of the 10th Irish Division followed. Mentioned in despatches on ten occasions, he retired as Sir John Longley in 1923. During the Second World War he served in the Dover garrison and died in 1953. He is remembered with a stained glass window in the chapel of the Church of All Saints at Kingston-on-Thames. Brigadier General Aylmer Hunter-Weston also went on to greater glory but of all the brigade commanders who fought on the Aisne his subsequent career has probably suffered the most from a bad press. His command of 29th Division at Gallipoli has been rather unfairly described by John Laffin as verging on the wilfully negligent which is slightly less offensive than another remark which accused him of being one of the most brutal and incompetent commanders of the First World War. Hunter-Weston returned from Gallipoli to an October 1916 parliamentary by-election in which he was elected to the House of Commons as the Unionist Member for North Ayrshire. He was appointed GOC VIII Corps when it was re-established in France in 1916 and commanded the corps during the Somme offensive. On 1 July 1916 his divisions attacked in the northern sector of the battlefield and failed to capture any of their objectives. Again his leadership and artillery fire plan was called into question. Hunter-Weston continued in politics after the war being elected again for Bute and North Ayrshire in 1918. He resigned from the army in 1919 with a knighthood, and from parliament in 1935. This complex and single-minded individual of whom history has been generous in its criticism, died in 1940 following a fall at his ancestral home in Hunterston.

Edward Northey, the commanding officer of 2/KRRC, had a far less chequered career. He was in command of 15 Brigade by 1915 but was wounded during the Second Battle of Ypres. On his return he was sent to East Africa to command the Nyasa-Rhodesian Field force. He was knighted and promoted to major general in 1918 and two years later became governor of British East Africa – the modern day Kenya. He also died in 1953. Francis Towsey the commanding officer of 1/West Yorkshires who was wounded on 20 September, regained the confidence of Sir Douglas Haig and after two successful temporary appointments to brigade command was appointed to command 122 Brigade which he led during the Battle of the Somme in 1916. He died aged 83 in May 1948. Major Christopher Griffin who led the Lancashire Fusiliers was wounded four times during the Great War and died in 1957 having retired as a brigadier general with the DSO and bar.

For many others surviving the war intact was reward enough. Lieutenant Arthur Griffith, the gunner subaltern who won a DSO with his 71/Battery guns at Cour de Soupir Farm, retired as a major. He was wounded at Cour de Soupir Farm and again on two other occasions. In addition to his DSO he was mentioned in despatches four times. He died aged 46 in hospital after an operation. Lieutenant William Synge who fought with the King's Liverpool regiment retired as a captain and apart from writing up his experiences of the Great War, he put pen to paper again in 1926 with the publication of *The Story of the World at War* and in 1952 wrote *The Story of the Green Howards 1939–45*. He died in 1968 aged 72. Another officer who turned to writing was Lieutenant Arthur Mills. Mills came from a family of authors, his brother George was the author of *Meredith and Co* and *King Willow* whilst his father, Arthur, wrote *India in 1858* which is still in print! Promoted to captain, Mills was wounded at La Bassée and during his convalescence in 1916 wrote *With My Regiment: From the Aisne to La Bassée* and *Hospital Days*. At his wedding to Lady Dorothy Walpole in 1916, her wedding ring was reputed to have been made from a bullet which had been removed from his ankle. Mills eventually became known as an author of cheap crime and adventure novels.

The Eton-educated Lieutenant Evelyn Jack Needham of the Northamptonshire Regiment was mentioned in despatches for his work on the Chemin des Dames on 14 September. He retired with the rank of major having spent the final period of the war in the RFC and wrote *The First Three Months – The Impressions of an Amateur Infantry Subaltern* in 1936. His brother Robert also served in the same regiment but was taken prisoner later in the war, Evelyn died in 1956 aged 68 and his brother – who remained unmarried – twelve years later in 1968.

Christopher Baker-Carr the volunteer driver with the Royal Automobile Club also recorded his story in print after the war and wrote *From Chauffeur to Brigadier* in 1930. The former Rifle Brigade officer was soon brought back into service and after establishing the Machine Gun School at St Omer he laid the foundations for the formation of the Machine Gun Corps. By 1916 he was in command of a battalion of tanks and a year later was appointed a brigadier general in command of the first brigade of tanks. Awarded the DSO in 1916 he survived the war and died near Norwich in January 1949. Cranley Onslow's brief appearance on the Aisne with the Bedfordshires led to a period of recuperation before he was back in France in January 1915 commanding the 2nd Battalion. Awarded the DSO and a CMG in the King's Birthday Honours list of 1915, he was wounded again at the Battle of Loos. He was back again in January 1916 commanding the 1st Battalion, finally being promoted to full lieutenant colonel in February. At the Battle of Messines he commanded 7 Brigade. Brigadier General Onslow was mentioned in despatches three times and died in December 1940. Tragically his son Captain Geoffrey Onslow was killed on 1 June 1940 at Dunkirk.

The irrepressible Lieutenant James Hyndson who had played cricket for England and Surrey before the war, was promoted to captain in March 1915 and survived the war to write his experiences of serving with the Loyal North Lancs in *From Mons to the First Battle of Ypres* which was published in 1932. Sadly he died three years later in February 1935 aged only 42. Another cricketer was Lieutenant Hon Lionel Tennyson who was captain of the Hampshire side from 1919–1932. He succeeded his father to the title of Lord Tennyson in 1928 having retired from the army with the rank of major. He was wounded on three occasions and mentioned in despatches twice. In 1933 he published his autobiography *From Verse to Worse*. He died in 1951 aged 61. The title went to his son Mark Aubrey Tennyson.

Gerald Whittuck of the Somerset Light Infantry rose to become brigade major of 129 Brigade in 1918 and finished the war as a major. He was described as a, 'capable officer, with a *sangfroid* that nothing could disturb', an accolade earned in May 1918 when he once again found himself on the Aisne. He remained in the army and served in the Second World War as a brigadier general.

Lieutenant Gerald Lowry who served with the Royal Irish Rifles was shot in the head and blinded on 25 October 1914. Promoted to captain two days after he was wounded he was taken off the active list and placed on half pay in 1915. In 1925 he qualified as an osteopath and wrote of his experiences in *From Mons to 1933*. John Lucy who served with Lowry as a corporal in the Irish Rifles was commissioned shortly afterwards and rose to become a lieutenant colonel. Lucy's commanding officer, Lieutenant Colonel Wilkinson Bird was less fortunate, he was badly wounded on the Aisne resulting in the loss of a leg, a misfortune shared by Major Tom Bridges who had a leg amputated in 1917 when commanding the 19th Division at Ypres. Whereas Wilkinson Bird was content to retire, Bridges was clearly not. In 1922 Lieutenant General Sir George Tom Molesworth Bridges was appointed governor of South Australia, a position he held until 1927. Bridges died in November 1939 but not before he had written several books including his autobiography *Alarms and Excursions*. Young Ben Clouting who followed Bridges up the hill at Paissy on 20 September also survived the war and lived to the ripe old age of 93, finally passing away in August 1990.

Alexander Johnston, the 7 Brigade signalling officer, eventually rose through the ranks to command 10/Cheshires in August 1916, a year later he was promoted again and appointed to command 126 Infantry Brigade but within days of taking up his new post he was badly wounded. He finished his war having been mentioned in despatches five times and with a DSO and bar. A first-class county cricketer before the war, Johnston's legacy of the Great War was a permanent limp; nevertheless he continued to play cricket after the war until 1933. He died in December 1952. Lieutenant Arthur Acland, the adjutant of 1/DCLI, also rose to battalion command but had to wait until 1934 before he was appointed. Prior to that he was mentioned in despatches seven times and won a Military Cross and the DSO. He was appointed lieutenant general in 1941, retiring from the army a year later. He died in 1980.

Jock Marden after being wounded near Paissy on 20 September, was back with the regiment on 30 October in time to take part in the last attempt by Allenby's cavalry to hold the Messines Ridge. Wounded again in the head on 19 November he was invalided to England where he remained for the rest of the war. Invalided out of the army at the end of hostilities, Marden turned his attention to skiing, winning the British Championship in 1926. Two years later in 1928 he died attempting to make the first winter ski ascent of Mount Aconcagua in

South America which, at 6,962 metres, is the highest mountain beyond the Himalyas. He is buried in the small Climber's Cemetery at Punte del Inca.

Others were content to forget the war years as much as they could and, barring Second World War service, attempted to settle down to a more normal existence. Lieutenant Cecil Brereton, the gunner subaltern who served with 68 Battery, retired as a major and died on his 65th Birthday in October 1953, whilst Jack Hay continued to serve as a dispatch rider until 1917 when he joined the RFC as an observer. He saw service in the Second World War as a squadron leader, retiring with the rank of wing commander in 1946. Hay died in 1978. Sergeant Reeve ended his war as BQMS in 315 Brigade RFA, Sergeant Bradlaugh Sanderson of the KRRC was wounded at Ypres and after leaving the British Red Cross hospital at Hale near Altrincham he arrived home at Holmfirth on sick leave early in 1915. His diary was first published in the *Holmfirth Express*. Corporal Cuthbert Avis who fought with the Queen's on the Chemin des Dames returned to the battalion after recovering from his wounds, was promoted to sergeant and discharged in 1921. Another diarist, Sergeant John McIlwain of the Connaught Rangers ended his war with the rank of colour sergeant having been awarded the French *Médaille Militaire* which was gazetted in August 1918. He was wounded at Ypres in November 1914 and later served with the 5th Battalion on the Gallipoli Peninsula in 1915.

Of the seven Victoria Cross winners, three were later killed in action and four went on to survive the war. Apart from Captain Harry Ranken who is buried in Braine Communal Cemetery, Captain William Johnston was killed by a sniper on 8 June 1915 south of Ypres and is buried at Perth Cemetery (China Wall) and Ernest Horlock was drowned on 30 December 1917 when the SS *Aragon* was sunk 10 miles off Alexandria. Battery Sergeant Major Horlock – as he was then – was one of the 610 on board who were drowned. He is buried at Alexandria War Memorial Cemetery. As for the survivors, if we exclude William Fuller who was discharged in 1915 as unfit for further service and lived until he was 90, the other VC recipients did not fare so well. Ross Tollerton was promoted to sergeant and after the war became the janitor at Bank Street School, Irvine. He died in May 1931 aged 41. The man whose life he saved, James Matheson also died a young man in February 1933. George Wilson died of tuberculosis in Craigleigh Hospital, Edinburgh, in April 1926 aged only 39 and eight years later, William Dobson, the Coldstream guardsman, who won his cross near Cour de Soupir Farm, died aged 49. He is buried at Ryton Cemetery, County Durham.

Lieutenant Cyril Martin, the RE officer who first inspected the bridge at Vailly won the Victoria Cross at Spanbroekmolen in 1915 when he volunteered to lead a bombing party, despite being wounded before he started; he continued the attack and held a section of enemy trench for two and a half hours until ordered to retire. He later achieved the rank of brigadier general serving in the Second World War as Chief Engineer in Iraq. He died in August 1980. Kenneth Godsell the young RE officer who took such delight in watching Brigadier Gleichen's horse swimming the river won a DSO and MC and survived the war as did Jim Pennyman, the KOSB officer who was badly wounded at Missy. Bernard Young of 9/Field Company, who wrote so descriptively of his experiences and spent most of his time on the Aisne building and repairing bridges, was another survivor and eventually, after an illustrious career spanning two world wars, retired as a major general and died in 1969.

Sadly the two RFC pilots who worked so hard to introduce the use of wireless transmission from the air did not survive. Both men remained with the RFC and continued their work in developing wireless, Captain Baron Trevenen James MC was killed on 13 July 1915 during a solo test flight over enemy lines in an aircraft from 6 Squadron and Lieutenant Colonel Donald Swain Lewis DSO was killed on 10 April 1916 by the very guns which he had been spotting for – a tragic case of 'friendly fire'. Lewis is buried at Lijssenthoek Military Cemetery and James is commemorated on the Arras Flying Service Memorial. Sergeant Major Victor Laws who was attached to the 'Pom-Pom' unit at Bucy-le-Long, returned to 3 Squadron and began a long career developing air photography. After serving in both world wars, he retired in 1946 with the rank of group captain and died in 1975. Kenlis Atkinson returned to the RFA and won a Military Cross in September 1918 near Cambrai whilst in command of a battery of CLXXVII Brigade guns. William Read remained in the RFC becoming commanding officer of both 45 and 216 Squadrons. He won an MC in 1916 and the new award of the DFC was made in 1919 and a year later he was awarded the Air Force Cross and bar. James McCudden, the young mechanic who flew with Baron James, became one of the most celebrated air aces of the war. He was killed on 9 July 1918 whilst in command of 60 Squadron. On his death, aged 23, he had accounted for fifty-four enemy aircraft and had been awarded the Military Medal, Military Cross and bar, DSO and bar and in March 1918 was posthumously awarded the Victoria Cross.

Captain Henry Jackson returned to the ground in 1915 and a year later was commanding 8/Bedfords, he finished his war as a major general in command of 50th Division where he found himself once again on the Aisne in May 1918, this time facing the German Blücher-Yorck offensive. He was awarded the DSO and mentioned in despatches on eight occasions. Sir Henry Jackson died in 1972 having reached the grand old age of 93. Captain Hubert Rees, a company commander with 2/Welch, was another officer who would return to the Aisne in 1918, this time in command of 150 Brigade and serving under Henry Jackson in the 50th Division. On the opening day of the Blücher-Yorck offensive 150 Brigade was surrounded giving Rees little alternative but to surrender. Before he was transferred to Germany and captivity he was taken to meet the Kaiser on the Craonne plateau, a meeting during which the Kaiser was said to have been amused that Rees was Welsh – the same nationality as Lloyd George. Rees died in 1948.

Captain Arthur Osburn, the medical officer attached to 4/Dragoon Guards, won a DSO and retired from the RAMC as a lieutenant colonel. He wrote of his experiences in *Unwilling Passenger* and died in 1952 aged 75. Gerard Kempthorne was eventually repatriated in 1915 as was Captain Robert Dolbey who was captured near La Bassée with the KOSB in October 1914. Dolbey also wrote a book describing his time on the Aisne and his subsequent captivity, *A Regimental Surgeon in War and Prison* was published in 1917. Bertie Ratcliffe the West Yorkshire officer who was captured on 20 September and later escaped from the train near Crefeld, was awarded the Military Cross and apparently had tea with the king who wanted to hear of his escapades. Private John Cooper was not invited to tea neither was Sergeant Edward Facer but both men received the Military Medal in 1920 in recognition of their successful escape.

Sir John French who commanded the BEF on the Aisne continued clinging to command until the failures at Aubers Ridge, Festubert and Loos forced Lord Kitchener to replace him with Sir Douglas Haig in December 1915. Ideally this should have taken place before the BEF moved to Flanders. Sadly for General Sir Horace Smith-Dorrien 1915 was not a good year either. The tensions between him and Sir John came to a head after Smith-Dorrien advocated a tactical withdrawal in April 1915 to consolidate the front line at Ypres. Sir John was still bearing a grudge over Le Cateau and used Smith-Dorrien's suggestion of a withdrawal to remove him, accusing him of having a pessimistic outlook. To add insult to injury, several days later Sir John accepted the advice of General Herbert Plumer – Smith-Dorrien's replacement – to perform a withdrawal almost identical to the one which Smith-Dorrien had recommended. Smith-Dorrien died in August 1939 following a car accident.

If there is a final line which can be drawn under the Aisne campaign of 1914 it is perhaps contained in the words of Frederick Coleman, the RAC volunteer driver as he headed towards Flanders with 2 Cavalry Brigade: 'The Aisne we had reached with such sanguine hopes twenty-one days before was still the high water mark of our advance'.

Notes on Sources

Introduction

1. For a greater understanding of the Battle of Mons and Le Cateau see *Retreat and Rearguard 1914* by Jerry Murland.

Chapter 1

2. Sergeant Evelyn Guy Whiteman is buried at Perreuse Château Franco British National Cemetery at Signy-Signets. Grave Reference: 1.D.34. Lance Corporal William Ticehurst is buried at Pécy Communal Cemetery.
3. Bridges, *Alarms and Excursions*, p.93.
4. Herwig, *The Marne 1914, The Opening of World War 1 and the Battle Which Changed the World*, p.xii.
5. Ibid, pp.221–2.
6. Ibid, p.222.
7. Cited in Barnett, *The Sword Bearers*, p.98.
8. Ibid, p.101.
9. Colin Robert Ballard was commanding officer of the 1st Norfolks in August 1914 when, along with the 1st Cheshires, 2nd Cavalry Brigade and 119 Battery, RHA, he fought in the rearguard action at Audregnies on 24 August. He was wounded in 1916 whilst commanding 57 Infantry Brigade. He retired from the army in 1923 and died in 1941. His book, *Smith-Dorrien* was published in 1931.
10. The 3rd and 6th Cavalry Brigades had been detached from the Cavalry Division and were now under the command of Hubert Gough. On 16 September they became part of the 2nd Cavalry Division.
11. Herwig, The *Marne 1914, The Opening of World War 1 and the Battle Which Changed the World*, p.xv.
12. Captain John Clive Darling was the signalling officer of 20/Hussars in 1914. He was awarded the DSO and mentioned in despatches. He finished the war as a major and wrote the history of the regiment. He died in 1933, aged 45.
13. Wyrall, *The History of the Duke of Cornwall's Light Infantry 1914–1918*, p.54.
14. Gleichen, *The Doings of the Fifteenth Infantry Brigade*, p.62.
15. Dolbey, *A Regimental Surgeon in War and Prison*, p.33.
16. Figures cited by Sir John French to Lord Kitchener in TNA WO 33/713.
17. Astil, *The Great War Diaries of Brigadier General Alexander Johnston*, p.19.
18. Anglesey, *The History of the British Cavalry Volume 7*, p.185.

19. Ibid, Campbell's account, p.185–6.
20. Lamb, *Country Life*, Vol. 38.
21. Gleichen, *The Doings of the Fifteenth Infantry Brigade*, p.62.
22. Private Papers of C L Brereton. IWM Dept. of Documents, 86/30/1.
23. Young, *Diary of an RE Subaltern*.
24. War Diary of 20/Field Ambulance, TNA WO 95/129.
25. Captain Robin Grey and Captain Robert Albany Boger of 5 Squadron RFC were shot down and taken prisoner on 5 October 1914.
26. Private Papers of C L Brereton. IWM Dept. of Documents, 86/30/1.
27. Astil, *The Great War Diaries of Brigadier General Alexander Johnston*, p.21.
28. Private Papers of A Reeve. IWM Dept. of Documents, 90/20/1.
29. Ballard, *Smith-Dorrien*, p.210.

Chapter 3
30. Barnett, *The Sword Bearers*, p.101.
31. Bidwell & Graham, *Fire-Power*, p.41.
32. Griffith, *Battle Tactics of the Western Front*, p.13.
33. Carl Philipp Gottfried von Clausewitz was the son of a retired lieutenant and first encountered war as a 12-year-old lance corporal in 1793, eventually attaining the rank of major general. He is famous primarily as a military theorist interested in the examination of war. He wrote a careful, systematic, philosophical examination of war in all its aspects, as he saw it and taught it. The result was his principal work, *On War*, the West's premier work on the philosophy of war.
34. Clausewitz, *On War*.
35. Bloem, *The Advance from Mons*, p.183.
36. Ibid, p.153.
37. Three of these battalions were deployed to escort prisoners.
38. War Diary of Adjutant of IR 53/3 found in TNA WO 95/1566.
39. Von Poseck, *The German Cavalry 1914 in Belgium and France*, p.122.
40. Further reinforcements would arrive within twenty-four hours in the shape of two battalions released from Maubeuge and two 8-inch howitzer batteries.
41. The I Corps War Diary, TNA WO 95/588.
42. The Private Papers of J L Mowbray, IWM Dept. of Documents, 82/16/1.
43. Brigadier General Phillip Howell was killed in action on 7 October 1916. He is buried at Varennes Military Cemetery, near Albert, grave reference: I.B.37.
44. Evans and Laing, *The 4th (Queen's Own) Hussars in the Great War*, p.18.
45. Wilson took over command of the 4th Division on 9 September from Major General Thomas Snow who was injured in a riding accident. Brigadier General Frederick Anley was given command of 12 Brigade.
46. Young, *Diary of an RE Subaltern*.
47. Captain Frank Fisher, Lieutenant Horatio John Vicat and Sergeant William Burr are commemorated on the La Ferté-sous-Jouarre Memorial.
48. Walker, *From the Curragh to the Aisne 1914*.
49. The Personal Diary of Kenneth Godsell, RE Archive.
50. 54-year-old Major General Hubert Ian Wetherall Hamilton was killed on 14 October 1914 and is buried at Cheriton (St Mary's) Churchyard in Kent.
51. Osburn, *Unwilling Passenger*, p.142.
52. The Private Papers of Captain B J N Marden. IWM Dept. of Documents, 14292.

53. Needham, *The First Three Months*, p.53.
54. The Diary of Corporal J N R Perks.
55. The 50-year-old Lieutenant Colonel Alexander William Abercrombie died in captivity on 5 November 1915. He is buried at the Berlin South Western Cemetery. Grave Reference: IX.A.7.
56. Dutchmen is a term used throughout the Gordon Lennox diary and would appear to be a corruption of Deutscher or Deutscherman.
57. Private Diary of Major Bernard Gordon Lennox, Grenadier Guards Archive.

Chapter 5

58. Gordon Corrigan, *Mud, Blood and Poppycock*, p.199.
59. Private Papers of Lord Tennyson. IWM Dept. of Documents, 76/21/1.
60. 4th Division War Diary, TNA WO 95/1439.
61. Typescript diary held in the Somerset Light Infantry Archive.
62. Bloem, *The Advance from Mons* p.193.
63. C J Griffin DSO, *The Lancashire Fusiliers' Annual 1916*, No. XXVII. pp.84–88.
64. Private Papers of C L Brereton. IWM Dept. of Documents, 86/30/1.
65. Company commanders during the attack were as follows: Captain J E S Woodman – A Company, Second Lieutenant J Evatt – B Company, Lieutenant A J W Blencowe – C Company and Lieutenant J Fulton – D Company.
66. 25-year-old John Sydney Paulson is buried in St Marguerite Churchyard.
67. 2/Battalion Lancashire Fusiliers War Diary, TNA WO 95/1495.
68. 4th Division War Diary, TNA WO 95/1439.
69. Sergeant Charles Dorey and Rifleman Charles Spindler are buried at Vauxbuin French National Cemetery, grave references: III.E.7 and III.E.6. The Sergeant Walker referred to is probably 5653 Sergeant Walker who was later discharged from the army.
70. Private Papers of Lord Tennyson. IWM Dept. of Documents, 76/21/1.
71. Lieutenant Kenneth Morley Loch (1890–1961) served with 68/Battery until 1916 when he became an instructor in gunnery, at School of Instruction for Royal Horse Artillery and Royal Field Artillery until returning to active service in Italy during 1918. Between the wars Loch was involved in air defence preparations for Britain and the British Empire. From the beginning of the Second World War until 1941, Loch was Director of Anti-Aircraft and Coastal Defence. He retired with the rank of lieutenant general.
72. Private Papers of C L Brereton. IWM Dept. of Documents, 86/30/1.
73. Cited by Macdonald in, *1914*, pp.302–3.
74. Haldane, *A Brigade of the Old Army, 1914*, p.107.
75. Private Papers of C L Brereton. IWM Dept. of Documents, 86/30/1.
76. Manuscript diary held in the Somerset Light Infantry Archive.
77. XXXVII Brigade RFA War Diary, TNA WO 95/1467.
78. Second Lieutenant Arthur Beddone Read is buried at Vailly British Cemetery. Grave Reference: IV.G.12. He was 23-years-old.

Chapter 6

79. Major J E C Livingstone-Learmonth. His brother, Captain J N C Livingstone-Learmonth was killed at Gallipoli on 24 August 1915.
80. 108/Battery War Diary, TNA WO 95/542.
81. The Diary of JBW Pennyman. Teeside Archives, U.PEN/7/150.

82. 2/Bridging Train War Diary, TNA WO 95/4999.
83. This view was disputed by Major General George Addison in 1935 who had previously served as a captain with 23/Field Company in September 1914. Addison maintained that the divisions advancing on the Aisne would not have welcomed the addition of the bridging trains and to have 'sub-allotted' them earlier would have been a grave error of judgement. However, evidence would seem to suggest that a more comprehensive bridging plan may have contributed to greater success on the battlefield.
84. Gleichen, *Infantry Brigade 1914,* p.80.
85. Ibid, p.81.
86. 1/East Surrey War Diary, TNA WO 95/1563.
87. Crookenden, *The History of the Cheshire Regiment, in the Great War,* p.24.
88. Private Papers of CC Onslow. IWM Dept. of Documents 86/9/1.
89. The Diary of JBW Pennyman. Teeside Archives, U.PEN/7/150.
90. Ibid.
91. Dolbey, *A Regimental Surgeon in War and Prison,* p.55.
92. The Diary of JBW Pennyman. Teeside Archives, U.PEN/7/150.
93. Private Papers of CC Onslow. IWM Dept. of Documents, 86/9/1.
94. 1/East Surrey War Diary, TNA WO 95/1563.
95. The Private Diary of Cyril Helm. Western Front Association 2008.
96. Ibid.
97. Brereton, *The Great War and the RAMC,* p.246.
98. Private papers of CC Onslow. IWM Dept. of Documents, 86/9/1.
99. The Diary of JBW Pennyman. Teeside Archives, U.PEN/7/150.

Chapter 7
100. Rushton was recommended for the Victoria Cross along with Sergeant William Boyd for bringing in the badly wounded Lieutenant R Phillips whilst under fire, at Mons on 23 August. Neither awards were made, Boyd was taken prisoner at Le Cateau and 26-year-old Frederick Hornby Lever Rushton MC was killed in action on 14 September. He is commemorated on the la Ferté–sous-Jouarre Memorial.
101. The rather bizarre events which led up to the incident involving the Gordon Highlanders at Audencourt are detailed in several histories and accounts. *The Official History* covers the incident on pp.187–88 as do Nigel Cave and Jack Sheldon in *Le Cateau,* pp.107–8.
102. Simpson, *The History of the Lincolnshire Regiment 1914–1918.*
103. Private Papers of G A Kempthorne. IWM Dept. of Documents, 79/17/1.
104. Ewing, *Royal Scots 1914–1919,* Vol. 1.
105. Cited in, *The Die-Hards in the Great War,* Vol. 1, p.56.
106. Cited in, *The Die-Hards in the Great War,* Vol. 1, p.59.
107. Captain George Clarke Briggs was 36-years-old. He is buried at Vailly British Cemetery. Grave Reference: III.A.26.
108. Private Papers of G A Kempthorne. IWM Dept. of Documents, 79/17/1.
109. Edmonds, *Military Operations – France and Belgium 1914.* p.351.
110. Darling in his history of the 20th Hussars quotes 13 September but Anglesey in *A History of the British Cavalry* states it was 15 September.
111. Darling, *20th Hussars in the Great War,* p.38.
112. Private Papers of B C Myatt, IWM Dept. of Documents, 97/4/1.
113. Lucy, *There's A Devil in the Drum,* p.168.

114. Ibid, pp.170–1.
115. Lowry, *From Mons to 1933*.
116. Darling, *20th Hussars in the Great War*, p.38.
117. The two officers were Second Lieutenants Richard Henry Cole Magenis aged 27 and Henry Poyntz Swaine, aged 24. Both men are commemorated on the La Ferté-sous-Jouarre Memorial. Henry Magenis had only been with the battalion for twenty-one days.
118. Lowry, *From Mons to 1933*.
119. The Lincolns war diary suggests this attack took place at midnight, but this is not mentioned in other accounts. There may of course have been several attacks but as the Lincolns were out of the firing line it is easy to understand how these events became blurred.
120. 8/Field Ambulance War Diary, TNA WO 95/1407.
121. Ibid.
122. Definition: a fold of the tissue lining the abdomen which surrounds the organs.
123. 8/Field Ambulance War Diary, TNA WO 95/1407.

Chapter 8
124. Hanbury-Sparrow, *The Land Locked Lake*.
125. This is almost certainly the Maison Brulée referred to in the *Official History* which was situated on the eastern side of the l'Oise à l'Aisne Canal. The current location on modern maps does not, however, match the location on 1914 maps. The building was not reconstructed after the war.
126. Hanbury-Sparrow, *The Land Locked Lake*.
127. Synge, *From the Marne to the Aisne – The Diary of an Infantry Subaltern*, p.109.
128. Marval is in all probability a mis-spelling of Malval.
129. William Stirling Bannatyne was killed on 24 October 1914 and is commemorated on the Menin Gate Memorial, Ieper. He was 45-years-old.
130. 1/King's Liverpool Regiment War Diary, TNA WO 95/1359.
131. Ibid.
132. Hanbury-Sparrow, *The Land Locked Lake*.
133. I Corps War Diary, TNA WO 95/588.
134. Tilleul de Courtcon is at the junction of the track running north along the Moussy spur with the minor road leading to the Chapelle de Courtecon. It is situated on the Chemin des Dames just over a mile west of the Cerny-en-Laonnois crossroads.
135. Private Diary of Major Bernard Gordon Lennox, Grenadier Guards Archive.
136. 2/Connaught Rangers War Diary, TNA WO 95/1347.
137. Although the family name of this officer was Pickersgill-Cuncliffe, he is referred to as Cuncliffe in George Jeffrey's account of the fight at Cour de Soupir and in the Grenadiers' history. For the sake of clarity I have continued to refer to him as Cuncliffe. However the CWGC lists him as John Reynolds Pickersgill-Cuncliffe. He is buried at Soupir Communal Cemetery, grave reference: B.4.
138. 2/Connaught Rangers War Diary, TNA WO 95/1347.
139. Major Sir Torquhil George Matheson, 5th Baronet of Lochalsh, was commanding the battalion as the Commanding Officer, Lieutenant Colonel Fielding, was in temporary command of the brigade at the time.
140. Craster, *Fifteen Rounds a Minute*, p.84.

141. 31-year-old Captain Alwyn Bertram Robert Raphael Gosselin DSO, was killed in action on 7 February 1915. He is buried at Cuinchy Communal Cemetery. Grave Reference: II.D.23.
142. Lieutenant Cecil Francis Aleck Walker, Grenadier Guards.
143. Lieutenant Granville Charles FitzHerbert Harcourt-Vernon, Grenadier Guards.
144. Private Diary of Major Bernard Gordon Lennox, Grenadier Guards Archive. Captain Lord Heneage Greville Finch Guernsey, Irish Guards, is buried at Soupir Communal Cemetery. The CWGC gives no grave reference. 25-year-old Captain Lord Arthur Vincent Hay, Irish Guards, is buried at Soupir Communal Cemetery, grave reference: A.5. 25-year-old Lieutenant Richard William Gregory Welby, Grenadier Guards, was killed in action on 16 September 1914 and is also buried at Soupir Communal Cemetery, grave reference: B.2.
145. XXVI Brigade War Diary, TNA WO 95/1325.
146. Captain William Cecil Holt Cree died of wounds on 24 October 1914 and is buried at Falmouth Cemetery, Cornwall, grave reference: I.B.58.
147. 36 Brigade War Diary, TNA WO 95/1325.
148. Ibid.
149. Craster, *Fifteen Rounds a Minute*, p.86.
150. I Corps War Diary, TNA WO 95/588.
151. Osburn, *Unwilling Passenger*, p.144.
152. 11/Hussars War Diary, TNA WO 95/1109.
153. Victor Aloysius Lentaigne is commemorated on La Ferté-sous-Jouarre Memorial.
154. Private Papers of J McIlwain. IWM Dept. of Documents, 96/29/1.
155. 24-year-old Frederick William des Voeux is buried at Soupir Communal Cemetery, grave reference: B.3. So too is 23-year-old Richard William Mark Lockwood, Coldstream Guards, grave reference: A.6.
156. 23-year-old Richard William Mark Lockwood is buried at Soupir Communal Cemetery, grave reference: A.3.
157. 26-year-old Percy Lyulph Wyndham is commemorated on the La Ferté-sous-Jouarre Memorial.
158. Lieutenant Hon Edward Wyndham Tennant was killed in action on 22 September 1916 and is buried at Guillemont Road Cemetery. Grave Reference: I.B.18. Tennant became well known as a war poet, his *Worple Flit and other poems* was published posthumously by Blackwell in 1916.
159. Charles Dalton LRCP died of his wounds in L'Hôpital Farm on 18 September 1914. He is the only casualty of the Great War buried at the Veil-Arcy Communal Cemetery.
160. Assistant Director of Medical Services.
161. Brereton, *The Great War and the RAMC*, p.222.
162. In January 1914 Calmette launched a campaign against Minister of Finance Joseph Caillaux, who had introduced progressive taxation and was known for his pacifist stance towards Germany. During this campaign *Le Figaro* published numerous letters from the Minister's private correspondence. Caillaux's second wife, Henriette, alarmed that the newspaper would also make public a love letter proving their relationship was taking place during his first marriage, entered Calmette's office on 16 March 1914 and shot him. Calmette died instantly. Caillaux resigned his post

the next day, but during a highly publicised trial later in the year Henriette was acquitted, a verdict which caused riots in the streets of Paris.

163. Extract from an unsigned diary found in WO 95/1226.

164. The Private Papers of J McIlwain, IWM Dept. of Documents, 96/29/1.

Chapter 9

165. Bond, *The Royal Engineers Journal*, September 1938.

166. The Private Papers of Captain B J N Marden. IWM Dept. of Documents, 14292.

167. Captain Douglas Keith Lucas Lucas-Tooth, 9/(Queen's Royal) Lancers, is buried at Moulins New Communal Cemetery, grave reference: 1. His eldest brother, 35-year-old Captain Selwyn Lucas Lucas-Tooth, Lancashire Fusiliers, was killed on 20 October 1914 and is buried at Le Touquet Railway Crossing Cemetery, grave reference: A.10. Tragically another brother, 34-year-old Major Sir Archibald Leonard Lucas Lucas-Tooth was killed on 12 July 1918 serving with the Honourable Artillery Company. He is buried at Aubigny Communal Cemetery, grave reference: V.B.4.

168. 2 Cavalry Brigade losses on 24 August 1914 were 234 officers and men killed and wounded. The battle at Audregnies is described in the author's book on the retreat from Mons, *Retreat and Rearguard 1914*.

169. 2/KRRC War Diary, TNA WO/951272.

170. Sanderson, *A Holmfirth Soldier's Diary*.

171. The Private Papers of Captain B J N Marden. IWM Dept. of Documents, 14292.

172. 34-year-old Riversdale Nonus Grenfell is buried at Vendresse Churchyard. His twin brother, Francis Octavius Grenfell, also of 9/Lancers, was killed in action on 24 May 1915. He is buried at Vlamertinghe Military Cemetery, grave reference: II.B.14. Francis was awarded the Victoria Cross at Audregnies on 24 August 1914. The Grenfell twins were from a notable military family. Their maternal grandfather was Admiral John Pascoe Grenfell and other relatives included their uncle, Field Marshal Francis Grenfell, 1st Baron Grenfell. An older brother, Lieutenant Robert Septimus Grenfell, 21st Lancers, was killed in a cavalry charge during the Battle of Omdurman in 1898. Three other brothers, Cecil Alfred, Howard Maxwell and Arthur Morton Grenfell, all reached the rank of Lieutenant Colonel. A cousin, Lieutenant Claude George Grenfell was killed at Spion Kop during the Boer War and two other cousins Julian Grenfell, the poet, and his brother, Gerald William Grenfell, were also killed in the Great War.

173. Captain Augustus Ernest Cathcart, aged 39 is buried at Paissy Churchyard, grave reference: Sp Memorial 1. Second Lieutenant Stuart Davison is buried at Vendresse British Cemetery, grave reference: I.J.14.

174. Sanderson, *A Holmfirth Soldier's Diary*.

175. 1/Loyal North Lancs War Diary, TNA WO 95/1270.

176. Lieutenants Herbert Reuben Loomes and George Henry Goldie were killed on 14 September 1914 and are commemorated on the La Ferté-sous-Jouarre Memorial.

177. 1/Loyal North Lancs War Diary, TNA WO 95/1270.

178. Both Walter Reginald Lloyd and Richard Howard-Vyse are commemorated on the La Ferté-sous-Jouarre Memorial.

179. 1/Loyal North Lancs War Diary, TNA WO 95/1270.

180. An account of this rearguard action can be found in the author's *Retreat and Rearguard 1914*.
181. 1/Queen's Own Cameron Highlanders War Diary, TNA WO 95/1264.
182. Ponsonby, TNA WO/95/1236.
183. Ibid.
184. Needham, *The First Three Months–The Impressions of an Amateur Infantry Subaltern*.
185. Ibid.
186. 37-year-old Captain Lionel Theopilus Allason was killed in action on 7 October 1914. He is commemorated on the La Ferté-sous-Jouarre Memorial.
187. 1/Loyal North Lancs War Diary, TNA WO 95/1270.
188. Sanderson, *A Holmfirth Soldier's Diary*.
189. 22-year-old Arthur Dennis Harding died of wounds received at Geluvelt on 30 October 1914. He is buried at Ypres Town Cemetery. Grave Reference: E2.10.
190. The Battle of Inkerman was fought during the Crimean War on 5 November 1854 between the armies of Britain and France against the Imperial Russian Army. The battle broke the will of the Russian Army to defeat the Allies in the field, and was followed by the Siege of Sevastopol. The fighting was characterized by small parties of troops, fighting mostly on their own initiative due to the misty conditions, earning the engagement the name 'The Soldier's Battle'.
191. 1/Loyal North Lancs War Diary, TNA WO 95/1270.
192. 41-year-old Alfred Henry Maitland commanded A Company and is commemorated on the La Ferté-sous-Jouarre Memorial.
193. See An Officers Letters from 1914 at http://www.westernfrontassociation.com/great-war-people/48-brothers-arms/300-off-letter-1914.html
194. Captain Alastair Hugh Mackintosh and Lieutenant Hector William Lovett Cameron are commemorated on the La Ferté-sous-Jouarre Memorial. 20-year-old Second Lieutenant Alastair John Greville Murray is buried at Montcornet Military Cemetery, grave reference: L.8. CSM John Wood is buried at Vendresse Churchyard. Hector Cameron's death is described by Private Arthur Burgess in Chapter 14.
195. Quoted in Edmonds, *Military Operations – France and Belgium 1914* p.364.
196. 38-year-old Captain Mark Haggard died of wounds in 15 September 1914 and is buried at Vendresse British Cemetery, grave reference: I.G.11.
197. The names of Lord George Stewart Murray, Lewis Robert Cumming and Reginald G Don are commemorated on the La Ferté-sous-Jouarre Memorial. Lieutenant Colonel Adrian Grant-Duff is buried at Moulins New Communal Cemetery. 20-year-old Nigel John Lawson died of wounds in Edinburgh on 12 September 1914. He is buried at the Edinburgh Western Cemetery, grave reference: I.110.
198. Gerard Frederick Freeman-Thomas was 21-years-old when he was killed and is commemorated on the La Ferté-sous-Jouarre Memorial.
199. 51-year-old Ernest Henry Montresor and Sergeant George William Hutson are commemorated on the La Ferté-sous-Jouarre Memorial.
200. Naval and Military Press, *Soldiers Died in the Great War* database.
201. 46-year-old Walter Reginald Lloyd is commemorated on the La Ferté-sous-Jouarre Memorial.

Chapter 10
202. Edmonds, *Military Operations France and Belgium 1914*, p.384.
203. Cited in Ousby, *The Road to Verdun*, p.37.
204. Mills, *With My Regiment*, p.47.
205. Major Anthony Drummond Boden's name is commemorated on the La Ferté-sous-Jouarre Memorial. There is no record of a MacKenzie of the 3/RB being killed.
206. The Private Papers of E R Meade-Waldo. IWM Dept. of Documents, 76/227/1.
207. Private Diary of Major Bernard Gordon Lennox, Grenadier Guards Archive.
208. James Laidlaw Huggan is commemorated on the La Ferté-sous-Jouarre Memorial.
209. Ronald Francis Simson was 24-years-old and is buried at Moulins New Communal Cemetery, grave reference: 2. He was the first Rugby Union international to be killed in the Great War.
210. Harry Sherwood Ranken is buried at Braine Communal Cemetery, grave reference: A.43.
211. The name of William Ormsby Wyndham Ball is commemorated on the La Ferté-sous-Jouarre Memorial. He was 24-years-old.
212. Needham, *The First Three Months*, p.58.
213. Manuscript diary held in the Somerset Light Infantry Archive.
214. Needham, *The First Three Months*, p.60.
215. Robert Burton Parker was 35-years-old and is commemorated on the La Ferté-sous-Jouarre Memorial.
216. Needham, *The First Three Months*, p.61.
217. John Arkdeen Savage is commemorated on the La Ferté-sous-Jouarre Memorial. John Henry Stephen Dimmer was awarded the Victoria Cross for his actions on 12 November 1914 at Klein Zillebeke in Belgium. Dimmer later achieved the rank of lieutenant colonel. He was killed in action at Marteville, France on 21 March 1918. His Victoria Cross is displayed at the Royal Green Jackets Museum, Winchester, England.
218. Needham, *The First Three Months*, p.62.
219. Cosmo George Gordon is buried at Vailly British Cemetery, grave reference: II.E.7.
220. The Private Papers of J G Stennett. IWM Dept. of Documents, 6655.
221. Dawson Warren is buried at Paissy Churchyard, grave reference: 1. Charles Edward Wilson is buried next to him.
222. Astil , *The Great War Diaries of Brigadier General Alexander Johnston*, p.26.
223. Lucy, *There's a Devil in the Drum*, p.193.
224. Astil, *The Great War Diaries of Brigadier General Alexander Johnston*, p.27.
225. This man is probably Private 6080 R J Stagg, whose death is recorded by CWGC as 22 September 1914 and is buried at Vailly British Cemetery, grave reference: Sp Memorial 11. Gaskell may not have known at the time the man was still alive but died of wounds two days later. Captain Henry Clendon Collis Reynolds was 30-years-old and is commemorated on the La Ferté-sous-Jouarre Memorial.
226. Private papers of C H Gaskell IWM Dept. of Documents, 99/55/1.
227. Ibid.
228. Astil , *The Great War Diaries of Brigadier General Alexander Johnston*, p.27.
229. Synge, *From the Marne to the Aisne*, p.121.

230. Ibid.
231. Lieutenants James Adam Hamilton Fergusson, Evan Ronald Horatio MacDonald and Colin Landseer McKenzie were buried that evening in the same grave with Lieutenant John O'Connell on the ridge behind the HLI positions. The bodies were never recovered and their names are commemorated on the La Ferté-sous-Jouarre Memorial.
232. Lieutenants Geoffrey Russell Fenton and Raymond Montgomerie Henderson are commemorated on the La Ferté-sous-Jouarre Memorial. Second Lieutenant Robert Burton Benison is buried at Vendresse British Cemetery. Grave Reference: III.C.7. Major William Sarsfield is buried at Vailly British Cemetery. Grave Reference: II.C.11.
233. Private Diary of Major Bernard Gordon Lennox, Grenadier Guards Archive.
234. Major Billy Congreve – as he was in 1916 – was killed in action on 20 July 1916 and is buried at Corbie Communal Cemetery Extension, grave reference: I.F.35. At the time of his death he had been awarded the DSO and MC, the posthumous award of the Victoria Cross was gazetted in October 1916.

Chapter 11
235. Osburn, *Unwilling Passenger*, p.153.
236. Thomas Gilliat Meautys is buried at Vendresse British Cemetery, grave reference: III.J.10. He was 25-years-old.
237. Private Papers of C Rainbird. IWM Dept. of Documents, 02/39/1.
238. The officer in question was Lieutenant George Vyvyan Naylor-Leyland, aged 22, of the Royal Horse Guards. He died of wounds on 21 September 1914 and is buried in Vendresse Churchyard Cemetery, grave reference 1. He was the son of Sir Herbert Scarisbrick Naylor-Leyland and had been mentioned in despatches.
239. The Private Papers of Captain B J N Marden. IWM Dept. of Documents, 14292.
240. POW Report, TNA WO 161/95/98.
241. Ibid.
242. 1/West Yorkshire War Diary, TNA WO 95/1618.
243. The Private Papers of Captain B J N Marden. IWM Dept. of Documents, 14292.
244. Bridges, *Alarms and Excursions*, pp.96–7.
245. Cited by Van Emden in, *Tickled to Death to Go*, p.74.
246. 1/West Yorkshire War Diary, TNA WO 95/1618.
247. Cited by Sheffield in, *The Chief – Douglas Haig and the British Army*.
248. Frederick Coleman, *From Mons to the Marne with General French*, p.194.
249. Edmonds, *Military Operations France and Belgium 1914*, p.396.
250. Captain Robert Frank Hawes is buried at Vailly British Cemetery. Grave Reference: I.A.10. He was the first officer of the Leicesters to die in action in the Great War.
251. Lieutenant Charles Paterson, *War Diary of the 24th (SWB)*. SWB Museum Archive. W.18.66.
252. The Diary of Major G Ward. SWB Museum Archive W.2.48.
253. Ibid.
254. The names of Major Glynne Everard Welby, Lieutenants Charles Cadwell Sills and George Prescot Blackall-Simonds are commemorated on the La Ferté-sous-Jouarre Memorial. George Simonds had only been with the

battalion for five days before his death in action. Lieutenant John Cadwallader Coker is buried at Vendresse British Cemetery., grave reference: I.B.8.

255. The Diary of Major G Ward. SWB Museum Archive W.2.48.

256. Captains Douglas Miers, Allan Cameron, Lieutenants Napier Cameron, and John Crocket, RSM Burt and Private R Brown are buried at Bourg-et-Comin Communal Cemetery. Lieutenant Kenneth Meiklejohn is buried at Vendresse British Cemetery, grave reference III.C.4. The remaining men are commemorated on the La Ferté-sous-Jouarre Memorial.

257. Ewen James Brodie was killed at Ypres on 12 November 1914. His name is commemorated on the Menin Gate Memorial.

258. From an account found in TNA WO 95/1399.

Chapter 12

259. Astil, *The Great War Diaries of Brigadier General Alexander Johnston*, p.25.

260. Maze, *A Frenchman in Khaki*, p.65.

261. Private Diary of J V Hay. RAF Museum Archive, AC 78/22/1.

262. Interestingly, Lieutenant Kenlis Atkinson, 4 Squadron RFC, mentions in his diary account that during the evening of 16 September, 'all guns of the 1st Army [I Corps] turned onto German position'. He was unable to observe this but Lieutenant R G Small reported the bombardment was a, 'terrific and a beautiful sight'. Whether this was the first concentration of artillery on the Aisne is not clear.

263. The Private Papers of J L Mowbray, IWM Dept. of Documents, 82/16/1.

264. Gunners H W Fuller (D.9.) and J R Smith (D.7.) died of wounds on 26 September at Soupir Château and are buried at Soupir Churchyard Cemetery.

265. Sergeant Herbert William Shadbolt died of wounds received in this premature explosion on 4 October 1914. He is buried at Braine Communal Cemetery. Grave Reference: B.6.

266. The Private Papers of J L Mowbray, IWM Dept. of Documents, 82/16/1.

267. Private Diary of Major Bernard Gordon Lennox, Grenadier Guards Archive. The 1/Siege Battery War Diary records four rounds being fired at the trench on 6 October.

268. The Private Papers of J L Mowbray, IWM Dept. of Documents, 82/16/1.

269. I Corps War Diary, TNA WO 95/588

270. Osburn, *Unwilling Passenger*, p.146.

Chapter 13

271. Major Hubert Dunsterville Harvey-Kelly was shot down and killed on 21 December 1916 whilst flying as Commanding Officer of 56 Squadron. He is buried at Brown's Copse Cemetery, Roeux – Special Memorial 7.

272. The use of the word 'our' infers that the British artillery was engaged in this action although it would appear that the action was entirely French.

273. I Corps War Diary, TNA WO 95/588.

274. Captain C H Darley, 3 Squadron, developed Pretyman's photographic work and by early 1915 the squadron was photographing and mapping entire lengths of the German trench systems.

275. McCudden, *Flying Fury*, p.5.

276. Terraine, World War One and the RAF, RAF History Society, No. 12/1994.

277. War Diary of Lieutenant W R Read. RAF Museum Archive, DC/73/76/1.

278. War Diary of Lieutenant K P Atkinson found in TNA AIR 1/719/33/1/1.

279. Private Papers of Sir Henry Jackson. IWM Dept. of Documents, 95/06/17.

280. Haldane, *A Brigade of the Old Army 1914*, p.103.

281. War Diary of Lieutenant W R Read. RAF Museum Archive, DC/73/76/1.

282. Ibid.

283. The Private Papers of J L Mowbray, IWM Dept. of Documents, 82/16/1.

284. Cited by Dye in, No. 9 (Wireless) Squadron 1914–1914. *Cross and Cockade International* 35/2/2004.

285. The Moffat referred to in WO 161/99/91 by Private Burgess was probably 8412 Private Thomas Moffatt. Makae is probably a misspelling of 'Mackie' or 'Mackay/McKay'.

Chapter 14
286. POW Report, TNA WO 161/95/40.

287. POW Report, TNA WO 161/98/526.

288. POW Report, TNA WO 161/95/40.

289. POW Report, TNA WO 161/98/526.

290. POW Report, TNA WO 161/99/91.

291. POW Report, TNA WO 161/95/99.

292. POW Report, TNA WO 161/95/61.

293. Ibid.

294. POW Report, TNA WO 161/95/98.

295. POW Report, TNA WO 161/95/98.

296. This was probably Major Arthur David Nicholson, the son of Major General Stuart Nicholson, the Colonel Commandant of the Royal Artillery. Nicholson died in captivity on 24 September 1915 and is buried at Cologne Southern Cemetery. Grave Reference: VIII.E.18.

297. POW Report, TNA WO 161/95/21.

298. POW Report, TNA WO 16196/11.

299. Ibid.

300. POW Report, TNA WO 161/95/98.

Chapter 15
301. Casualties are defined as men who were killed, wounded or missing in action. Any man who failed to answer his name at roll call and was not confirmed dead or wounded was deemed to be missing until he was confirmed dead or a prisoner of war.

Appendix I

Order of Battle – British Expeditionary Force September 1914

I Corps – Lieutenant General Sir Douglas Haig

1st Division – General Officer Commanding – Major General S H Lomax

Brigades	Battalions	Artillery	Engineers	Field Ambulance
1 (Guards) Brigade	1/Coldstream 1/Scots Guards 1/Black Watch 1/Cameron Highlanders	XXV Brigade (113, 114, 115 Btys) XXVI Brigade (116, 117, 118 Btys)	23 Field Company 26 Field Company 1/Signal Company	1/Field Ambulance 2/Field Ambulance 3/Field Ambulance
2 Infantry Brigade	2/Royal Sussex Regiment 1/Loyal North Lancs 1/Northamptonshire Regiment 2/King's Royal Rifle Corps	XXXIX Brigade (46, 51, 54 Btys) XLIII Howitzer Brigade (30, 40, 57 Btys) 26/Heavy Battery RGA		
3 Infantry Brigade	1/Queen's Royal West Surrey 1/South Wales Borderers 1/Gloucestershire Regiment 2/Welch Regiment		*Divisional Mounted Troops* A Squadron 15/(The King's) Hussars 1/Cyclist Company	

2nd Division – General Officer Commanding – Major General C C Monro

Brigades	Battalions	Artillery	Engineers	Field Ambulance
4 (Guards) Brigade	2/Grenadier Guards 2/Coldstream Guards 3/Coldstream Guards 1/Irish Guards	XXXIV Brigade (22, 50, 70 Btys) XXXVI Brigade (15, 48, 71 Btys) XLI Brigade (9, 16, 17 Btys)	5/Field Company 11/Field Company 2/Signal Company	4/Field Ambulance 5/Field Ambulance 6/Field Ambulance
5 Infantry Brigade	2/Worcestershire Regiment 2/Ox and Bucks Light Infantry 2/Highland Light Infantry 2/Connaught Rangers	XLIV Howitzer Brigade (47, 56, 60 Btys) 35/Heavy Battery RGA		
6 Infantry Brigade	1/King's Liverpool Regiment 2/South Staffordshire Regiment 1/Royal Berkshire Regiment 1/Kings Royal Rifle Corps		*Divisional Mounted Troops* B Squadron 15/(The King's) Hussars 2/Cyclist Company	

II Corps – General Sir Horace Smith-Dorrien (after 17 August 1914)

3rd Division – General Officer Commanding – Major General H I W Hamilton

Brigades	Battalions	Artillery	Engineers	Field Ambulance
7 Infantry Brigade	3/Worcestershire Regiment 2/South Lancashire Regiment 1/Wiltshire Regiment 2/Royal Irish Rifles	XXIII Brigade (107, 108, 109 Btys) XL Brigade (6, 23, 49 Btys) XLII Brigade (29, 41, 45 Btys) XXX Howitzer Brigade (128, 129, 130 Btys) 48/Heavy Battery RGA	56/Field Company 57/Field Company 3/Signal Company	7/Field Ambulance 8/Field Ambulance 9/Field Ambulance
8 Infantry Brigade	2/Royal Scots 2/Royal Irish Regiment 4/Middlesex Regiment 1/Gordon Highlanders			
9 Infantry Brigade	1/Northumberland Fusiliers 4/Royal Fusiliers 1/Lincolnshire Regiment 1/Royal Scots Fusiliers		*Divisional Mounted Troops* C Squadron 15/(The King's) Hussars 3/Cyclist Company	

5th Division – General Officer Commanding – Major General Sir C Fergusson

Brigades	Battalions	Artillery	Engineers	Field Ambulance
13 Infantry Brigade	2/King's Own Scottish Borderers 2/Duke of Wellingtons Regiment 1/Queen's Royal West Kent 2/King's Own Yorkshire Light Infantry	XV Brigade (11, 52, 80 Btys) XXVII Brigade (119, 120, 121 Btys) XXVIII Brigade (122, 123, 124 Btys) VIII Howitzer Brigade (37, 61, 65 Btys) 108/Heavy Battery RGA	59/Field Company 17/Field Company 5/Signal Company	13/Field Ambulance 14/Field Ambulance 15/Field Ambulance
14 Infantry Brigade	2/Suffolk Regiment 1/East Surrey Regiment 1/Duke of Cornwall's Light Infantry 2/Manchester Regiment			
15 Infantry Brigade	1/Norfolk Regiment 1/Bedfordshire Regiment 1/Cheshire Regiment 1/Dorsetshire Regiment		*Divisional Mounted Troops* A Squadron 19/(Queen Alexandra's Own) Royal Hussars 5/Cyclist Company	

III Corps – Major General W P Pulteney (formed in France on 31 August 1914)

4th Division – General Officer Commanding – Major General T D'O Snow (Landed in France on 22/23 August 1914)

Brigades	Battalions	Artillery	Engineers	Field Ambulance
10 Infantry Brigade	1/Royal Warwickshire Regiment 2/Seaforth Highlanders 1/Royal Irish Fusiliers 2/Royal Dublin Fusiliers	XIV Brigade (39, 68, 88 Btys) XXIX Brigade (125, 126, 127 Btys) XXXII Brigade	7/Field Company 9/Field Company 4/Signal Company	11/Field Ambulance 12/Field Ambulance 10/Field Ambulance
11 Infantry Brigade	1/Somerset Light Infantry 1/East Lancashire Regiment 1/Hampshire Regiment 1/Rifle Brigade	(27, 134, 135 Btys) XXXVII Howitzer Brigade (31, 35, 55 Btys) 31/Heavy Battery RGA		
12 Infantry Brigade	1/King's Own 2/Lancashire Fusiliers 2/Inniskilling Fusiliers 2/Essex Regiment		*Divisional Mounted Troops* B Squadron 19/(Queen Alexandra's Own) Royal Hussars 4/Cyclist Company	

6th Division – General Officer Commanding – Major General J L Keir (Landed in France on 9 September)

Brigades	Battalions	Artillery	Engineers	Field Ambulance
16 Infantry Brigade	1/East Kent Regiment 1/Leicestershire Regiment 1/King's Shropshire light Infantry 2/York and Lancaster Regiment	II Brigade 21,42,53 Btys XXIV Brigade 110,11,112 Btys XXXVIII Brigade	12/Field Company 38/Field Company 6/Signal Company	16/Field Ambulance 17/Field Ambulance 18/Field Ambulance
17 Infantry Brigade	1/Royal Fusiliers 1/North Staffordshire Regiment 2/Leinster Regiment 3/Rifle Brigade	24,34,72 Btys XII Howitzer Brigade 43,86,87 Btys		
18 Infantry Brigade	1/West Yorkshire Regiment 1/East Yorkshire Regiment 2/Notts & Derby Regiment 2/Durham Light Infantry		*Divisional Mounted Troops* C Squadron 19/(Queen Alexandra's Own) Royal Hussars 6/Cyclist Company	

19th Infantry Brigade (formed from lines of communication troops at Valenciennes on 22 August)

General officers commanding	Battalions	Background
Initially the brigade was under the independent command of Major General L G Drummond. Colonel B E Ward assumed command of the brigade after Drummond was wounded on 27 August, relinquishing command on 3 September 1914, when Brigadier General F Gordon was appointed.	1/Devonshire Regiment 2/Royal Welch Fusiliers 1/Cameronians 1/Middlesex Regiment 2/Argyll and Sutherland Highlanders	Infantry brigades were generally deployed as part of an infantry division. However the role of 19 Brigade in August 1914 was to hold key towns and bridges along the route that connected the BEF to its supply bases on the coast. Hence the term 'lines of communication'. At Mons for example, 1/Middlesex were ordered to hold bridges and locks over the canal in anticipation of the general advance. In this manner it became embroiled in the retreat. On 25 August they were called upon to support the cavalry near Haussy before moving on to Solesmes and Le Cateau. At Le Cateau, the brigade was used on the right flank and was in action with 2/Suffolks on the Montay Spur. However, although it remained independent as such, it served o supply reinforcement troops for the remainder of the retreat and was later attached to 6th Division. The brigade continued in this role until May 1915 when it finally found a permanent home with the 27th Infantry Division.

Cavalry Corps – Major General E H Allenby

Brigades	Regiments	Horse Artillery	Engineers	Field Ambulance
1 Cavalry Brigade	2/Dragoon Guards (Queen's Bay's) 5/Princess Charlotte's) Dragoon Guards (11/(Prince Albert's Own) Hussars	III Brigade RHA D and E Batteries III Brigade Ammunition Column	1/Field Squadron RE 1/Signal Troop	1/Cavalry FA 2/Cavalry FA 3/Cavalry FA
2 Cavalry Brigade	4/(Royal Irish) Dragoon Guards 9/(Queens Royal) Lancers 18/(Queen Mary's Own) Hussars	VII Brigade RHA I and L Batteries VII Brigade Ammunition Column		4/Cavalry FA
3 Cavalry Brigade	4/(Queen's Own) Hussars 5/(Royal Irish) Lancers 16/(The Queen's) Lancers			
4 Cavalry Brigade	Composite Household Cavalry Regiment 6/Dragoon Guards (Carabiniers) 3/(King's Own) Hussars			
5 Cavalry Brigade	2/Dragoons (Royal Scots Greys) 12/(Prince of Wales's Own) Lancers 20/Hussars	J Battery RHA and Ammunition Column	4/Field Troop 5/Signal Troop	5/Cavalry FA

Appendix II

The Aisne Cemeteries

There are some twenty-six cemeteries north and south of the river Aisne which contain casualties of the 1914 fighting. Below, in alphabetical order, are the locations and references to some of the individuals mentioned in the text who are buried on or near the battlefield. The memorial at La Ferté-sous-Jouarre, although much further south, has been included as it commemorates so many of the Aisne dead of 1914. For more precise information on the location of each cemetery visit the Commonwealth War Graves Commission website at: www.cwgc.org.

Cemetery	Location	Detail
Bourg-et-Comin Communal Cemetery	Bourg can be reached on the D967 which runs south from Cerny to meet the D925. The communal cemetery is located in the centre of town.	There are eleven identified burials here, all of 1914 vintage and with one exception, the result of two separate incidents. The 4/Dragoon Guards casualties incurred on 13 September when taking the bridges at Bourg are here: Captain G Fitzgerald, Lance Corporal W Baker, Corporal F Chapman and Private H Savory. There are also six Cameron Highlanders from the cave disaster of 25 September 1914: Captain D Miers, Captain N Cameron, Captain A Cameron, Private J Brown and RSM G Burt, and although not technically a Cameron Highlander, Lieutenant J Crocket, RAMC.
Braine Communal Cemetery	Braine is southeast of Chassemy on the D14. Once in the town turn left onto D1320 and follow signs for the cemetery.	Braine was taken by 1 Cavalry Brigade on 12 September and there are three casualties of that action here: Captain G Springfield, Captain B Stuart & Corporal E Medlam. Thereafter, it was the home of No. 5 Casualty Clearing Station and the majority of the seventy-eight identified casualties are from that period, many of whom are

Cemetery	Location	Detail
		commemorated on special memorials. Buried here is Captain H Ranken VC who died of wounds on 25 September 1914, Lieutenant G Hutton (19 September 1914) from 3/Signal Company who drowned whilst attempting to swim the river with a telephone cable and Sergeant H Shadbolt, 2/Siege Battery, who died of wounds received after a premature explosion.
Bucy-le-Long Communal Cemetery	Situated north of the village on the D95.	There are two 1914 burials here, Rifleman S Cridland killed on 25 September 1914 and Rifleman A Hammond who was killed on 24 September 1914. Both men were serving with 1/Rifle Brigade.
Chauny Communal Cemetery, British Extension	From the town centre head north along Avenue Victor Hugo on the D 937. Turn right onto Rue Ernest Renan and the communal cemetery is on the right hand side.	The cemetery was begun after the Armistice when casualties from the surrounding area were brought in, the majority are from 1918, but fifty-six of the identified 437 burials are from 1914. Five officers and eight men of the Sherwood Foresters are buried here, all casualties of 20 September 1914 when the battalion re-took the West Yorkshires' trenches.
Ciry-Salsogne Communal Cemetery	The village is southeast of Sermoise and the cemetery is situated on the outskirts of the village.	Three soldiers from 121/Battery, RFA are buried here. Driver W Martin and Gunner W Woods were probably killed by shellfire on 14 September 1914, with Gunner F Calow dying of wounds two days later. At the time, 121/Battery were east of Sermoise near to the point where the Mezieres road bends southwest.
Crouy-Vauxrot French National Cemetery	Crouy is northeast of Soissons on the D304. Enter Crouy on the Avenue du General Patton and turn left on Rue Maurice Dupuis and in just over half a mile you will find the cemetery on the right.	There are now fifty burials here, twenty of which are unidentified. All were brought in after the Armistice, including twenty-five Seaforth Highlanders who were previously buried at Bucy-le-Long and killed between 14 September and 4 October 1914. Amongst the dead here is Lieutenant Colonel Sir

Cemetery	Location	Detail
		E Bradford the commanding officer of the Seaforths who is more than twice the age of 18-year-old Private A Paterson who was killed on 15 September1914.
Filain Churchyard	The village is just north of the Chemin des Dames on the D 152. The Churchyard is beside the church in the centre of the village.	There are three 1914 casualties buried here: Private T Brown, Royal Scots Fusiliers and Private H Chitty, Royal Fusiliers, both killed on 22 September. Private E Tyas of the Lincolnshire Regiment was killed on 20 September.
La Ferté-sous-Jouarre Memorial	The memorial is situated in a small park on the south-western edge of the town, on the south bank of the River Marne just off the main road to Paris. The Memorial Register is kept at the Town Hall.	The La Ferté-sous-Jouarre Memorial commemorates nearly 4,000 officers and men of the British Expeditionary Force who died in August, September and the early part of October 1914 and who have no known grave. Names are listed on the memorial by regiments in order of precedence, under the title of each regiment by rank, and under each rank alphabetically.
Longueval Communal Cemetery	Longueval Barbonval is south of Bourg on the D 976. Go through the village and where the road takes a left hand bend bear right along Rue des Forneaux.	The nineteen casualties here are all victims of shellfire and were killed when the 9/Lancers billets in the town was shelled on 29 September 1914. All are NCOs and enlisted men except Second Lieutenant G Taylor-Whitehead.
Montcornet Military Cemetery	From the town centre at Montcornet turn right following the signs for Rethel. Where the road forks, bear right and follow the CWGC sign.	Over half the 100 burials here are unidentified and the cemetery holds casualties from 1914 and the 1918 German offensive. There are only thirteen casualties here from the 1914 campaign which includes men from the West Yorkshire Regiment, Rifle Brigade, KRRC, Cameron Highlanders and Black Watch.
Moulins New Communal Cemetery	Situated on the left as you enter the village from Vendresse, the graves are in the far northeastern corner of the cemetery.	The ten burials include Lieutenant Colonel A Grant Duff, the Black Watch commanding officer who was killed on 14 September 1914 and Captain D Lucas-Tooth of 9/Lancers killed on the same day. The Scottish rugby union international, Lieutenant

Cemetery	Location	Detail
		R Simpson, who was killed on 15 September 1914 with 16/Battery RFA is also buried here.
Paissy Churchyard	In the rear left hand side of the churchyard in Paissy village.	There are five BEF soldiers here: Captain A Cathcart, 2/KRRC, killed on 14 September 1914; Lieutenant Colonel D Warren, 1/Queen's and his adjutant, Captain C Wilson, both killed on 17 September 1914; Gunner T Connor from 135/Battery, killed on 17 September 1914 and Private C Kenward of 2/Royal Sussex, killed on 21 September 1914.
Pargnan Churchyard	Pargnan is just north of Oeuilly on the D 893. The church and its churchyard sit above the village.	There are six burials here, four of which are identified. Very much a gunners' cemetery as all four identified casualties are from 26/Heavy Battery and 118/Battery. The youngest, and possibly one of the youngest casualties of 1914 on the Aisne is Gunner B Brandon of 26/Heavy Battery, aged 17, killed on 25 September 1914. Gunner J Ellison who was killed on 6 October 1914 served with the same battery. The two remaining casualties are from 118/Battery, Driver W Smith, killed on 25 September 1914 and Driver J Chamberlin, killed on 6 October 1914.
Rozieres Churchyard	The church is in the centre of the village of Rozieres-sur-Crise, 4km south of Soissons.	There are twelve identified burials here all killed between 14–20 September 1914. The youngest is 21-year-old Private J Burns killed on 20 September serving with 2/Argyll & Sutherland Highlanders.
Serches Communal Cemetery	Serches is on the D952 from Vénizel. The cemetery is on the left as you enter the village on the Rue de la Grenouillère.	There is only one casualty buried here, Private P Thompson, King's Own Scottish Borderers who died on 22 September 1914. Quite possibly he was buried here en route to the casualty collecting station at Le Mont de Soissons farm. The D 952 was regularly swept by German shellfire.

Cemetery	Location	Detail
Sissone British Cemetery	The cemetery is east of Sissone on the D 18.	The cemetery was made after the Armistice when casualties were brought in from the Chemin des Dames and surrounding area. There are ten 1914 casualties of the Aisne fighting here, a number of whom were killed in the fighting of 20 September.
Soupir Churchyard	Located behind the church in Soupir village.	The burial ground for the Field Ambulances based at La Cour de Soupir Farm and Château. Thirty 1914 burials including some of the casualties from the quarry at Cour de Soupir on 16 Sept, these include Lieutenant H Mockler-Ferryman, Lieutenant R Worthington and 18-year-old Second Lieutenant P Girardot, all from the Ox and Bucks Light Infantry. Gunners H Fuller and J Smith from 1/Siege Battery are also buried here, victims of a premature explosion.
Soupir Communal Cemetery	Turn right opposite the church along the Rue de Paris and then turn right again up a steep narrow road marked with a CWGC plaque. This road leads up to the Communal Cemetery.	There are sixteen named burials all brought in after the Armistice from their original burial ground. All are officers and men from the Guards Brigade except Major Arthur Green, Brigade Major of 17 Brigade. Notable Guards casualties include: Captain Lord Arthur Hay; Captain Lord Guernsey; the Captain Hon William Cecil; Lieutenant John Pickersgill-Cuncliffe; Lieutenant Richard Welby; Second Lieutenant R Lockwood and Lieutenant Frederick Des Voeux. Six private soldiers rest alongside their officers.
Soupir French National Cemetery No 2	Leave Soupir in the direction of Chavonne on the D88. The cemetery is at the junction with the D925.	There are two unidentified soldiers here in graves 1898 and 1899. Both were killed in September 1914.
St Marguerite Churchyard Cemetery	The cemetery is beside the church in the village centre.	Of the six burials here five are Lancashire Fusiliers. Private W Gratrix was killed on 13 September 1914, Corporal E Slough on 14 September, Private J Murphy and Second Lieutenant J Paulson on 17

Cemetery	Location	Detail
		September and Private C Brooks on 25 September. Two men were killed attempting to bring in the wounded Paulson after he had been hit by shellfire; one of these may have been Private Murphy.
Vauxbuin French National Cemetery	The cemetery is 4km southwest of Soissons along the N2.	The British plot was made up after the Armistice from casualties brought in from surrounding areas. There are some 300 British burials here over half of which are unidentified and only fifty-five are casualties from the Aisne in 1914. Here you will find 18-year-old Second Lieutenant G Amos, the KOSB subaltern who was killed at Missy on 14 September 1914 and the two 1/Rifle Brigade casualties of 13 September mentioned by Lieutenant L Tennyson – Sergeant C Dorey, the platoon Sergeant of No. 7 Platoon and Rifleman C Spindler.
Vailly British Cemetery	The cemetery is west of the town centre on the D925.	The cemetery was made after the Armistice when graves were brought in from other burial grounds and from the battlefields. The majority of those buried here died in September 1914.There are 675 burials here of which 370 are identified. Here you will find Captain R F Hawes of the 1/Leicesters,; Lieutenant A Read of the Somersets; Captain G Briggs of the Royal Scots Fusiliers; Captain T Wright, the Royal Engineer VC winner and Major W Sarsfield, the commanding officer of the Connaughts. Other burials include Lieutenant H Hopkins, the medical officer attached to the Devonshire Regiment; Brigadier N Findlay, CRA to 1st Division and RSM MacWhinnie, one of the first KOSB casualties of the battle. You will also find a number of Connaught Rangers here, testament to their fight at La Cour de Soupir on 14 September and Second Lieutenant Cosmo Gordon of the Northamptons who died of his wounds on 17 September.

Cemetery	Location	Detail
Vendresse British Cemetery	Situated halfway along the D967 between Cerny and the village of Vendresse-Beaulne.	Another concentration cemetery containing casualties from both 1914 and 1918. There are over 700 British burials here, over half of which are unidentified and of these, 245 are from 1914. Here you will find Lieutenant T Meautys who was killed on 20 September 1914 during the attack on the West Yorkshires' trenches, a further eight casualties from the attacks of 20 September are buried here, including: Major A Robb of the Durham Light Infantry and Lieutenant J O'Connell, the RAMC doctor attached to the Highland Light Infantry. Another casualty killed in the cave disaster of 25 September was Lieutenant K Meiklejohn , the Cameron Highlander's adjutant who was killed eleven days after the Royal Sussex adjutant, Lieutenant Hon H Pelham, the son of the Earl of Chichester. He died alongside his colonel on the Chemin des Dames. Also here is Second Lieutenant R Benison of the Connaught Rangers, killed on 20 September 1914 and Lieutenant J Coker of the South Wales Borders who was killed in the attack of 26 September. Here also is the nephew of novelist Rider Haggard, Captain M Haggard, who was carried to safety by VC winner Lance Corporal W Fuller of 2/Welsh.
Vendresse Churchyard	The churchyard is at the rear of the church, which can be found in the centre of the village.	There are over eighty casualties from 1914 buried here, over half of which are unidentified. Amongst the more notable are: Captain Rivy Grenfell of 9/Lancers; Major J Johnston who commanded 115/Battery RFA and Major J Carpenter-Garnier of the Scots Guards. Also here is the unfortunate Lieutenant G Naylor-Leyland of the Royal Horse Guards, whose trench Jock Marden took over on 20 September.

Cemetery	Location	Detail
Viel-Arcy Communal Cemetery	The village is just northeast of Brazne on the D22.The cemetery is near the centre of the village.	There is only one BEF burial here, that of Lieutenant Colonel Charles Dalton, the RAMC officer who was wounded at Verneuil Château on 19 September 1914 and died of his wounds in the nearby CCS.
Villers-en-Prayeres Communal Cemetery	The village is south of Bourg on the D 22. In the village turn right at the war memorial onto Rue des Marrionners.	There were two dressing stations in the village in 1914 and the thirty-three men buried here probably died of their wounds after their evacuation from the battlefield.

Bibliography

Unpublished sources

The National Archives
Unit War Diaries in WO 95.
Service Records in WO 339.
Personal Papers in WO 106 and CAB 45.
Prisoner of War Reports in WO 161.

Private Papers
The Private Papers of C L Brereton.
The Private Papers of A V Spencer.
The Diary of K B Godsell.
The Diary of C Helm.
The Diary of D Lloyd-Burch.
The Private Papers and letters of R H Owen.
The Private Papers of G A Kempthorne.
The Diary of Major Lord Bernard Gordon Lennox.
The Private Papers of J McIlwain.
The Private Papers of A Reeve.
The Letters of R H Owen.
The Diary and Private Papers of J B W Pennyman.
The Private Papers and letters of N L Woodroffe.
The Private Papers of C S A Avis.
The Private Papers of J L Mowbray.
The Private Papers of C C Onslow.
The Private Papers of B C Myatt.
The Private Papers of J G Stennet.
The Private Papers of E R Meade-Waldo.
The Diary of J V Hay.
The Private Papers of W Edgington.
The Private Papers of Lord Tennyson.
The Private Papers and letters of Sir Henry Jackson.
The Diary of W R Read.
The Private Papers of G H Gaskell.
The diary of G B C Ward.

Published Sources

Books
The Marquess of Anglesey, *A History of the British Cavalry 1816–1919* (Vol. 7), Leo Cooper, 1973–1982.
Edwin Astil, *The Great War Diaries of Brigadier General Alexander Johnston 1914–1917*, Pen & Sword, 2007.
R Barker, *A Brief History of the Royal Flying Corps in World War 1*, Robinson, 2002.
Correlli Barnett, *The Sword Bearers – Studies in Supreme Command in the First World War*, Hodder & Stoughton, 1986.
Lt Colonel F S Brereton, *The Great War and the RAMC*, Constable 1919.
C Ballard, *Smith-Dorrien*, Constable, 1931.
S Bidwell and D Graham, *Fire-Power- The British Army Weapons & Theories of War 1904–1945*, Pen & Sword, 2004.
Walter Bloem, *The Advance From Mons*, Tandem, 1967.
Sir Tom Bridges, *Alarms and Excursions*, Longmans, 1938.
Lord Carnock, *The History of the 15th The King's Hussars 1914–1922*, Crypt House Press, 1932.
Frederick Coleman, *From Mons to Ypres with General French*, A L Burt Company, 1916.
Sir Arthur Conan Doyle, *The British Campaign in France And Flanders 1914*, Hodder & Stoughton, 1916.
J M Craster, *Fifteen Rounds a Minute*, Pen & Sword, 2012.
A Crookenden, *The Cheshire Regiment in the Great War*, Privately published, 1956.
J C Darling, *20th Hussars in the Great War*, Privately published, 1923.
R V Dolbey, *A Regimental Surgeon in War and Prison*, John Murray, 1917.
J Dunn, *The War The Infantry Knew*, Abacus, 1994.
Sir J E Edmonds, *Military Operations France and Belgium 1914 Vol. 1*, Macmillan, 1926.
H Evans and N Laing, *The 4th (Queen's Own) Hussars in the Great War*, Gale and Polden, 1920.
General Sir M Farndale, *History of the Royal Regiment of Artillery-Western Front*, Royal Artillery Institution, 1986.
Anthony Farrar-Hockley, *Death of an Army*, Arthur Barker, 1967.
Nikolas Gardner, *Trial by Fire*, Praeger, 2003.
H Gibb, *Record of the 4th Royal Irish Dragoon Guards in the Great War 1914–1918*, Canterbury, 1925.
Paddy Griffith, *Battle Tactics of the Western Front*, Yale University Press, 1994.
Brian Gillard, *Good Old Somersets – An Old Contemptible Battalion in 1914*, Matador, 2004.
Stair Gillon, *The KOSB in the Great War*, Thomas Nelson, 1930.
Gerald Gliddon, *VCs Handbook*, Sutton, 2005.
Count E Gleichen, *The Doings of the Fifteenth Infantry Brigade*, Blackwood, 1917.
Sir Aylmer Haldane, *A Brigade of the Old Army 1914*. Edward Arnold, 1920.
Lord E Hamilton, *The First Seven Divisions*, Hurst & Blackett, 1916.
A A Hanbury-Sparrow, *The Land Locked Lake*, Arthur Barker 1932.
Basil Liddell Hart, *History of the First World War*, Book Club, 1973.
Holger H Herwig, *The Marne 1914*, Random House, 2011.
Brigadier General Sir Archibald Home, *The Diary of a World War I Cavalry Officer*, Costello, 1985.
Rudyard Kipling, *The Irish Guards in the Great War – Volume 1: The 1st Battalion*, Leonaur, 2007.
J T Long, *Three's Company, A History of No.3 (Fighter) Squadron RAF*, Pen & Sword, 2005.
Gerald Lowry, *From Mons to 1933*, Simpkin and Marshall, 1933.
J F Lucy, *There's a Devil in the Drum*, Faber and Faber, 1938.
Lynn MacDonald, *1914*, Michael Joseph, 1987.
Major General T Marden, *A Short History of the 6th Division*, Hugh Rees, 1920.
C V Maloney, *Invicta, With the 1st Battalion The Queen's Own Royal West Kent Regiment in The Great War*, Nisbet & Co., 1923.

Arthur Mills, *With My Regiment – From the Aisne to La Bassée*, Heinemann, 1915.

Jerry Murland, *Retreat and Rearguard 1914*, Pen & Sword, 2011.

Paul Maze, *A Frenchman in Khaki*, Heinemann, 1934.

Evelyn J Needham, *The First Three Months*, Gale and Polden, 1936.

Arthur Osburn, *Unwilling Passenger*, Faber and Faber, 1932.

Ponsonby, F, *The Grenadier Guards in the Great War of 1914–1918*, Macmillan, 1920.

M von Posek, *The German Cavalry 1914 in Belgium and France*, Naval & Military Press, 2007.

Major General H L Pritchard, (Editor) *History of The Corps Of Royal Engineers (Volume 5)*, Institute of Royal Engineers, 1951.

Sir W Raleigh, *War in the Air, Volume 1*, Clarendon Press, 1922.

Sir J Ross of Bladensburg, *The Coldstream Guards 1914–1918*, Oxford University Press, 1928.

Gary Sheffield and John Bourne, *Douglas Haig War Diaries and Letters 1914–1918*, Orion, 2005.

Andy Simpson, *The Evolution of Victory*, Donovan, 1995.

C R Simpson, *History of the Lincolnshire Regiment 1914–1918*, The Medici Society,1931.

James Taylor, *The 2nd Royal Irish Rifles in the Great War*, Four Courts, 2005.

Richard Van Emden, *Tickled To Death To Go*, Spellmount, 1996.

The War Office, *Battle of the Aisne 13th-15th September, 1914 – Tour of the Battlefield*, H M Stationary Office, 1934.

Everard Wyrall, *The Gloucestershire Regiment in the War 1914–1918*, Methuen, 1931.

Everard Wyrall, *The History of the Duke of Cornwall's Light Infantry 1914–1919*, Methuen & Co. 1932.

Everard Wyrall, *The Diehards in the Great War*, Harrisons and Sons, 1926.

H C Wylly, *History of the 1st & 2nd Battalions The Leicestershire Regiment in the Great War*, Gale and Polden. 1928.

Articles

Captain H A Baker, History of the 7th Field Company, RE, During the War 1914–1918, *RE Journal*, June, 1932.

Brigadier General C J Griffiths, Crossing the Aisne, *The Lancashire Fusiliers Annual 1916*, Number XXVIII.

W A Synge, From the Marne to the Aisne – The Diary of an Infantry Subaltern, *Army Quarterly*, January and May, 1935.

Brigadier General G Walker, From the Curragh to the Aisne, 1914, *R E Journal*, April, 1919.

Major B K Young, The Diary of an RE Subaltern with the BEF in 1914, *RE Journal*, December, 1933.

Index